Personnel Management

Third Edition

Margaret Attwood
and
Stuart Dimmock

MACMILLAN
Business

First published by Pan Books Ltd as *Introduction to Personnel
Management* in the Breakthrough series in 1985

Published by Macmillan 1989
MACMILLAN PRESS LTD
Houndmills, Basingstoke, Hampshire RG21 6XS
and London
Companies and representatives
throughout the world

ISBN 0-333-65006-9

A catalogue record for this book is available
from the British Library.

This book is printed on paper suitable for recycling and
made from fully managed and sustained forest sources.

11 10   9   8   7   6   5   4   3
06 05 04 03 02 01 00 99 98

Typeset in Great Britain by
Aarontype Limited
Easton, Bristol

Printed and bound in Great Britain by
Creative Print and Design Group (Wales), Ebbw Vale

Macmillan Business Masters

Personnel Management

Third Edition

Macmillan Business Masters

Company Accounts (3rd edn) Roger Oldcorn
Economics S. F. Goodman
Financial Management (3rd edn) Geoffrey Knott
Management (3rd edn) Roger Oldcorn
Marketing Geoff Lancaster and Paul Reynolds
Operations Management (2nd edn) Howard Barnett
Personnel Management (3rd edn) Margaret Attwood and Stuart Dimmock

To Bill, Abi and Jonathon

Contents

Introduction

This book is about the search for success in the management of people at work. Unfortunately, in the past, more attention has been given to the mismanagement of employees and the reasons for this than to the development of criteria for success in personnel management. Any attempt to generate universal prescriptions for effectiveness in this area of management is likely to be misleading. What appears to stimulate work of both high quality and quantity in one organisation may not be successful elsewhere. Nor should we assume that other nations have all the answers. Once, everything American was thought likely to be the key to industrial utopia. Then many people were excited by Japanese management techniques. Now we recognise that the search for excellence is long and difficult.

This book is not a panacea for all ills. It attempts to assist the new personnel specialist or manager to develop competence in this area. It encourages more experienced practitioners to question established techniques. On the basis of such analysis it should be possible to develop strategies and practices relevant to the circumstances of the particular organisation. Management is a lonely business; there are no guaranteed steps to effectiveness. Yet, paradoxically, no problem is unique. We hope to emphasise the complexity of good personnel management practice and the rejection and questioning, where relevant, of current employment practices.

While writing this book we have learnt the difficulty of deciding how much emphasis to give to each topic. Of necessity the results reflect our own values, experiences and interests. The further reading section at the end of the book gives limited advice for the extension of knowledge in this area of management. Experience, especially if reflected upon and shared with other practitioners, is at least as important.

MARGARET ATTWOOD
STUART DIMMOCK

1 Definitions of Personnel Management

'Personnel management' is that part of management concerned with the man-agement of people at work. However, like many things in life, reality is more complex: for example, in recent years the term 'human resource management' has frequently been used in preference to 'personnel manage-ment'. In this introduction we shall examine this change together with some other initial definitions.

- Most organisations have a specialist personnel department which gives support to managers and supervisors, who have direct responsibility for the management of people.
- A wide range of people – personnel specialists, line managers and super-visors – practise personnel management.
- There are a number of specialist management techniques which together comprise personnel management.
- The practice of personnel management varies greatly from one organ-isation to another.

This chapter examines each of these four points. By the end you should have a general awareness of the nature and complexity of personnel management and of some of the reasons for this.

1.1 The Structure and Organisation of a Personnel Department

The function of a personnel department is to assist with the acquisition, development and retention of the human resources necessary for the success of the organisation. It is unhelpful to imply that there is one best design for a personnel department. In this section we examine some of the options.

Particularly in large multi-establishment companies this is likely to be headed by a member of the board of directors. This should make easier the task of the personnel department in encouraging the effective management of the organisation's employees, in that its head will have ready access to the chief executive. In large organisations, where there is generally considerable emphasis on the development of formal personnel policies, the involvement of the head of the personnel function in board-level decision-making should help to ensure that these are supportive of business strategy.

The structure shown in Figure 1.1 could be that of the senior personnel posts in a multi-establishment organisation. Within the structure shown, the *personnel director* would have responsibility for:

- Formulating the organisation's personnel policies and overseeing their implementation by both members of her/his department and other managers.
- Advice to other board members on personnel matters.
- Management of the personnel department.

The *industrial relations adviser* would be likely to carry responsibility for:

- Formulating industrial relations policies in conjunction with the personnel director.
- The provision of advice, guidance and information to the divisional personnel managers (and, through them, to other managers) on industrial relations.
- Guidance to all managers on employment legislation.

Depending on the structure of industrial relations in the company, there might also be an advisory or an executive role in trade union negotiations. If, as is increasingly the case, the organisation concerned either does not recognise trade unions or engages in collective bargaining only for a small proportion of its workforce, then the term employee relations rather than industrial relations may be used to describe this aspect of personnel work.

The *group employee development adviser* would be responsible for:

- The formulation of policies for the development of the organisation's human resources, in conjunction with the personnel director.
- Advice, guidance and information to the divisional personnel managers (and, through them, to other managers and employees) on training and development.

Fig 1.1   Organisation structure for a personnel department

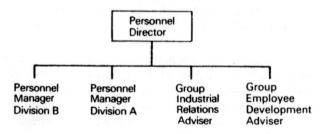

The divisional personnel managers would provide a day-to-day personnel service covering all aspects of personnel management, industrial relations and employee development, for their division. It would also be necessary for them to provide information to the personnel director and the advisers, to allow policies to be formulated and monitored satisfactorily for the organisation as a whole.

It should be stressed that it is difficult to generalise about the specialisms within a personnel department which exist, or indeed should exist, in any organisation at any time. This will depend upon such factors as:

- size;
- profitability;
- status of the personnel function;
- nature of the market for the organisation's products;
- nature of the labour force from which workers are recruited;
- expectations and values of senior management.

When unemployment was very low in the late 1960s through to the mid-1970s trade union power increased. The work of many personnel managers became dominated by industrial relations. Since then the emphasis has shifted towards ways in which the personnel function can contribute to greater organisational efficiency and effectiveness.

The increasing use, from the late 1980s, of the term 'human resource management' in preference to 'personnel management' can be seen as an indication of this shift in focus. However, it should not be taken as a universal change. For some personnel departments it may represent little more than re-labelling, but for others it marks a definite decision to move away from the ideas of the late 1960s and 1970s when personnel was sometimes pictured as the conscience of the organisation, or the mediator between management and employees.

By comparison, human resource management (HRM) is a philosophy about the purpose of personnel and the contribution it can make to an oganisation's business objectives. The philosophy emphasises four things. The first is that personnel is totally integrated into management and acts in its interests. Second, it takes a strategic view of the employees or human resource, that is to say it identifies the ways in which key factors, such as the values, skills, activities and rewards of employees need to be shaped or adapted in order to achieve the organisation's business objectives. Third, it works to ensure that these factors are achieved from the organisation's human resource. Fourth, by this approach it demonstrates the function's financial contribution to the organisation's success.

This business-orientated approach does not necessarily imply a tougher, more restrictive attitude to employees. Indeed HRM is frequently concerned to find ways to increase people's sense of involvement in their work and their department and organisation. Nor does the introduction of HRM mean that the actual work of personnel practitioners has undergone significant change.

It is simply that, within an HRM philosophy, the work of personnel has become more tightly focused on the achievement of organisational objectives. Major current concerns of personnel practitioners therefore include:

- the improvement of selection systems;
- employee communication and consultation mechanisms;
- training to improve current job performance including relations with customers;
- management development;
- performance review systems;
- value for money in personnel policies including the sub-contracting of some services to other organisations.

To assess the importance accorded to specialisms within personnel management it is useful to examine advertisements for jobs. We selected three from a recent copy of *Personnel Management*. They were:

1 Training manager for a major retailer, developing and designing management courses, managing external training policy and practice and ensuring that the company's training service is cost-effective and meets the needs of its operations.
2 Recruitment officer responsible for the co-ordination of recruitment of managerial and other senior staff for the London sites of an industrial caterer.
3 Compensation and benefits analyst for a financial services organisation with particular responsibility for the maintenance of the job evaluation system and for the undertaking of salary and benefits surveys.

Your list may differ from this, since there is now a plethora of personnel specialisms. All the personnel activities covered by this book may be carried out by specialist personnel staff or by generalists, whose work covers the whole range of personnel, training and industrial relations activities for a department or a whole organisation. In some small companies in particular there may be no specialist personnel department, the services required being provided intermittently or regularly by a specialist consultancy. In other small organisations the personnel department may be staffed by a single employee with responsibility for everything from visiting sick staff to the provision of safety goggles.

Detailed organisation of the personnel function cannot be prescribed easily. However, if personnel management activities are to be effectively carried out, it is important that line managers feel that their immediate needs are being met, as well as that attention is being given to longer-term matters. If the personnel specialist finds that longer-term considerations are constantly relegated to the bottom of the filing tray, one can safely assume that something is wrong!

1.2 **Who Practises Personnel Management?**

Personnel management forms part of every manager's job as well as being the particular concern of the specialist. What tasks do personnel specialists undertake?

1.3 **Personnel Roles and Responsibilities**

In practice the specialist role may take a number of forms:

- audit;
- executive;
- facilitator;
- consultancy;
- service.

The audit role

Personnel specialists have responsibility for ensuring that all members of management carry out those parts of their roles concerned with the effective use of human resources.

The executive role

Personnel management is part of every manager's job, but some personnel activities are carried out by specialists rather than by line managers or supervisors. Factors which seem to influence the division of responsibilities include potential economies of scale if the activity is carried out by specialists, the need for 'expert' knowledge, organisational tradition and the preferences of both specialists and line managers. For example, it seems that personnel specialists tend to maintain a high profile in those areas of work which they see as most important and prestigious. Employee relations falls into this category.

The facilitator role

Many personnel management activities require considerable skills and knowledge if they are to be carried out effectively. One of the responsibilities of personnel specialists is to see that those who practise such activities, as part of a more general managerial role, are equipped to do so. Attempts by personnel practitioners to carry out this task may lead to conflict between themselves and line managers.

The consultancy role

Managers may confront a variety of problems as they attempt to supervise employees. These may include motivation difficulties, lack of training or pay grievances. The individual manager may meet a particular problem infrequently and, therefore, may need advice in order to resolve it successfully. In this area the role of the personnel specialist can be equated with that of an internal management consultant.

The service role

Managers need information on which to base decisions about the deployment of their staff. The personnel specialist can provide, for example, statistics on pay rates nationally, by industry or by occupation. Because of the increasing complexity of employment legislation, there is often a need for information on the interpretation of such laws by the courts as well as the detail of the law itself.

To become familiar with this categorisation of the roles and responsibilities of personnel specialists, you may find it helpful to talk to members of the personnel department in your own organisation or one with which you are familiar. Seek information on the tasks they are undertaking in their efforts to support managers. Can you categorise their roles in the way I have suggested? You may find this difficult since my categorisation of the work of the personnel specialist is not definitive. There will be overlap in particular cases between roles. For example, in the area of advice on employment legislation, there will often be little distinction between 'service' and 'consultancy'. At times one role will assume greater significance at the expense of others; for example, when the organisation is experiencing severe financial difficulties, pressure on indirect costs, of which a personnel department is one, may restrict the more creative aspects of the work of specialists, in particular those which here I have labelled, 'facilitator' and 'consultancy'. It is false to assume that personnel specialists should always operate in one particular way. Far better that those involved in personnel management recognise the potential variations in the specialist role and can diagnose what might be the optimum division of labour between specialists and line managers.

Exercise 1

Below are listed a number of activities carried out by personnel specialists. Into which category – audit, executive, facilitator, consultancy, service – does each fall?

1 Negotiating the introduction of a new grievance procedure with trade union representatives.

2 Running a workshop for managers on the skills of performance appraisal interviewing.

3 Checking that annual performance appraisal interviews have been carried out.

4 Discussing possible ways of improving a problem employee's attendance and timekeeping with the immediate manager.

5 Compiling and circulating labour turnover statistics to departmental managers.

6 Interviewing applicants for jobs in the computer department with the departmental manager.

1.4 Universal Good Practice in Personnel Management: A Myth for Students or a Reality for Practitioners?

Personnel management's central concern is the efficient utilisation of one of the resources available to an organisation: its employees. In this way, it can be equated with other functions of management – finance, production or marketing.

Some people would argue that personnel management is simply a collection of people-management techniques which can be used in all organisations. However, if you remember our discussion of the influences on the specialisms which exist within the personnel function, you will doubt the validity of this view. Unfortunately, although there are books which purport to provide answers to all problems of dealing with employees, there is little universal good practice in this area of management. Techniques which appear to assist in the effective utilisation of staff in one organisation may fail elsewhere. For example, where a company has a history of strikes, employees may react with hostility to managerial proposals on new working practices; where industrial peace has been the norm for years, and relationships between management and workers have been good, there probably would be much less distrust of identical proposals.

The ways in which business decisions are made affect personnel policies and practices. The latter are often an expression of senior management's values about the development and maintenance of the employment relationship and, as such, are major determinants of the organisation's 'culture'. Hence, no universal principles govern the formulation of personnel policies and techniques. However, there are certain basic headings and guidelines which together may be said to comprise personnel management. These usually include:

- recruitment and selection;
- training;
- performance appraisal;
- wage and salary systems and administration;
- employee relations;
- welfare and counselling.

Such activities may be the responsibility of a specialist department, or of managers or supervisors, or both.

The Institute of Personnel and Development (IPD) says that personnel management is that part of the management process concerned with:

> recruiting and selecting people; training and developing them for their work; ensuring that their payment and conditions of employment are appropriate, where necessary negotiating such terms of employment with trade unions; advising on healthy and appropriate working conditions; the organisation of people at work, and the encouragement of relations between management and work people.

No matter what the organisational context, it is always necessary for someone to have responsibility for the movement of people into, through and out of an organisation, if the human resource is to be effectively managed. However, the detailed organisation of such responsibilities, for example between managers or supervisors and specialists, and the specific techniques utilised will differ from organisation to organisation. This passage of people through organisations is the integrating theme of this book.

1.5 **Is Personnel Management a Profession?**

Personnel specialists have sought to become recognised as professional in the same way as members of other professions – law, medicine and accountancy, for example.

In the UK, much of this debate has centred around the role of the Institute of Personnel and Development (IPD), which has developed a rigorous and lengthy training scheme for entry to membership. Does this mean, therefore, that personnel specialists are professionals? Sociologists have examined the process by which occupational groups achieve professional status. A quotation will help us:

> Professionalisation might be defined as a process by which an organised occupation, usually but not always by virtue of making a claim to special esoteric competence and to concern for the equality of this work and its benefits to society, obtains the exclusive right to perform a particular kind of work, control, training for and access to it, and control the right of determining and evaluating the way the work is performed. (E. Freidson, *The Professions and Their Prospects*, London, 1973)

How does the work undertaken by personnel specialists measure up to such yardsticks of professionalism?

Firstly, personnel management is not the exclusive preserve of personnel specialists. It is undertaken by most managers as part of their role in managing employees. Personnel specialists do not exercise autonomy over their own work, which is determined for them by more senior management within the general framework of corporate goals. Personnel specialists may feel that they occupy the role of 'piggy in the middle', caught between the organisational goals of profit of efficiency and the needs of employees. However, when there is redundancy there is usually no doubt that the personnel specialist is part of the management team and must assist other managers in the efficient running of the organisation.

Secondly, the IPD's examination scheme, though well accepted both in industry and in higher education, does not regulate entry to the occupation in the way that medical, legal or accountancy training does. Indeed many personnel practitioners are not members of the IPD. A reasonable conclusion is that personnel management is not a profession; rather it has become a well-developed function of management.

Exercise 2

Which of these statements are true and which are false?

1 Personnel management is only undertaken by trained specialists. *True or false?*
2 There are textbooks which will tell intending personnel specialists or line managers everything they need to know about techniques which will lead to effective human resources utilisation in their own organisation. *True or false?*
3 It is possible to define personnel management under a number of broad headings concerned with the management of working people. *True or false?*
4 Though its status as a profession is in doubt, personnel management is a well-developed function of management. *True or false?*
5 There is no one best design for the organisation structure of a personnel department. *True or false?*

2 Planning for People in Organisations

The focus of this chapter is the techniques available to plan the process whereby people enter, move through and leave organisations, in accordance with the overall business objectives. Management's choice of a human resource strategy will depend on the values held by those in positions of power within the organisation. In most private-sector companies employment policies are usually geared to corporate goals of profit and growth. Here the planning of human resources becomes a search for those individuals who now and in the future will contribute most to the success of the organisation. By contrast some organisations have developed equal opportunities policies and practices. These have considerable implications for the planning of human resources in that they aim, over time, for the population of the organisation to come to resemble that of the local community which the authority serves.

2.1 What is Human Resource Planning?

A number of planning techniques have been developed to help managers answer the question: 'How many staff do we need both now and in the future?' By the end of this chapter you should be able to explain the main stages of human resource planning and should have an awareness also of the role of the personnel department in this.

Colin's Cars is a successful sports car manufacturer. Suppose that you are the member of the personnel department charged with assessing both the company's future demand for labour and its likely availability. Factors that you would need to investigate are listed below.

Factors influencing the demand for labour:
- The objectives of the company and its future plans.
- Market demand for the company's sports cars.
- The technology used by the company.
- The product range or numbers of models produced.

- The productivity per employee.
- The degree to which components are 'bought in'.
- The level of stock.

Factors influencing the supply of labour:
- Company policies in so far as they affect recruitment and selection, staffing levels, retirement and redundancy.
- The attractiveness of jobs in the company, including pay and other terms and conditions of employment.
- The skills available in the labour market.
- The price of houses in the locality.
- The age profile of the population from which the company draws its labour.
- Government legislation, for example on employees' rights.

Exercise 1

Why is the attractiveness of jobs in the company an important influence on the supply of labour?

We would need to know more about Colin's Cars and the state of the local and national economy to undertake a detailed staff planning exercise for the company. However, the company's demand for labour will be determined predominantly by the demand for its products. By contrast the demand for the services of the National Health Service can be considered to be almost infinite. Demand for staff by the NHS is determined predominantly by the level of government funding. The supply of labour to the NHS is influenced by the factors listed above. Through the NHS is a national employer, the ease with which individual health care authorities can attract and retain labour varies widely because of local labour market conditions. For example, house prices are higher in London and the South East than in the North. Even in such national organisations human resource planning must be undertaken locally as well as organisation-wide.

Some factors influencing the number of people available for work are short-term in character – the numbers of people currently seeking employment in the locality, for example; others are much more long term – changes in the birth rate or retirement age, for example.

Exercise 2

Can management control all the factors affecting the demand for and supply of labour?

Human resource planning: a summary

Human resource planning attempts to analyse likely influences on the supply of and demand for people, with a view to maximising the organisation's future performance.

Planning for people in organisations, then, involves trying to obtain:

- the right people
- in the right numbers
- with the right knowledge, skills and experience
- in the right jobs
- in the right place
- at the right time
- at the right cost.

It can be seen as an attempt to balance the demand for employees with the numbers available. However, it is not merely a 'numbers exercise' concerned with the *quantity* of human resources, it also involves issues related to the *quality* of human resources such as the requirements for training and development.

The process of human resource planning involves a distinct number of stages, which are shown in Figure 2.1.

Although the stages of the human resource planning process are shown in sequence in the diagram, stages 1 and 2, which involve an analysis of the organisation's past and present human resource on the one hand, and the corporate or business plan on the other, generally are undertaken in parallel. Other stages occur in sequence since each depends on adequate operation of the previous part of the process.

2.2 Stage 1: Analysis of Current Staff in the Organisation and Past Trends

To embark on the human resource planning process it is necessary to have certain 'key facts' about staffing in the organisation. These include:

- grade;
- job type, title or department;
- sex;
- age;
- length of service;
- skill or educational level.

Employers concerned to implement equal opportunity policies must collect this data by sex, ethnic origin and disability. Only when such information is available can the employment position of 'minority' groups be compared with that of other employees; barriers to their progression into more senior

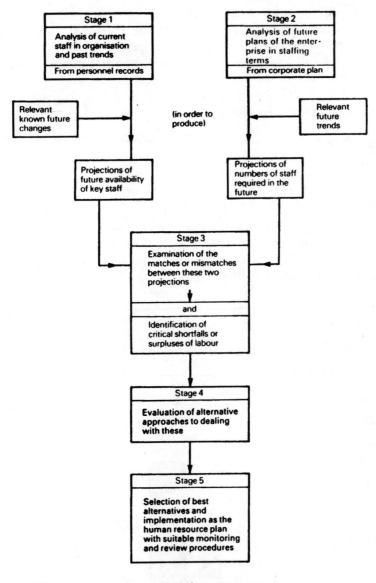

Fig 2.1   The human resource planning process

positions can be identified. In this way objectives for the achievement of equality of opportunity can be defined. On the surface this sounds very simple; in practice many employers have encountered difficulties, in particular with the collection of ethnic origin data because of the sensitivity felt by many employees of being categorised in this way. Further guidance on this issue is available from the Commission for Racial Equality.

Additionally statistics about the utilisation of labour, including labour turnover, working hours lost due to sickness and absence, the rate at which people are promoted and the productivity per person employed are needed. It is also helpful to analyse the ways in which these statistics have changed over the recent past.

Analysis of employees' age distribution

Exercise 3

Figure 2.2 shows the age distribution of pilots in Senior Airways in 1996. Pilots normally retire at 55. Examine the percentage of staff retiring in each year (scale 2). What is the problem for Senior Airways?

Age distributions can tell us something of problems due to retirements in the near future. An imbalance in the age structure also would exist if many people in senior positions were young.

Exercise 4

What are the human resource implications of this?

Fig 2.2   Age distribution of pilots in Senior Airways, 1996

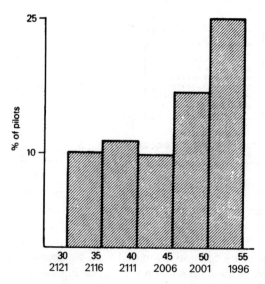

30	35	40	45	50	55	Actual age in 1996 (scale 1)
2121	2116	2111	2006	2001	1996	Retirement date (scale 2)

Analysis of length of service

The analysis of length of service also gives insights into the processes which underlie decisions by individuals to leave jobs or to stay in them.

Exercise 5

Figure 2.3 depicts the length of service of middle managers in Colin's Cars. From the graph you can see that middle managers are relatively new to their jobs. Why should this be a potential threat to the success of the company?

Analysis of labour turnover

If we analyse the behaviour of leavers in an organisation then we find that the shape of the length-of-service distribution for leavers (called the 'completed length of service' or CLS) takes the same shape in almost all cases.

Soon after the day on which the individual joins the organisation there comes an 'induction crisis'. The new employee has uncertainties about the decision to take the job. At this point, depending on a number of factors such as the availability of jobs elsewhere, a decision to leave may occur.

The induction crisis occurs anything from one month to two years after engagement, depending on such variables as the nature of the job and the organisation. If there is no severance, a period of mutual accommodation

Fig 2.3   Length of service of middle managers in Colin's Cars

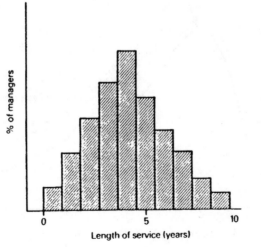

and adjustment goes on. Both management and the employee modify their expectations of the other. This period is given the term 'differential transit'.

A *second* induction crisis may occur from two to five years after the date of engagement. (It is often very small and sometimes may not occur at all.) In other words, after there has been mutual accommodation, there may still be feelings of concern. The new employee may have doubts about future job or career prospects or other aspects of work. Management may have concerns about the employee's performance. If this second induction crisis – the small peak – is surmounted, then the final period of 'settled connection' takes place during which the individual is much less likely to leave.

It is interesting to note that similar-shaped curves are obtained for most jobs or organisations, although the exact positions of 'X' and 'Y' in Figure 2.4 vary for particular organisations and jobs.

Other measures of labour turnover

Labour turnover index   Many companies use index measures of labour turnover, which express the number of leavers or 'stayers' as a percentage of those employed.

The labour turnover index is defined as:

$$\frac{\text{Number of leavers in a time period}}{\text{Average number employed during the period}} \times 100$$

Fig 2.4   The process of labour turnover

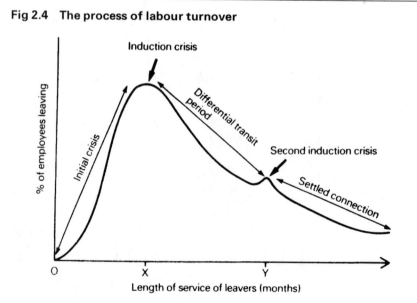

More accurately this might be referred to as an index of labour wastage since it is concerned only with the process whereby employees leave the organisation (wastage) and not with the leaving process and subsequent recruitment (turnover). You should also note that the choice of time period is left to the user (A year or a month is common.) The average number employed is usually the average of those employed at the end, i.e.

Average number employed =

$$\frac{\text{Number employed at start of period} + \text{number employed at end of period}}{\text{Total number of employees}}$$

Exercise 6

Lyttlewood Enterprises has 2350 employees at the beginning of January and 2450 at the beginning of February. During January 725 people left.
Average number employed in January = (2350 + 2450) ÷ 2 = 2400
What is the turnover index for January?

Labour stability index   Another index focuses on the stability of labour. The labour stability index is defined as:

$$\frac{\text{number of staff with more than } x \text{ periods of service}}{\text{number employed } x \text{ periods ago}} \times 100$$

It is customary to use this index for periods of one year.

Exercise 7

Smith's Supermarkets employ 250 staff of which 200 have more than one year's service. The business is contracting. One year ago they employed 300 people. To calculate the stability index, which figure would you put as the denominator of the equation?

Using the formula given above it is possible to calculate the stability index.

Stability index = (200 ÷ 300) × 100 = 66.6 per cent

Labour turnover and stability indices can be produced over time for any group of staff. You could choose to look at a particular department or factory, or at all the people employed on a certain job. The indices for such a group then can be monitored over time. Figure 2.5 shows a control chart which could be produced to monitor turnover. In this case it would be sensible to examine the reasons for the sudden and dramatic increase since October.

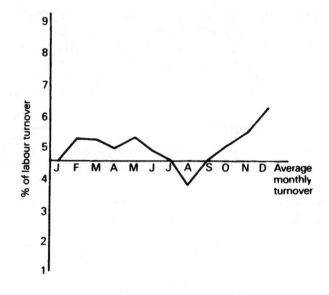

Fig 2.5   Control chart to monitor labour turnover

It is difficult to be certain of the causes of labour turnover. Often leavers are asked to complete a form giving their reasons for leaving, or an 'exit interview' is conducted. Psychologists have suggested that different reasons than those which are given for leaving cause people to look for other jobs. Figure 2.6 below shows a 'step model' for a sample leaver.

Exercise 8

In Figure 2.6 what was the *real* reason which caused the individual to look for another job? Was this the same reason as was given at the exit interview?

Fig 2.6   'Step model' for a sample leaver

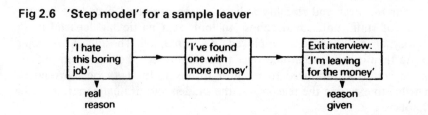

Despite the difficulties of ascertaining the 'real' reasons for leaving, it is useful to analyse labour turnover in this way. A useful classification is:

- dismissal;
- internal transfers (redeployment, promotion or demotion);
- death;
- sickness or ill-health;
- more money;
- more interesting work;
- pregnancy;
- domestic reasons (such as the move by a spouse to another area of the country);
- retirement;
- poor relations with a supervisor or workmates.

It is useful to see whether any patterns emerge amongst employees who leave.

Exercise 9

Suppose Smith's Supermarkets lost ten employees to Lyttlewood Enterprises within six months. What questions should senior management in Smith's Supermarkets ask?

This comparison process is important. Comparisons can be made within a company as well as with other organisations.

Other human resource information

Other analyses of staffing can help us monitor the results of employment policies. For example, in organisations where care is being taken to ensure that equal opportunities policies are put into practice, selection ratios by department or grade will be calculated to measure the proportion of applicants from ethnic minority groups, women and the disabled. Skills inventories can tell management about available staff skills, some of which may not be currently in use – for example, employees' use of foreign languages or computing skills.

Analysis of absenteeism and sickness using time-based ratios, such as:

- average number of days lost per year per employee, or
- number of spells of absence and their duration per year per employee

can be used to identify both 'problem' employees and 'problem' jobs or departments (by comparison with the average).

It also will be useful to compute the total number of working days lost per year due to absence or sickness for departments and for the organisation as a whole. This statistic, if computed annually, provides a useful monitoring device, which can be used to help shape policy either to reduce absence levels or, at least, to plan levels of staffing in such a way as to cause least disruption to services or production. It may seem odd to accept sickness or absence but, in some organisations, rates are as high as 5 per cent per day. To ignore these would result in intolerable disruption to service delivery or production.

Analysis of current staff and past trends: summary

The aim of this analysis in Stage 1 of the human resource planning process is to evaluate how many and what kinds of staff will be available in future. As a result a sort of human resource budget can be produced, as shown in Table 2.1.

Table 2.1 **Human resource budget of social workers, 1996**

Social workers in post 1996	84	
Expected leavers 1996–7 (10%)		8
Retirements (early)		1
		9
Net social workers available	75	
Sickness (5%)	4	
Staff available for work	71	

2.3 Stage 2: Analysis of the Organisation's Future Plans in Human Resource Terms

Exercise 10

Is it true that this stage of the human resource planning process cannot be carried out until Stage 1 has been completed?

At this point we need to ascertain:

- what the organisation's future plans are; and
- what these plans mean for the numbers of staff required to carry them out.

Here we are concerned with the corporate or long-range plans which set the scene for the organisation over a three- to five-year period. Many organisations have planning systems, while others improvise as they go along. All that is needed is some statement of work output in quantitative terms. For example:

- 'sales will be £1,000,000'; or
- 'outpatients will be 25,000 per annum'

The difficulty of corporate planning is the main reason for the problems associated with this stage of human resource planning. Corporate conditions are very volatile; any forecast, no matter how well it interprets business change, future productivity levels or social influences on the organisation, will be subject to the recessions or booms of the world economy.

The task of the human resource planner is to translate corporate plans into statements of workload and thence into numbers of employees required. There are techniques which assist the accuracy of this process.

Ratio-trend analysis

This is the easiest technique since it assumes that the relationship between the level of production and the number of people employed will remain roughly constant in future. It is a crude, though sometimes useful, method. That is, the relationships measured may change in future. There may be economies of scale as output increases; technological change is likely to increase productivity per employee. Suppose a clerical worker can handle 500 inquiries per month and there are 2,500 each month. This suggests that five staff would be employed. However, if you were computerising the system of dealing with inquiries, you might expect a 20 per cent increase in efficiency. This would mean that only four staff would be required. Such factors have to be considered carefully for each individual case.

Work study on organisation and methods (O & M) techniques in planning demand for human resources

A refinement of ratio-trend human resource demand forecasting uses work study and organisation and methods techniques. The output or sales forecast is converted into a production schedule in the way suggested above. This is then broken down into department-by-department, function-by-function or job-by-job work schedules for the period concerned.

To achieve this involves the analysis of a job into its component parts through the observation of the performance of a number of workers. An allowance is made for their different speeds of working in order to arrive at a standard time, to which are added allowances for relaxation or recuperation. In this way a forecast of the required staffing levels for various job categories can be derived.

Often organisations have specialist O & M or work study departments which can gather the information needed to use this method of human resource demand forecasting. The detail of these techniques is outside the scope of this book.

Activity sampling is a quick cheap method of producing standard data on which to base forecasts of future demand for staff. Sampling of the activities of a number of workers is continued until the observer feels that a representative sample has been achieved.

Generally the application of these techniques involves:

- the collection of data about the exact nature of the work being done;
- measurement of this work and examination of the methods used to seek improvements;
- comparison of work output between departments, and with other organisations where relevant.

Assessing future staffing levels using work measurement techniques is a very worthwhile exercise for repetitive jobs with a high degree of manual content which does not change frequently.

Managerial judgement in planning demand for human resources

It may be unrealistic to assume that the relationship between output or sales and the number of people employed will remain constant in the future.

Exercise 11

In your organisation, who might be able to guess with a reasonable degree of accuracy the number of people who will need to be employed on particular types of work in future?

Managerial judgement is not without its dangers as a basis for human resource planning. Managers may not be objective; some may be 'empire builders'; Therefore the result could be overstaffing. One useful method is for top management to prepare planning guidelines for departmental managers, possibly acting on the advice of personnel or other specialists. Managers can be told to think about some of the following:

- replacements for retirements, leavers, transfers and promotions;
- possible improvements in production;
- redeployment of existing manpower;
- planned changes in output levels;
- planned introduction of new methods and equipment;
- planned reorganisation of work;
- the impact of changes in employment law or collective agreements.

2.4 Stage 3: Analysis of the Matches or Mismatches between Human Resource Supply and Demand Forecasts

The results of the two previous stages of planning the human resource process can be represented in tabular form.

We now will consider ways of dealing with the mismatches, considering the two cases – shortages and surpluses – separately.

To decide whether or not a projected shortage of staff was critical to the achievement of the corporate plan you would need to answer the following two questions:

1 Is the work undertaken by the staff who are likely to be in shortage critical to the organisation's future success?
2 Does the gap between supply and demand get wider or narrower as we get further into the future?

We can define 'critical skills' as follows:

- A skill or job where recruitment is expensive or difficult.
- A skill or job where training or retraining of existing staff is impractical or costly.
- A skill critical to the effective functioning of the organisation; for example, salesmen in insurance brokerage, or pilots in airlines.

Then we need to see whether there is a clear trend in the development of staff shortages: that is, whether the projections increase or decrease in a regular pattern each year. We also need to see whether the absolute magnitude of the numbers is striking. Generally this would be the case if the shortage or surplus was more than about 10 per cent of the total staff employed. In the example for the hospital porters the small numerical shortage is 20 per cent of the total number of porters employed and there is a clear trend. It is necessary to look at strategies to deal with such mismatches.

Here we have discussed an example of a labour shortage. All too often these days the results of human resource planning reveal that the organisation will have a future labour surplus.

Table 2.2   **The difference between demand for and supply of hospital porters 1989–92**

Job category	Porters	1989	1990	1991	1992
Estimated demand		25	30	35	40
Estimated supply		20	17	15	10
Difference		−5	−13	−20	−30

2.5 **Stage 4: Evaluating the Options**

If there are likely to be too many staff in a given work area you would have to consider these options:

- Natural wastage.
- Redundancy (voluntary and compulsory).
- Redeployment (including training, if needed).
- Early retirement.
- Dismissal.
- A freeze on future recruitment.
- Part-time working or job-sharing.
- Elimination of overtime.
- Move to more labour-intensive methods or new products.
- Search for additional or new work.

If there were too few staff the options would be:

- Recruitment.
- Redeployment.
- Promotion or demotion.
- Extension of the contracts of those about to retire.
- Use of freelance, agency or temporary staff.
- Overtime.
- Productivity bargaining.
- Automation or the elimination of jobs.
- Increase capital investment to increase productivity (for example, by the introduction of new technology).

As you can see, there are a number of strategies to deal with each case of projected labour shortage or surplus. It is important to take into account the particular nature of the organisation, and of the environment in which it operates, before embarking on a strategy. Here is an extract from a document which evaluates the voluntary redundancy option where a future surplus of staff is projected. First the advantages of this strategy are assessed.

Voluntary redundancy: the options for Mike's Manufacturing

Advantages
1 Avoids compulsory redundancy.
2 Therefore should be acceptable to the trade unions (i.e. the company has a policy of 'no compulsory redundancy' with the recognised trade unions).
3 Will not subsequently damage the ability to recruit.
4 Voluntary redundancy agreement with trade unions already exists.
5 Therefore compensation payments for those who leave are already agreed.

6 Therefore scheme would be quick to set up and administer.
7 Likely that 5 to 10 per cent of staff will apply. This is within the target identified from the forecast of future staff surpluses.
8 Therefore this would give rapid reduction in wage costs.
9 Would allow some recruitment, when necessary.
10 No moral obligation to retrain or place staff who decide to volunteer for redundancy.

Before examining that part of the document which assessed the disadvantages of this strategy, here are a few comments on the use of the voluntary redundancy option. Many companies, when faced with surplus staff, use a strategy which combines natural wastage with a freeze on recruitment.

Exercise 12

If a freeze is placed on recruitment, turnover invariably falls. Why is this? (Look at the labour turnover section again).

Natural wastage, together with a recruitment freeze, may cause certain departments to suffer dramatically, and affect work capacity. Careful monitoring and control are necessary to manage the process.

The use of dismissal as a strategy for dealing with staff surpluses may seem an odd choice but overstaffed companies often 'toughen up' on offenders as a means of reducing staff. In these cases care must be taken to ensure that the unfair dismissal legislation is not breached Chapter 15, pp. 202–14.)

The move to labour-intensive methods may also seem strange, but one hi-fi manufacturer with surplus craftsmen modified a product to be hand-finished (raising the price accordingly) and thus improved productivity.

Taking on additional work is another ploy. A firm of travel agents introduced related services such as travel insurance and travel goods as a way of more effectively using staff.

Voluntary redundancy: the options for Mike's Manufacturing

Disadvantages
1 Only the good staff may decide to leave.
2 Some departments or units may be depleted.
3 Costly option, since agreed compensation payments are greater than those laid down in legislation (see Chapter 1).
4 It is not absolutely certain how attractive the scheme is to employees.

5 Difficulties of dealing with staff who volunteer for redundancy whom the company does not wish to lose.

Most of these points are self-explanatory. However, the option of raising retirement age (in selected cases) may need a little more discussion. An airline with pilot shortages did this, and obtained an average of three to five years' additional service from them. This gave a breathing space to train replacements.

Voluntary redundancy: the options for Mike's Manufacturing

Conclusions and Recommendations
Invite applications from employees for discussion purposes and the collection of data. Then make a more rational decision, based on better information on 'take-up' and costs.

Examining the possible solutions for human resource problems and analysing them carefully is a creative and exciting process which often pays dividends. It should be emphasised that what works in practice will depend upon the nature of the organisation.

Core or peripheral workforces?

A number of writers have questioned the idea that an organisation should directly employ all, or even most of its labour force. This is not a new idea. Sub-contracting work and labour has always been a feature of industry. Recently it has taken a new form. For example:

- Communications technology has reached the point where it can be inefficient for a company to pay for high office overheads when employees can work and communicate from their homes.
- Concentration on the main 'core business', where an organisation will decide to put some or all of its support services out to tender.
- The creation of a flexible workforce, employed on annual hours contracts which allows companies to flex production according to the pattern of demand for their goods and services.

The Transfer of Undertakings Regulations (discussed in Chapter 12) has tended to limit the possibilities of contracting out services to save money, which has been a feature of public services, such as local government and the National Health Service. Instead companies have begun to examine 'market testing' as a way of improving the quality of part of the business or the service they offer, by entering into a contracting relationship with another company which can do it better. Examples include a major rental company which contracts the whole of its computing needs to a specialist computer company, or a major computer company which contracts all its financial accounting services to a firm of accountants.

2.6 Stage 5: Selection of Best Alternatives and Implementation as the Human Resource Plan, with Monitoring and Review Procedures

The strategies most likely to assist the organisation to achieve its corporate plans should be written up as the human resource plan and analysed and costed in more detail. Clearly, like the corporate plan itself, it is based on assumptions or estimates which subsequently may prove wrong. Some of the scepticism about the value of human resource planning has arisen because of the failure to monitor trends, check assumptions and treat the plan as a flexible document not as a 'tablet of stone'.

The best way to consider a human resource plan is perhaps as a scenario or picture of what is felt to be likely to happen in the future based on the best evidence today. To operate without some kind of planning of human resources is at best risky and at worst destructive for the organisation in any kind of competitive or resource-limited environment. Therefore it is important that personnel specialists demonstrate its value. To do this, identify a problem relevant to the organisation which is capable of being investigated with available data, techniques and expertise. If the results of the exercise are presented to those who can act on its conclusions, the value of the contribution of human resource planning to the resolution of real business problems will become apparent and will emphasise the necessity to utilise it more widely.

Fig 2.7   Human resource planning – monitoring and review procedures

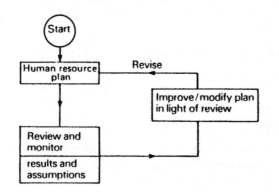

3 Recruitment and Selection

In this chapter we concentrate on the process of matching the characteristics of individuals to the demands of jobs. This is the purpose of recruitment and selection. As in other areas of personnel management you will find that unfortunately there are no easy prescriptions for success. Much depends on the knowledge and skills of those involved, whether line managers or personnel specialists. In addition, as you should recall from earlier in the book, any personnel technique needs to be relevant to and effective within the context of a particular organisation. Towards the end of the chapter you will be encouraged to examine how you might evaluate the effectiveness of recruitment and selection in an organisation.

3.1 How to Start

Suppose you opened a shop and decided that you needed an assistant. Before attempting to recruit someone to fill the position, you would need to answer these questions:

- What job do I want to be done?
- What kind of person do I think will do it most effectively?
- How can I find some people who might be suitable to fill the vacancy?
- What methods should I use to decide which one would best fit my requirements?

In broad terms the stages to be followed can be expressed as:

- defining the job to be done;
- defining the characteristics of the ideal candidate;
- attracting candidates;
- selecting candidates.

Before examining each in more detail it is necessary to emphasise the importance of good selection. 'Square pegs in round holes' are not conducive to effective or efficient management.

In the 1930s, when queues of unemployed people waited at the factory gates for work, foremen would choose, 'You, you and you'. Since then recruitment and selection techniques have developed in ways which help to give a better basis for decision-making. However, predictions about other people are subject to error. All recruiters run the risk of making mistakes.

Recruitment and selection must also be fair. Equality of access to jobs regardless of race, sex or disability is underpinned by legislation on the rights of prospective employees (see Chapter 5). While equal opportunities policies and practices are desirable on ethical grounds, they also contribute to effective employment practice: unfair discrimination reduces the number of potentially suitable candidates, thereby increasing the effort and the cost of recruitment.

3.2 Stage 1: Defining the Job to the Done

You might find it useful to draw a flowchart to assist you to define the steps necessary to complete this stage effectively. It should resemble Figure 3.1.

The need to link the early stages of recruitment and selection with the human resource planning process cannot be over-emphasised. When an employee leaves there is an opportunity to assess whether the job needs to be done at all or whether the work usefully could be reorganised.

Job analysis

The tasks which comprise the job must be analysed. This process is known as job analysis. The main steps involved are:

- identifying the tasks involved in the job;
- examining how, when and why tasks are performed;
- identifying the main duties and responsibilities of the job;
- noting the physical, social and financial conditions of the job.

Job analysis is a technique which generates basic information about the nature of tasks undertaken by employees. It can be used in many areas of personnel work. Five such areas are:

- Appraisal (see Chapter 7).
- Training systems (see Chapter 8).
- Payment systems (see Chapter 13).
- Job evaluation (see Chapter 13).
- Disciplinary interviews (see Chapter 15).

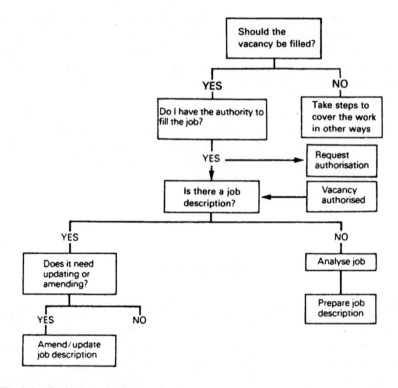

Fig 3.1   Defining the job to be done

Using job analysis you should be able to define the overall purpose or the role of the job in the organisation and the main tasks which the incumbent must carry out.

Management should ensure that clear, concise and accurate job descriptions are available for every position from that of the most senior executive to the most junior clerical worker. Where jobs require contact with the public or supervision of other staff, it is useful to make explicit the implications for post-holders of other human resource policies. For example:

> The job holder must carry out the tasks detailed above in compliance with the Company's equal opportunities policy.

Accurate job descriptions are the basic building blocks on which advertisements, interviews and other aspects of fair selection are constructed.

Here is a job description for the post of assistant children's librarian.

Greenfields County Council

Libraries Department

Job title: Assistant Children's Librarian.

Responsible to: Assistant Librarian (Children's and Schools' Services).
Purpose: To assist in the effective provision by the Council of children's and schools' library services.

1 General duties
    1.1 Undertake such professional duties as may be required by the Assistant Librarian (children's and schools' services).
    1.2 Assist in the promotion of the use of the library service and reading with young people and parents.
    1.3 Participate in children's book selection and reviewing.
    1.4 Assist with the organisation of in-library activities as may be directed by senior children's and schools' library staff.
    1.5 Participate in the activities of the schools' library service.
    1.6 Undertake duties at any of the Council's libraries as directed by the Assistant Librarian (children's and schools' services).

2 Staff
    2.1 Control and supervise the work of non-professional staff in the absence of senior colleagues.
    2.2 Assist with the promotion of effective on-the-job training.

3 Resources
    3.1 Display a professional interest in current resources appropriate to the Childrens' Schools' Services and submit suggestions for additions to stock through the Senior Children's Librarian.
    3.2 Assist readers in the effective use of library resources.

4 Contacts
    4.1 Assistant Librarian Children's and Schools' Services, Senior Children's Librarian.
    4.2 Teachers.
    4.3 Playgroups and play scheme organisers and staff.
    4.4 Children and parents.

5 Work origin
    5.1 Children and parents.
    5.2 Teachers.
    5.3 Senior Children's and Schools Services library staff.
    5.4 Playgroups.
    5.5 Parents' associations.
    5.6 Other departments and groups interested in work with children.

6 Work disposal
Same categories.

7 Circumstances
The post-holder will be located at the main library in the centre of Blanktown. There are also seven branch libraries in the surrounding district. The job holder will be required to work at these branch libraries from time to time.

You would find it useful to work through this job description to assess whether it gives all the information required to begin the recruitment and selection process. If you do this you will find that some information is lacking. Many local authorities have equal opportunities policies and therefore some reference to the need to ensure that efforts are made to meet the needs of children from all sections of the community would be a likely addition to the job description. Also, though we are told that the job holder reports to the Assistant Librarian (Children's and Schools' Services) we do not know to whom this latter employee reports. In section 5.3 of the job description we are told that the tasks to be undertaken by the incumbent of this job may originate from 'Senior Children's and Schools' Services staff'. However, we do not know how these positions are related to the one described here. An organisation chart to show the staffing of the libraries would be helpful as a supporting document. In addition the 'circumstances' section is rather vague. What are the hours of work? What are the main features of the libraries service? Since the next stage of the process involves the development of a pen picture of the ideal candidate for the job, it would be useful to have an idea of the context of the job and of its non-material rewards.

Thus, the 'circumstances' section might continue as follows:

7.1 *Working conditions*. Old main library. Small offices. Post-holder will share an office with the other Assistant Children's Librarian.

7.2 *Supervision received*. No close supervision. Main check is absence of complaints from originators of work.

7.3 *Consequences of error*. Receivers of service may be unaware of full range of services provided; delays in supply of books and teacher difficulties in schools may result.

7.4 *Difficulties*. Growing volume of work and enquiries. Pressure on schools' service in particular because of financial constraints on schools' ability to purchase new books.

7.5 *Satisfaction*. Interactions with children, young people and other users.

To be useful, job descriptions need to be full and accurate reflections of work done. A key task for personnel specialists and line managers is to ensure that job descriptions are regularly updated.

Exercise 1

List six features of an effective job description.

As organisations come to place more emphasis on the need for flexibility to meet continually changing business demands, there is a need to ensure that job descriptions are not overly rigid thus reducing rather than increasing the potential of staff to respond to changes in job requirements.

3.3 Stage 2: Defining the Ideal Candidate

Having prepared a job description for the vacancy under consideration, we now need to match the characteristics of the job with the characteristics of candidates who may apply for it. In order to undertake this process satisfactorily, we need a picture of the ideal candidate. Such a picture is called a 'person specification'. The aim of the person specification is to define the knowledge, skills and experience required to successfully execute the tasks summarised in the job description. Hence criteria listed in the person specification must be related strictly to job requirements. Decisions about candidates' suitability must be based on an assessment of their characteristics as compared with those laid out in the person specification.

Here is an example of a person specification for a personnel officer specialising in the recruitment of professional and managerial staff:

Job title:	Personnel Officer–Executive Recruitment	
	Essential	Desirable
Physical make-up	Well dressed Clear speech Articulate Good general health	
Attainments		
Education	Degree or equivalent qualification	Member of the Institute of Personnel and Development
Training	Selection testing course	
Job experience	Three years' experience of recruitment selection and more general aspects personnel work	Work in a similar industry/ organisation
General intelligence	Good verbal reasoning ability Logical thought Ability to analyse candidates' skills, etc. and relate these to job requirements	Good numerical ability
Specialised aptitudes	Good oral and written communication skills	
Interests	Evidence of some non-work related interests	Social activities

Job title:	Personnel Officer–Executive Recruitment	
	Essential	Desirable

Disposition		
Acceptability	Able to get on well with people of many different backgrounds Empathy with the requirements of the equal opportunity policy	
Independence	Able to make decisions within the recruitment budget	
Influence	Able to convince managers of the value of systematic and fair recruitment and selection methods	
Objectivity	Able to make sound judgements about job applicants	
Circumstances	Free to spend occasional nights away from home Clean driving licence	

This specification is based upon Rodger's Seven-Point Plan. (Professor Alec Rodger, *The Seven-Point Plan*, National Institute of Industrial Psychology, 1952.)

The 'Seven-Point Plan'

1 Physical make-up – health, physique, appearance, hearing and speech.
2 Attainments – educational and occupational attainments and experience.
3 General intelligence – ability to reason quickly and accurately, to learn quickly and to handle complex ideas.
4 Specialised aptitudes – manual dexterity, mechanical aptitude, verbal or numerical facility, artistic aptitudes.
5 Interests – intellectual, practical and constructional, physically active, social and artistic.
6 Disposition – personality characteristics such as steadiness and self-reliance, acceptability to others, relationships with others.
7 Circumstances – domestic circumstances.

Many organisations use this framework to assist in the systematic delineation of the myriad of requirements, which may comprise the profile of the ideal candidate for the job. However, those concerned with the implementation of equal opportunity policies must scrutinise the framework provided by the plan as well as the detailed content of any personnel specification to ensure that all requirements specified for entry to a job are relevant to the demands of effective job performance. It is common to express experience requirements in years, as in this example. This may be indirect discrimination against female candidates whose 'track records' are broken by periods of child-rearing. To guard against this it would be helpful to indicate what the good candidate would have been doing during those three years. If this can be done only in very vague terms, then the odds are that the requirement is invalid. Indeed, it may be preferable to avoid the use of the 'job experience' heading altogether relying on the specification of the knowledge and skills of the successful candidate.

The 'circumstances' heading may be likely to lead to unfair discrimination. Employers may be tempted to exclude candidates with family responsibilities. The yardstick must be the requirements of the job. In this case it is not unfair to stipulate that candidates must be able to spend occasional nights away from home, if this is vital to effective job performance.

A further danger, when writing a person specification, is that it may be expressed in the writer's own image or as an expression of the perceived characteristics of a previous successful incumbent. This is particularly dangerous where minority group members are very unlikely to have held the job previously – black sales representatives or female maintenance engineers, for example.

Many of those involved in recruitment and selection argue that the 'desirable' and 'essential' columns of a personnel specification are necessary in order to distinguish between those features of candidates deemed absolutely essential and those which provide the 'icing on the cake' which the employer is likely to be able to find within a pool of job applicants at times of labour surplus. While this may be a sensible aid in sifting large numbers of applications, it is more within the spirit of an equal opportunity policy to specify only the essential attributes of the successful candidate, since these should be easy to justify with reference to core job demands.

As we shall see in Chapter 5, the law does not give the disabled the same rights as ethnic minorities and women in the area of discrimination in access to jobs. However, fair employment practice should include the review of person specifications for potential discrimination against this group. Sadly there is an implicit tendency to assume that all suitable applicants are able-bodied. It is important to check that job requirements are strictly job-related. For example, a requirement that applicants must have high manual dexterity because the job involves the manipulation of objects may lead selectors automatically to reject disabled applicants. However, many such people have found ways to minimise the effects of their disability and may be able to cope well. Also it may be possible to overcome such requirements by obtaining special tools or equipment on permanent loan to that individual from the Disablement Advisory Service.

A good piece of guidance to those writing person specifications is that they should be as precise as specifications for machinery.

3.4 Stage 3: Attracting Candidates

Having written a person specification, it is necessary to encourage some people to become applicants.

Possible sources of applicants for jobs can be categorised as:

- Internal advertisements or analysis of personnel records.
- External advertisements.
- Employment agencies – private or public.
- Schools, colleges or other institutions providing training courses.
- Casual callers or writers of letters.
- Recommendations from existing employees.

Exercise 2

Equal access to jobs is a fundamental principle of equal employment practices. Which two of the sources of applicants listed above are likely to involve breach of this principle?

Internal advertising and its effect on the implementation of an equal opportunity policy needs very careful attention. For example, many organisations employ large numbers of women in secretarial and clerical jobs. These are likely to be 'cul-de-sac' jobs from which promotion is unlikely. By contrast relatively few women are employed in highly graded professional, managerial or technical occupations. Is it then more appropriate as part of equal opportunity policy implementation to advertise for these more senior posts internally or externally? A decision on this should be made only after a detailed analysis of the workforce and of relevant personnel practices.

Advertisements

As well as advertisements in the published media, employers use radio, television and computerised information systems such as teletext. Here we are concerned with the principles of effective recruitment advertising. These can be established by answering the following questions.

Where am I likely to find potential candidates?

You need to know where candidates are likely to be currently working or undergoing education or training, and where they live. Some candidates will be found in the local labour market, because their skills can be used by many employers; those who occupy specialist positions are part of a national labour market. There would be little point in a local solicitor advertising for a typist in a national newspaper!

How can I attract them to work for me?

A useful way to answer this is to put yourself in the candidate's shoes. What would be the attractions of this particular job? For example, imagine that you are a sixteen-year-old school leaver thinking of applying for a job in a supermarket as a checkout operator. The details you would require before accepting the job would be likely to include:

- Earnings (including any bonus).
- Perks, e.g. discount on goods, overalls, canteen, other staff facilities.
- Hours of work.
- Holidays.

Other information which you may like to have would include:

- Company name, size, location, etc.
- Conditions of work, rush hours, quiet times.
- Training.
- Promotion prospects.
- Job security.
- Notice periods.

Designing a recruitment advertisement is a marketing exercise in which the preferences of potential candidates should be compared with the features of the job (taken from the job description). Those aspects which are most likely to appeal can be emphasised.

If there are significant problems in recruiting candidates who equate to the requirements of the personnel specification, it is useful to consider the specific advantages and disadvantages of the job to identify the selling points. Additionally it is helpful if a recruitment advertisement obtains a brief profile of the ideal applicant.

There are no prizes for writing advertisements which attract the largest possible number of candidates. The aim should be to recruit the right quality of candidates. If the characteristics of the ideal candidate are succinctly expressed, then only suitable candidates are likely to apply. This should cut out some of the wasted effort involved in responding to a vast number of applicants, most of whom are unsuitable or marginal.

Five attributes of an effective advertisement are:

- A compelling headline.
- Interesting content.
- Clear, unambiguous information about the job and the likely candidate.
- Information on how to apply.
- Eye-catching design and typography.

External recruitment agencies

Several options are open to organisations that choose to use an external agency for recruitment purposes:

- government employment agencies – in the UK, the Job Centre or Professional and Executive Register (PER);
- private employment agencies;
- selection consultants to provide a shortlist of candidates;

- executive search consultants or 'head-hunters', who will contact suitable candidates direct;
- advertising agencies to design and place advertisements.

Some of these options can be expensive. selection consultants can charge up to 20 per cent of the annual salary of the job to be filled. However, those who use them often argue that they are cost-effective.

If employment agencies are used, their sources of applicants should be questioned as well as the ways in which they undertake initial screening to ensure that unfair discrimination does not occur through their actions.

Exercise 3

List six factors which influence the choice of a recruitment channel or source of applicants.

3.5 Stage 4: Selecting Candidates

Again it is useful to draw a flowchart for this stage of the recruitment and selection process, as in Figure 3.2. Variations are possible depending on the requirements of the organisation. For example, medical examinations may be used for older applicants, where jobs are particularly physically demanding and where safety is vital (e.g. airline pilots). In other cases medical history questionnaires are often sufficient. A further area of difference may be that of references. The important point to gain from the exercise lies in the design of a systematic assessment process.

Exercise 4

What objective is the employer trying to achieve in the selection process?

Shortlisting

For many jobs it is possible to eliminate the majority of candidates without even seeing them. Letters of application, *curricula vitae* and, above all, application forms can be used as screening devices. Letters of application and *CV*s are less likely to be vague if the advertisement is specific about the nature of the job and the person required to perform it; nevertheless, there are usually more problems in matching information thus received from applicants than if it is presented on a well-designed application form.

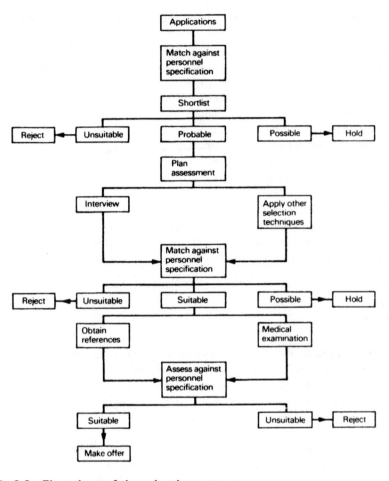

Fig 3.2   Flowchart of the selection process

By now you should be used to the notion that recruitment and selection techniques should be designed with an eye to the nature of the job and of the organisation. An application form is no different. For reasons of cost and simplicity most personnel practitioners find it adequate to use three or so basic types of form – for manual workers, routine non-manual jobs, and professional and managerial occupations.

You may find it useful to look at job advertisements in your local newspaper and to telephone a few organisations for application forms. Three types of information which all forms require are:

- personal details – name, address, date of birth, etc.;
- education;
- job history or work experience.

Other details may be required depending on the type of job and organisation.

Applicants must be asked only for personal information which is directly relevant to job requirements. Questions about marital status, numbers of children or place of birth are potentially unfairly discriminatory against women or members of ethnic minorities and should not be available to selectors. However, such data are needed to monitor the implementation of equal opportunity policies (see Chapter 2, pp. 12–13). To cope with the possibility of conflict here, many employers ask job applicants to complete a detachable slip describing their gender and ethnic origin. This is treated as confidential and separated from the rest of the application form prior to the consideration of candidates.

Care should be taken to ensure that the application form is not used as part of the selection process in an unfair manner. If literacy is a requirement of the job, this should be made explicit. Form-filling skills should be required only where they are job-related.

Interviewing

Nearly all selection procedures involve an interview, a fact that seems to be accepted or tolerated despite research evidence which casts doubt on both the reliability and the validity of this selection method. The interview provides many opportunities for stereotypes and prejudices to be used by selectors. The behavioural characteristics of the interview are summarised in Figure 3.3.

Distortions of perception are particularly likely when interviewing people of different social background, culture or gender. Since their roots are likely to be deep in the selector's psyche, they are likely to be difficult to eradicate. However, being aware of the nature of such psychological processes should be helpful.

The prevalence of race discrimination in selection may be related to the immediate visibility of the candidate's colour and the negative response of many interviewers to this. Similarly, black candidates and women (where the selector is male and white) are unlikely to benefit from the 'assumed similarity effect' where an interviewer establishes common ground with the candidate in certain ways and generalises this to other areas. This may be a particular problem for women and black people seeking to enter areas of work where in the past they have been few in number. Stereotyping involves assigning candidates to a class or category and then assuming behaviour characteristics associated with that group. For example, a belief that women are unreliable or black people dishonest is likely to lead to the categorisation of such individuals and their consequent rejection.

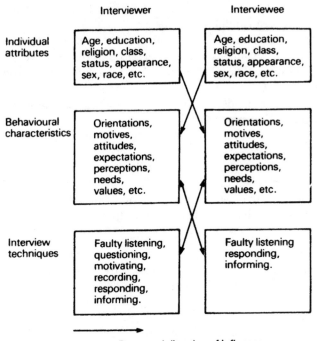

Fig 3.3   **The behavioural characteristics of the interview**

Basic guidelines to help interviewers avoid unfair discrimination in selection include:

1 All questions must be clearly related to job requirements (as described in the person specification).

2 Questions about family commitments or marriage and family plans should not be asked since they are likely to discriminate unfairly against female applicants.

3 Questions should not be asked to test ethnic minority candidates' understanding of UK customs or to check their fluency in English unless these are bona fide job requirements.

4 Where a job involves necessary unsocial or irregular hours, the full facts should be presented to all interviewees. Assumptions should not be made about the likelihood that women are less able to cope with the working hours. All candidates should be asked whether they have understood the requirements and will be able to conform to them, if appointed.

5 Interviewers should be trained on the effects which generalised assumptions about race or gender or marriage can have on selection decisions together with the relevant legal requirements.

6 Interviewers must keep interview notes, in order to make a fair comparison between candidates.

7 Reasons for rejection and selection both at the shortlisting stage and after interview must be recorded for later incorporation into the selection-monitoring process. These also should be available to candidates if required.

8 Performance of individual interviewers should be monitored by themselves and the organisation to ascertain the degree to which particular selectors are likely to select or reject 'minority' group candidates.

9 Attention also needs to be given to the less formal aspects of selection. Minority group candidates may be disadvantaged by lunchtime sessions in the pub aimed at the assessment of the candidate's social prowess. This is likely to be exacerbated if discussion at that time focuses on leisure interests.

These guidelines are merely a pointer to good interview practice, emphasising that equal opportunity policies provide a framework for the development of good personnel practice.

Questioning techniques
'Effective interviewers ask good questions.' This is one of the most important interviewing skills.

Open questions
One of the key purposes of selection interviewing is to elicit information to enable the candidate's characteristics to be matched against the personnel specification:

- 'Why did you apply for this job?'
- 'Why did you choose that course?'

Closed questions
These are questions to which the only answer can be, 'Yes', or 'No' or 'I don't know'. They may be used to check information or to get a definite response quickly. Effective interviewers ensure their use is restricted. An interview which relies heavily on these is rather wooden. A further danger is that such questions may push the candidate into false polarisations. For example the question, 'Did you enjoy your college course?' may provoke the answer, 'Yes', where the reality could be more complex. More garrulous or helpful candidates may expand the answer without prompting but the interviewer should be aware that control of the interview is being relinquished.

Probing questions
Sometimes the candidate's answers will lack depth or clarity: 'I left that job because I felt the career prospects were non-existent.' A probing question

following this might be: 'Why do you say that?' or 'What kind of career development did you want?' Sometimes the response to such a question will be slow. The interviewer should not rephrase the question or help the candidate in any other way. The time taken to reply probably indicates that it is an effective probing question.

Multiple questions

If the interviewer had asked both my probing questions at the same time this would have been a multiple question. These are faulty since the candidate can choose which question to answer. Again the interviewer is in danger of surrendering control of the situation.

Linking questions or statements

An interview should be a conversation with a purpose. One useful way of achieving this aim is for the interviewer to indicate, after completing a particular area of questioning, that it is time to look at another topic: 'Now that we've discussed your work experience, can we have a look at your activities outside work?'

Leading questions

These should be avoided in selection interviews since they are likely to feed the interviewer's own prejudices and desire to confirm early impressions: 'We are anxious to appoint someone who is good at dealing with the public. You'd be all right there, wouldn't you?' What fool is going to deny this?

Problem-centred questions

You may wish to gain an impression of the likely response of the candidate to particular situations: 'Could you tell me about the most difficult customer you had to deal with, when you were doing that Saturday job?' Such questions are very useful if relevant to the job in question and they can realistically be answered by the interviewee.

Discriminatory questions

These are illegal under anti-discrimination legislation (see Chapter 5) since they indicate an intention to discriminate on grounds of sex, marital status or race. Managers should ensure that all questions are job related: 'Are the hours required by this job likely to cause you any problems?'

Indirect questions

If candidates are asked 'Do you get on with other people?' control of the interview is being passed to the interviewee. It is probably better to ask about relationships with fellow workers or friends or for information on behaviour in particular circumstances. The interviewer can judge the applicants' relationships with others.

Exercise 5

Below is a list of questions which might be asked in a selection interview. What kind of question is each one? Could they be rephrased in any way for greater effectiveness?

1 'Did you leave school in 1969?'
2 'Did you get your professional qualification in 1973 and then decide that it was time to get a better job?'
3 'What made you decide to become an architect?'
4 'You said that you disliked your first job. Why was that?'
5 'I see that you spent three years working in West Africa. That'd be long enough for anyone, wouldn't you say?'
6 'What would you do if your spaceship crash-landed on the moon?'
7 'How good are you at making difficult decisions?'

Stress interviews

These attempt to simulate the stress generated by the job situation in order to assess whether the candidate would be able to cope. Some interviews for managerial positions are structured in this way. The problems of validity and reliability discussed earlier lead me to be sceptical about this approach. Indeed, with some candidates, they may be counter-productive. A friend of mine was shown into an office for an interview. Behind a desk sat a man obscured from sight by the newspaper he was reading. My friend waited. Presumably there was an attempt to create stress by the ambiguity of the situation. My friend was immensely irritated and left. Would he have been suitable for the job? Could an interviewer make an accurate judgement from his reaction to this situation? I doubt it?

Interview structure

To establish rapport early in the interview, it is useful to start the questioning in the candidate's 'home territory', for example asking for a description of the most recent job. Many experienced interviewers say that they have difficulty in ensuring that they always cover all the relevant ground during an interview. A checklist based, for example, on the headings of the 'seven point plan' or of the personnel specification is helpful. This may then form a basis for the interview structure. Details about the job can be given after obtaining information about the candidate. Time should be allowed for questions from the candidate.

Panel interviews

In the public sector in the United Kingdom, it is common to use panel interviews where a candidate faces several interviewers at once. Opinions differ as to whether these are more or less valid than one-to-one interviews. Broadly, the following principles should be observed:

- All participants should have a genuine claim to be involved.
- All interviewers should be skilled and experienced.
- Proper planning and co-ordination is vital.
- It is probably better to use a 'tight' structure, where each interviewer takes a particular role.

The don'ts of interviewing

Interviewers should not:

- keep the interviewee waiting;
- interview without systematic preparation and planning;
- allow the interview to be interrupted;
- ask trick, leading, multiple or discriminatory questions or too many closed questions.
- lose control of the interview to the interviewee;
- fail to give the candidate information about the job;
- take copious notes during the interview;
- display bias or prejudice;
- talk too much (probably not more than one-third of the interview time);
- allow the candidate to gloss over important points.

This list is not exhaustive and some of the points overlap.

Selection testing

Selection tests are used to provide a standardised, reliable, objective measure of applicants' skill. The evidence suggests that, properly used, they are of considerable value in predicting job performance.

Tests of capacity

Some jobs require the use of specialist skills. For example, aptitude tests have been devised to test the capacity of potential computer programmers. Manual dexterity tests are used to suit the demands of various jobs. These often consist of timed runs on work samples. Other tests of capacity may be more general. For example, many tests are concerned with mental agility. Other tests of capacity have been devised to measure clerical, mechanical and spatial abilities. The degree to which a candidate possesses a particular aptitude can be discerned by comparing test performance with norms for the relevant occupational group.

Tests of personality and attitude

These are the most controversial psychometric tests. It would be of enormous assistance to the personnel practitioner if valid and reliable tests were readily available to support interview data. This is not the case. Some tests show considerable promise but require highly developed interpretative skills.

Recently tests have had to be carefully scrutinised to ensure that they are not biased against minority groups. This poses some significant technical problems to the test constructor, especially where the test is to be applied to newcomers to a country or to those brought up within a community of different culture to that of the host society. Hence a decision to use tests should be very carefully taken. Claims of direct or indirect discrimination from ethnic minorities or women may be upheld by industrial tribunals if it can be proved that the test contains culture or gender bias which is not justified by job requirements (see Chapter 5).

Four situations in which it might be useful to use selection tests are:

- When large numbers of people must be recruited.
- When as a consequence of the numbers involved the use of tests would be cost-effective.
- When it is impossible to rely on educational qualifications as a predictor of job success.
- When sufficient time is available to validate the tests on the particular occupational group for which the test has been designed.

Assessment centres

Among the characteristics which neither the interview nor some pyschometric tests can assess accurately are candidates' social skills, including leadership ability. To meet this need, assessment centres have been developed as an attempt to simulate all or part of the job and the observe candidates' reactions to it. The origins of assessment centres lie in the War Office Selection Boards developed during the Second World War because of the need to select soldiers from the ranks for officer training.

The term 'assessment centre' is generally used to cover the assessment of a group of individuals by a team of judges using a comprehensive and integrated series of techniques, such as psychological tests, interviews and simulation exercises. Several assessors (usually senior managers specially trained in assessment skills) are used to assess the degree to which participants appear to possess dimensions of performance defined as significant in managerial positions in the organisation. A major use is the selection of employees for development.

Typically an assessment centre consists of:

- A leaderless group exercise in which candidates are given group tasks to undertake in a given time, for example the planning of a conference or the relocation of a factory. Assessors sit outside the group making notes on participants' behaviour. Attributes for assessment include assertiveness, influence and leadership. Sometimes this activity takes the form of a business game in which participants in teams must operate at a profit in a given market. Sometimes teams compete.

- A report-writing exercise in which participants, again under time pressure, write a report on their own jobs or on some other aspect of the business. Characteristics assessed include written communication skills, breadth of understanding and logical development of ideas.
- An in-tray exercise consisting of a sample of problems which a manager might find on his desk on a bad day. The aim is to test the ability to work under pressure, to delegate and to analyse and solve problems.

Other common elements of assessment centres include oral presentations, interviews and psychological tests of ability and personality.

To decide what activities to include in an assessment centre you would have to take into account such factors as:

- the characteristics of the job for which participants are being selected;
- the size of budget to run the assessment centre;
- the number of trained assessors available.

Characteristics tested during assessment centres

A detailed and accurate personnel specification is an essential prerequisite of an assessment centre. The activities to be included should be designed to test the characteristics of the ideal candidate laid down in this specification. For example, it would be futile to include an oral presentation if such a skill is not a requirement of the job. Where candidates are being chosen for development rather than immediate promotion, it will be necessary to take account of this in selecting dimensions for assessment. Frequently, as we saw above, activities can be chosen which test more than one dimension.

The cost of assessment centres

Assessment centres are not worth doing unless done well. The costs involved include the time of those who design and run the centre as well as those who train the assessors. These can be considerable since assessment centres usually last from two days to a week and involve one assessor for every two or three candidates. In addition external consultants are frequently hired to design and oversee the process.

Assessor training

Assessors should be:

- familiar with the jobs for development to which candidates are being considered;

- committed to management development and to the use of assessment centres as part of this;
- prepared to give sufficient time both to training as assessors and to involvement in assessment centres.

Training is vital. Managers do not generally possess the skills of recording and reporting verbal and non-verbal behaviour. In addition they must develop common definitions of assessment dimensions and of associated rating scales. Training usually involves assessors doing the exercises as assessees and discussing ratings. They also may observe assessment centres.

The development value for senior managers who act as assessors can be considerable: they are likely to take improved interviewing, observation and assessment skills back into the workplace.

The developmental value of assessment centres
At the end of the assessment centre, assessors pool their judgements. The centre may be used simply to accept or reject candidates. More often it is a basis for the counselling of participants as an aid to the planning of their career development. Hence, participation can be of developmental value: for example, assessees can get a better understanding of what a manager does and of the qualities needed to be a successful manager. Through the assessment centre they learn about their strengths and weaknesses and become better equipped to make more informed career development decisions.

Reliability and validity of assessment centres
Research indicates that assessment centres, if well designed and well run, are better predictors of future job performance than interviews alone.

References

Reasons for the use of references in selection include:

- To supplement information elicited by the use of other selection methods.
- To check the veracity of the candidate's statements.

In practice this area is fraught with problems. Applicants are unlikely to name referees who will indicate their unsuitability for a job. Some people suggest for this reason that references from a previous employer, who is less likely to gloss over the problem areas, should be used. Will this always be so? Probably not. Some employers will simply lack awareness of the job. The more unscrupulous may deliberately mislead, by writing either a glowing reference about an employee they wish to lose or an unfavourable one about an employee they wish to retain.

Three ways in which references may be made more reliable are:

- Ask a previous employer for factual information only (dates of employment, job title, reason for leaving, etc.).
- Check doubtful information by telephone.
- Provide a structure or short questionnaire for the referee to follow.

3.6 The Follow-Up Process

Once the candidate has started work, those involved in recruitment and selection are tempted to heave a sigh of relief and turn to other problems. This is unwise. Two types of follow-up system should be designed:

- individual follow-up or induction (see Chapter 4);
- evaluation of the recruitment and selection process to ensure that mistakes are avoided in future.

Evaluation procedures

It is necessary to evaluate the effectiveness of the recruitment and selection process:

- To seek improvements in policies and procedures.
- To calculate costs. Recruitment and selection are an expensive part of personnel management practice.
- To provide feedback into human resource planning. For example, it may be difficult to fill certain jobs; this will require questions to be answered about the nature of the jobs and of the people required to perform them.
- To ensure that unfair discrimination is not taking place.

Rigorous evaluation of the effectiveness of procedures will provide useful information. However, it must be emphasised that this is a difficult exercise. An example will indicate some possible reasons for this. If a company recruits graduates and a large proportion leave within a year, where does the fault lie? In the recruitment and selection process? In the training programme? In the nature of the tasks they are required to perform? In the salaries paid? Or may the reason be demand for their skills elsewhere in the labour market? Evaluation will need to be in depth rather than a superficial analysis only of recruitment and selection procedures and practices.

On p. 28 at the beginning of this chapter, we defined the recruitment and selection process as consisting of four stages:

- defining the job to be done;
- defining the characteristics of the ideal candidate;
- attracting candidates;
- selecting candidates.

Procedures need to be designed to evaluate each stage, such as the following questions:

Stage 1   Is the job description an accurate representation of the tasks which the job holder performs?
Stage 2   Is it possible to recruit candidates who match the personnel specification's description of the ideal candidate?
Stage 3   What is the cost of recruitment advertising as a proportion of the annual payroll? (Costs in different years and in the same year in different departments will be useful.)
Stage 4   How do assessors' judgements at the time of selection compare with candidates' actual performance in the job?

Evaluation of recruitment and selection by obtaining the answers to such questions is a very useful way to get a 'feel' for the validity of the whole process.

3.7 **Managerial Roles in Recruitment and Selection**

In Chapter 1 we discussed the respective roles of personnel practitioners and other members of management in personnel management.

Exercise 6

List five terms which we used there to describe the role of personnel specialists in the management of people at work.

Recruitment and selection activities of personnel specialists can be described in terms of five general roles. An example from each area is listed below:

Audit   Checking to establish that job description supplied by managers reflect the true nature of the tasks.
Executive   Placing advertisements in the local or the national press.
Facilitator   Ensuring that line managers and other involved in recruitment and selection have the necessary knowledge and skills to play their part in this activity effectively.
Consultancy   Advice to managers on selection decisions.
Service   Providing managers with response rate data on recruitment advertising to enable joint decisions to be made on the most effective way to attract a pool of applicants.

4   Introducing the Individual to the Organisation

4.1 What is Induction?

In this chapter we focus on the new employee's early 'life' with the organisation. This process of entry to jobs is commonly termed 'induction'. By the end of this chapter you should be familiar with the methods of helping employees to cope with a new job in a strange organisation. However, it is also important that you understand the reasons for giving attention to this stage of employment.

Studies have shown that where attention is given to induction the rate of labour turnover among new employees is lower. The existence of what has been termed the 'induction crisis' gives us a rationale for the development of techniques which aim generally to ease the entry of the individual into the organisation (see Chapter 2, p. 16).

Ways of reducing the effects of the induction crisis

- Get better information about candidates during recruitment and selection. This should improve selection decisions.
- Give candidates better information about the job on offer. To some degree people select themselves for jobs. This may include information which will cause candidates to withdraw or to refuse an offer of employment, should one be forthcoming. Some advertisements for social workers, for example say: 'What to be run off your feet, overworked, under-appreciated?... Then join our busy team.' In this way new recruits at least know what to expect.
- Be honest about training and career development. Some organisations have a tendency to over-glamorise the opportunities on offer. For example, one organisation I know have, in the past, given graduate entrants a very generalised impression of an international career with rapid progression from one job to another in the early years. Recently, they have been much more explicit about the roles which graduates can

expect to perform during the first five years of their employment. This should ensure that there is less of a gap between expectations and reality.
- Improve the induction process. (This is covered later in this chapter.)

Should the induction crisis be eliminated?

Many organisations which are resourceful in 'tying people to the organisation with golden chains', such as low-cost mortgages or non-contributory pension schemes, then regret the absence of turnover. Labour turnover does have positive aspects for the organisation. For example, it:

- Allows new blood into the organisation.
- Eliminates 'dead wood'.
- Creates opportunities for promotion.
- Reduces labour costs. Often employees who leave are near the top of the salary scale; new appointees start lower down.
- Creates flexibility for restructuring of work.

4.2 **The Induction Process**

The aims of the induction process are:

- To make the new employee efficient as quickly as possible.
- To encourage the new employee to become committed to the organisation and thus less likely to leave quickly.
- To familiarise the new employee with the job so that the feeling of being 'out of place' is quickly dispelled.

Those who have worked in organisations for some time forget what it felt like to be new. They take for granted their ways of working, the language they use at work and the accepted ways of dealing with colleagues, superiors, subordinates and clients. Departments, committees and other working groups are frequently referred to by initials.

Recently I have been involved in an organisation with an 'IR' group. My own background led me to believe that this was an 'industrial relations group'. I was wrong! 'IR' in this case stood for information retrieval' – very confusing to the newcomer! Another example of the 'taken-for-granted' nature of organisational life comes from some research I did in the hairdressing industry. A new trainee in a high-class salon was asked by a stylist to buy some sandwiches for an important client from a neighbouring snack bar. She returned with them in a paper bag and gave them to the client, not realising that this was unacceptable behaviour. Someone who 'knew the ropes' would have transferred the sandwiches to a plate before delivering them! Her embarrassment at this and other incidents led her to seek other employment.

From such stories as these you should realise the importance of giving attention to the induction process. New employees usually want to do a 'fair day's work for a fair day's pay'. They want to be accepted by their colleagues and to feel generally comfortable in the organisation and in their job. Management wants workers who will quickly become efficient and committed. The aim of the induction process is to meet the needs of both parties in a mutually acceptable way.

Though this aim is probably universally applicable, induction programmes must be designed to fit the characteristics of the job and of its organisational context. For example very small companies are unlikely to organise formal induction courses or to give employees printed handbooks. Nevertheless, attention should be given to the types of information required by the new employee.

Imagine that you are a receptionist at Brown's Hotel. It is your first day. What questions would you want to ask today as part of the process of becoming familiar with your job and the company for which you work? Possible questions might be:

- To whom do I give my income tax form, birth certificate, work permit, or any other information which my new employer requires?
- Do I have to sign in when I arrive for work each day, and if so, where?
- From whom do I collect my pay and when?
- Where do I eat my lunch and at what time?
- Do I get a coffee or tea break? When? Who relieves me?
- Where are the toilets and washing facilities?
- Whom do I need to meet to do my job effectively – my boss, heads of departments in the hotel, etc.?
- Where do I go or whom do I ask for help, if I cannot answer telephone or other queries?
- How do I operate the hotel switchboard, the word processor and any other equipment necessary for me to perform my job efficiently?

Whether you would need answers to all these questions depends on the information given to you during selection and your familiarity with similar work.

To summarise, on the first day it is necessary to ensure that new employees:

- do not feel lost or foolish;
- do not endanger themselves or other people because they are not given vital safety information.

Provided that this is done, there are no other hard-and-fast rules about this stage of the induction process. It is generally unwise to communicate a great deal of information orally to new employees at this time. The stress of the first day in a new environment can be equated with 'culture shock'. The danger is that little will be remembered. It is wise to provide written 'back-up' to vital information communicated orally, for this reason. An employee handbook containing the following information is useful:

- Brief description of the organisation – numbers employed, locations, products, etc.
- Basic conditions of employment – pay scales, holidays, pension arrangements, hours of work.
- Sickness arrangements – notification, pay, certification.
- Disciplinary and grievance procedures.
- Trade union membership and collective bargaining arrangements.
- Staff purchase arrangements and other 'perks'.
- Travelling and subsistence arrangements.
- Medical and welfare facilities.
- Canteen facilities.
- Health and safety arrangements.
- Education and training policies and facilities.

This list is by no means exhaustive. The content of employee handbooks varies depending on such organisational characteristics as numbers employed, jobs performed and managerial policies and practices. Handbooks need not be glossy and should be written clearly and concisely with the information needs of the employee as the focus.

4.3 **Induction for Senior Staff**

It is not only ordinary staff who benefit from systematic induction to an organisation. Senior managers, and even directors, may also experience feelings of lack of belonging and disorientation on joining a new organisation. Employee handbooks may contain some information which is of limited relevance to these people. However, this is no excuse for neglecting the process by which such people become members of an organisation. They may have the competence to fulfil the demands of the job. However, particularly where people come from different organisational cultures, they may find it difficult to 'fit in'. For example, many senior private-sector managers have found entry to senior roles in the public sector very problematic. Some have never been accepted and valued by colleagues and have left under a cloud.

4.4 **Induction Training**

Many organisations run induction courses as a formal mechanism for the induction of new employees.

Exercise 1

What three factors would the personnel manager of Brown's Hotel have to take into account in deciding whether or not it would be useful to design a formal induction training course?

Content and timing of induction training courses

If it is decided that such a course might be beneficial to some or all new employees, careful attention must be given to content and timing. A good starting point is: What does the new entrant want to know and when? The needs of new entrants differ considerably. For example, new members of management probably require more detailed information about organisation structure, policies and practices than will more junior clerical staff or manual workers. There are probably disadvantages in arranging for new employees to attend off-the-job induction courses too early. Initially it is likely that they will be keen to familiarise themselves with the immediate requirements of the job which they are to perform. However, in a relatively short time they should be ready to know more about the organisation in which they work.

Suppose that, as the training officer for Happy Days, you have been asked to design a one-day induction programme for new employees of Brown's Hotel. The programme could include:

- The structure of the Happy Days Group and of Brown's Hotel.
- Tour of the hotel.
- Pay arrangements, including sick pay and holiday arrangements.
- Company employment policies.
- Training and promotion practices and opportunities.
- Open forum. (Any questions?)

Having sketched out a design for an induction programme, it will be necessary to ensure that it fits the needs of new employees. One way of doing this is to run one or more 'pilot' courses which are carefully evaluated by both trainees and others with a direct interest in the area. (For further information on methods of evaluating training programmes see Chapter 8.)

Attention should also be given to the training methods utilised to convey information to new employees. These usefully could include:

- Film or videotape.
- Tape/slide presentation.
- Written handout supplemented by question and answer session.
- Lecture.

Departmental induction

A more informal induction process is probably just as important as a training course. For the new employee it may be far more important, at least in the initial stages of employment with an organisation, to get to know one's colleagues and the nature of one's job, than to be given more general information about the employing organisation. In a large organisation it is likely that the personnel or training department will carry responsibility for the formal part of the induction process, but line managers and supervisors should not abdicate responsibility for the less formal process. The importance of paying attention to the early period of a new employee's 'life' with an organisation should be stressed to line managers. Far too often, in my experience, new people are left to 'find their own feet', spending time reading documentation or aimlessly wandering around trying to get information. Little wonder that many go through an 'induction crisis'! New employees should at least be welcomed by their departmental manager even if – as commonly occurs – the immediate supervisor is mainly responsible for introducing the new employee to the job and to workmates. In small companies where it would not be economic to organise a formal induction course, it is even more vital that someone (probably the supervisor) is responsible for introducing each new employee to the organisation. A checklist of items to be covered would be a useful aid to ensure this is carried out effectively.

4.5 Roles in Induction

Line managers, supervisors, fellow workers, personnel and training staff all have a role to play in the induction of new workers. One activity which may be carried out by each of these is listed below:

Departmental managers: Welcoming new employees to the department.
Supervisors: Explaining the job to the new employee and providing support during the initial period.
Fellow workers: Making the new employee feel welcome and comfortable in the work group.
Personnel staff: Explaining conditions of employment very early in the employment of the newcomer.
Training staff: Designing induction courses or other training aids relevant to the needs of new employees.

4.6 A Final Word

Throughout this chapter we have stressed the need to design induction procedures with the perspective and needs of the new employee in mind. To ensure that this has been achieved it will be useful to review systematically the experiences of newcomers and other relevant employees (for example, supervisors, training and personnel specialists) in order that unsatisfactory elements can be changed. Many organisations do not do this; there is a plethora of film and video material about organisations which is either too remote from the newcomer's likely experience or so facile that it leads only to mockery! New employees might be prepared to voice such criticisms if only they were asked to speak!

5 The Law and the Rights of the New Employee

In order to be able to work within the law so far as employment is concerned you must understand the basic framework of the English legal system. Therefore we begin this chapter with an examination of the legal framework of employee rights in the UK. This is also a vital 'building block' for the work that you will do in Chapters 12 and 15. The rest of this chapter focuses on the ways in which the law influences the rights of the new employee. We shall examine relevant areas of the law on race and sex discrimination, the rights of trade unionists, the disabled and those who have been convicted of crimes. This is followed by a discussion of the rights and obligations of employers and employees when there is a contract of employment between them.

In the area of employment law, it is normally sufficient for managers to be aware of the main *statutory* provisions. This book can merely scratch the surface in this area; it is not intended to turn you into a lawyer. You should be aware of the limits of your knowledge if you are called on to make decisions which might affect employees' legal rights, and should be prepared to ask for specialist advice.

Four sources of such assistance are:

- Your organisation's personnel department.
- The Advisory, Conciliation and Arbitration Service (ACAS).
- Advisory services run by consultancies or professional bodies such as the Institute of Personnel and Development.
- A regularly updated employment law case book.

5.1 The Legal Framework of Employees' Rights

Employment law contains provisions relating both to collective bargaining, or the rights of employees as trade unionists, and to the rights at work of individual employees. In this book we are concerned mainly with the latter area.

Employees' legal rights are not only created by Acts of Parliament or statutes. They come also from case law. The English legal system can be distinguished from that of most other countries by the extent to which judges and tribunals are bound to follow the decisions of judges in higher courts unless they feel that the facts of the previous cases were substantially different. For this reason such judgements are called case law. Thus, in making decisions, members of tribunals and judges are bound by decisions made in higher courts; this is known as 'judicial precedent'.

The role of ACAS in individual rights legislation

The Advisory, Conciliation and Arbitration Service automatically receives copies of all individual legal claims to tribunals except those which are concerned only with redundancy compensation. Normally employees must make claims within three months of the occurrence of the event which forms the basis of their complaint. ACAS has specialist conciliation officers to assist in employment law cases. Often this official contacts the parties or their representatives and tries to help them reach a settlement before the case goes to a tribunal. Suggestions made at this stage are based on experience of the likely outcome if the case goes to a tribunal. About half the cases raised by employees result in a settlement at this stage.

Industrial tribunals

If conciliation fails, the case will go to a tribunal. Tribunals which are organised on a regional basis consist of a legally qualified chairman and two 'side members', representing the two sides – employers and employees – of industry. These are selected from a panel drawn up by the Secretary of State for Employment from nominations from the Trades Union Congress, the Confederation of British Industry, the Department of Employment and other bodies. In practice nominees often have trade union, personnel management or other relevant work experience.

Tribunal procedure is relatively informal. Employees are often represented by trade union officials and employers sometimes use legal representatives. Tribunal decisions do not set precedents in making decisions. Tribunals are bound by decisions of higher courts but not of other industrial tribunals. They do not normally award 'costs' in favour of the winning party, though they may do so where one party has acted 'frivolously or vexatiously'.

Appeals against tribunal decisions

If there is an appeal on a point of law against the Tribunal's decision, the case will go to the Employment Appeal Tribunal (EAT) and hence to the Court of Appeal and ultimately to the House of Lords and the European Court if the case touches on an aspect of European law.

The Employment Appeal Tribunal was established in 1975 specifically to deal with appeals from industrial tribunals and other aspects of labour law. As compared with other courts of law, its procedures are relatively informal, but it has all the powers of the High Court. On each case heard, there will be a judge and normally two lay members drawn from a panel of people with specialist knowledge of industrial relations.

Figure 5.1 charts the progress of an individual's claim against an employer for unfair dismissal, race or sex discrimination or for breach of any other employment right on which tribunals have jurisdiction.

In recent years the European Community (EC) law has had an increasing impact on UK employment issues. Proposals for European legislation are based on the principles of the Articles contained in the main EEC treaty, the Treaty of Rome 1957. In general, the legislation seeks to develop these principles, some of which provide for the health and welfare of employees, that were agreed by member states and are the means to create a framework for achieving a common market. The main instruments for developing these principles are Directives. These are the equivalent of Acts of Parliament for the Community's member states.

EC law is the supreme law in the Community, and where there is a conflict between UK law and Community law, the latter prevails. This means that it is possible for cases to be appealed to the European Court of Justice (ECJ), a fact which the House of Lords recognised in 1989, when it ruled that UK courts are under a duty to follow the practice of the ECJ and that they must give a purposeful construction to European Directives. Rulings of the ECJ are binding on the Community's member states. This means that decisions about a case in one state will apply to similar situations throughout the community.

5.2 **The Law and the Rights of Job Applicants**

Job applicants are protected from discrimination by employers on the grounds of:

- sex;
- marital status;
- colour;
- race;
- ethnic or national origin
- disability.

The main statutes here are the Sex Discrimination Acts 1975 and 1986, the Race Relations Act 1976 and the Disability Discrimination Act 1995, which came into effect in December 1996.

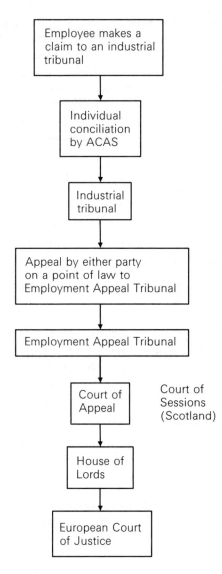

Fig 5.1   The possible progress of an employment law case from inception

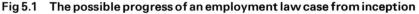

In Northern Ireland employees must not discriminate against job candidates on religious grounds, most specifically because they are catholics or protestants (Fair Employment (NI) Act 1989). More generally, the Employment Act 1990 requires employers not to discriminate against job applicants on grounds of either membership or non-membership of a trade union.

A great deal of detailed guidance on sexual and racial discrimination is given in the Codes of Practice published by the Commission for Racial Equality and the Equal Opportunities Commission. While failure to meet the requirements of these Codes is not directly actionable in law, individuals can cite relevant sections of the Code as evidence of bad management practice. Disabled people are similarly protected from the end of 1996 by the Disability Discrimination Act. Detailed guidance on discrimination against disabled persons is provided in the Code of Practice published by the Department of Education and Employment.

5.3 **What is Discrimination?**

Three kinds of discrimination are defined in law.

(1) **Direct discrimination**

Suppose you saw a notice board like this advertising vacancies outside a factory:

**BLOGGS ENGINEERING LIMITED
VACANCIES**

JOINER
HGV CLASS 1 DRIVER
UNIVERSAL MILLER

BLACKS AND WOMEN NEED NOT APPLY

You would probably be very surprised, since such overtly discriminatory behaviour tends to be unacceptable today. Indeed, such a notice is illegal in that it indicates that Bloggs Engineering Limited intends to treat black and female applicants for jobs less favourably than other people. That is direct discrimination.

(2) **Indirect discrimination**

WANTED HOSPITAL PORTERS

Applicants must be able to pass an
English language test and lift very
heavy objects

ST FLORENCE'S HOSPITAL

How would this advertisement fare under the anti-discrimination legislation? It could be argued that it is indirect discrimination; that is, the job requirements specified may favour one sex or racial group more than another. This would be the case if:

- the proportion of people of a particular racial group or sex who could comply with the job requirements specified was considerably smaller than the proportion of people outside those groups; *and*
- St Florence's Hospital could not justify the conditions.

In this example the hospital would need to demonstrate that it was necessary and not merely convenient for porters to speak English to the standard required by the test. Previous cases have shown that employers cannot automatically justify on health and safety grounds the non-selection of applicants who speak poor English. Of course, staff must be able to understand safety instructions and safety notices, but is the testing of applicants' proficiency in English the *only* way of ensuring that the requirements of the Health and Safety at Work Act are met?

Exercise 1

How else could St Florence's ensure that their porters could understand safety instructions and safety notices?

Is it also indirect discrimination, this time against women, to require applicants to lift heavy weights? This would depend on whether it could be proved that fewer women than men could meet the test of strength laid down by the hospital for entry to the job. If this was the case, then St Florence's would have to demonstrate that the nature of a porter's job required applicants to be able to lift the weights specified. Entry requirements must be justifiable and not merely convenient.

(3) Victimisation

The third type of discrimination outlawed by the legislation is where employees are treated less favourably by their employer on the grounds that they:

- brought proceedings;
- gave evidence;
- assisted the Commission for Racial Equality or the Equal Opportunities Commission;
- made allegations against the employer in good faith under the anti-discrimination legislation.

Segregation

The Race Relations Act also makes it illegal to segregate workers on racial grounds. Segregation by sex is not specifically prohibited.

5.4 Coverage of the Anti-Discrimination Legislation

The Sex Discrimination, Race Relations and Disability Discrimination Acts apply to all aspects of employment. In this chapter we examine in detail only their relevance to recruitment and selection decisions.

Recruitment

Employers must not unlawfully discriminate against potential employees in any of the following ways:

- in the general arrangements for filling a vacancy: for example, a supervisor should not tell a personnel officer to recruit 'a man to replace Tom';
- in deciding who to appoint to fill a vacancy: for example, by rejecting or omitting to consider applications from members of ethnic minorities;
- in offering different terms and conditions of employment depending on the sex or race of applicants: for example, by offering women lower rates of pay than men;
- by not holding the selection interview in a room which is accessible to a person in a wheelchair, when it was known that an applicant used a wheelchair.

The most obvious effect of the Sex Discrimination Act in particular has been in the field of recruitment advertising. This is because of the requirement in the legislation that there should be nothing in the wording of advertisements to suggest that jobs are open to some groups and not to others.

Selection

The method of filling vacancies can be discriminatory. As indicated in Chapter 3, p. 36, word-of-mouth recruitment has been legally tested and found to be a form of indirect discrimination.

Exercise 2

Why is word-of-mouth recruitment a form of indirect discrimination?

Since many potential employees approach organisations by telephoning or calling in 'on spec', it is important that personnel department secretaries, receptionists and other employees in 'gatekeeping' roles understand their responsibilities in law.

Interviews are likely places for discriminatory behaviour. In Chapter 3, p. 41–2, we have drafted some guidelines which aim to promote fair interviewing practices.

Indirect discrimination in recruitment

One of the most important cases so far has been *Price* v. *Civil Service Commission.* The case related to the age barrier of 28 for direct entry into the Executive Officer grade of the Civil Service. Belinda Price was 36. She claimed that her exclusion was indirect discrimination on the grounds of sex. Far fewer women than men could comply with this condition since, at this period of their lives, many women are out of the labour market while raising children. It was accepted that it was desirable for the Civil Service to ensure that a proportion of external candidates entering the Executive Officer grade was drawn from the lower age groups to maintain a balanced career structure, but it was held that there were alternative, non-discriminatory ways of achieving this.

Genuine occupational qualifications (GOQs)

It is quite lawful to look for workers of a particular sex or racial group in order to fill well-defined jobs.

When being a man or a woman is a qualification for the job
An example of a GOQ here would be lack of separate sleeping arrangements or toilet facilities where the job requires employees to 'live in' and it would be unreasonable to ask the employer to provide alternative accommodation.

Exercise 3

List four further examples of job where sex is a GOQ.

Where race is a genuine occupational qualification for the job
The principles here are the same as outlined above. An example would be a waiter in a Chinese restaurant.

It is up to management to justify the existence of a GOQ, if it is challenged by someone who feels unreasonably excluded from a job as a result.

Other groups protected from discriminatory recruitment decisions

The Rehabilitation of Offenders Act 1974

Under this Act an individual is allowed to 'wipe out' some 'spent' offences after a specified period. Depending upon the sentence imposed, a conviction for an offence is said to be spent between six months and ten years after the offence was committed, provided that no further serious offence was committed during the rehabilitation period. Potential employees in the position need not normally disclose their spent conviction when applying for a job. However, this is not the case for doctors, dentists, opticians, vets, nurses, midwives, health or social workers, teachers, lawyers, legal clerks, accountants, policemen, probation officers or traffic wardens.

5.5 The Contract of Employment

Once the employer makes an offer of employment to an individual and this is accepted, a contract of employment comes into existence. This need not take the form of a written document, though it is customary for it to do so. The details of the contract are known as its terms and conditions. A contract of employment can be seen as an exchange of work for wages. For it to be a legal exchange, neither party should feel that they made the contract under duress and each should be free to enter into it. A contract of employment would lack legality, for example, if a boss threatened physically to harm a potential employee who refused an offer of employment. Also, if either side misrepresented themselves prior to the contract being agreed, the contract would be invalid. For example, if an applicant claimed to possess a qualification specified for entry to a job and subsequently this proved not to be so, the employer would be legally justified in dispensing with her/his services.

Every employer has a legal obligation to provide its employees with a written statement setting out the main particulars of the employment within 8 weeks of the commencement of employment. Since November 1993 these have been as follows:

- The name of the employer and employee.
- The place of work or if the employee is required to work at various places, an indication of this, and the address of the employer.
- The date employment began.
- Where employment is not permanent, the period for which it is expected to continue or, if it is a fixed term, the date when it is to end.
- The scale and method of pay and the intervals at which it will be paid.
- Any collective agreements which directly affect the terms and conditions of employment.

- Any terms and conditions relating to hours of work.
- Holiday entitlement, including public holidays and the ways in which holiday pay is accrued.
- Sick pay and the procedures for reporting sickness.
- Pension arrangements.
- Length of notice which employee and employer must give.
- The title of the job for which the person is employed.
- Disciplinary rules and the procedure.
- The grievance procedure.
- Details of additional pay and benefits to those working outside the UK and any terms and conditions relating to their return to the UK.

In addition, the Trade Union Reform and Employment Rights Act 1993 requires employers to put certain of these terms and conditions – i.e. names of employer/employee; date employment commenced; rate and intervals of pay; hours of work; holiday entitlement and place of work – into a document called 'the principal statement'.

Moreover, whilst an employer may refer employees to the documents for details of sick-pay arrangement, pension rights, collective agreement and disciplinary and grievance procedures, these must be readily accessible to be read in working hours.

The significance of the written statement

The written statement is not a contract of employment, although it is often believed to be so. As said earlier, the contract is the existence of a relationship between employer and employee and it need not be in writing. However, employees who do not receive a written statement within 8 weeks of their engagement, or who receive particulars they believe are incorrect, can take the matter to an industrial tribunal for an order that the employer provide one. The written particulars are important to both parties, since either could experience a serious disadvantage in the courts if a legal case arose out of the contract.

Not all workers must have written statements. The major exclusions are:

- Husbands and wives of employers.
- Crown servants
- Employees who work wholly or mainly outside the UK.

Before 1993 those who worked less than 16 hours a week and had not been employed by the same employer for at least 5 years were also excluded.

Since November 1993, however, all employees who work a minimum of 8 hours per week are entitled to receive a written statement. This change aptly demonstrates the effect of European Court of Justice decisions on UK law, which has traditionally excluded part-timers (less than 16 hours per week) from a range of employee rights. It seems clear that it is becoming increasingly difficult to justify different treatment of part-time staff. Because most part-timers are women, questions have been asked as to whether the UK law is indirectly discriminating against women and therefore incompatible with the EC Directive on Equal Pay. This means that it would now be unwise to distinguish between full and part-timers in any aspects of employment.

Express and implied terms of a contract of employment

All contracts of employment contain 'express' conditions. These are those conditions which are expressed verbally or in writing. There are also 'implied' terms which are assumed to form part of every contract of employment under the common law. These are general obligations to be followed by employers and employees.

Employees' general obligations
An employee's implied duties can be summarised as follows:

- to be ready and willing to work;
- to obey reasonable orders;
- to use reasonable care and skill;
- to conduct herself/himself in the interest of the employer;
- to show good faith to his employer.

Employer's general obligations
These include the duty:

- to pay agreed wages;
- not to make deductions from wages without employees' consent;
- to provide work (in some cases);
- to obey the law.

Exercise 4

What are the two main types of law which determine employees' rights at work?

As we saw earlier in the chapter, managers are mainly concerned with employees' statutory rights. These are sometimes called 'property' rights, since they are said to have established that workers have rights to occupy their job or property undisturbed and not to have it taken away without the operation of certain legal processes. In this sense it is argued that workers' rights, as regards the 'ownership' of their jobs, are analogous to the rights of individuals to other material possessions – houses, cars and other consumer goods, for example.

Another way of regarding legislation on the rights of the individual worker is to see it as a minimum 'floor' of rights. That is, many employers employ people on terms which are more favourable than those which the law requires them to provide. Often this occurs where collective bargaining has been highly developed for many years.

5.6 **Summary: Case Study**

To check your understanding of the subject matter of this chapter, we have written a case study, in which you are asked to examine the legal implications of a manager's actions in recruiting a new member of staff. Read it through and then answer the questions listed at the end.

Save Easy Building Society

John Baker is manager of the Middleford branch of the Save Easy Building Society. Middleford is a quiet but prosperous country market town with little manufacturing industry. The Save Easy Building Society is one of the country's

---

> *MUMS PLEASE NOTE!*
> **THE SAVE EASY BUILDING SOCIETY**
> *needs a*
> **Part-time**
> **Cashier/Typist**
>
> You will work mainly with the public, selling the Society's savings and mortgages services as well as answering telephone queries and general office duties. On-line computer terminals are used for cashiering and all necessary training is provided.
>
> Would *you* like to be an important member of our team? Hours of work are 11.00 a.m. to 3.00 p.m. with additional hours as required (by mutual agreement). Saturday mornings are worked on a rota basis.
>
> Please apply for an application form to: J. E. Baker, Branch Manager, Save Easy Building Society, 2 Golden Square, Middleford, MF1 1DT.

---

largest building societies with offices in most major towns. Its smaller branches, of which the Middleford branch is typical, are staffed by a manager, usually male, and three or four part-time cashier/typists. The latter are usually married women, often with children, because the hours of work often suit their needs. One of John Baker's staff leaves and he needs to find a replacement. He places the advertisement shown opposite in the *Middleford Gazette*.

Six women telephone for application forms. From her voice, John deduces that one is black. He tells this applicant that the position has been filled. He feels justified in this action when he imagines the expressions on the faces of some of his clients if they were served by a black cashier. He would deny personal racial prejudice. When he was assistant manager of a branch in Pottington in the Midlands, he was happy to have black cashiers. But not here in Middleford! The clients would not be happy! Also, the job entails much telephone work and he found the applicant difficult to understand over the telephone.

Subsequently, four women complete application forms. One is fifty-five years old. He rejects her as too old for the job. With the advent of computer technology, she would not be able to cope. He notes that the other three applicants have school-age children and he calls them all for interview. From previous experience he has come to the conclusion that the most important characteristic of an effective member of staff is stability. People who leave disrupt efficiency. He is a man who likes a comfortable routine both in work and outside. He is a great believer in family life. It is most important that applicants have the support of their husbands and good childcare arrangements. The prospect of having to recruit a temporary replacement to cover a period of maternity leave fills him with horror! It is therefore his normal practice, when he interviews applicants for jobs, to ask about these personal matters.

On this occasion one of the applicants objects to his questioning. She tells him that her private life is none of his business and promptly leaves the office. He reassures himself with the thought that she is some kind of cranky feminist.

The next interviewee has worked as a cashier in a large engineering company. The experience is probably relevant to the demands of work in the branch,he feels. However, further conversation reveals that she was a trade union representative in that company. Well, that rules her out – John Baker is decidedly opposed to having left-wing extremists working for him!

He offers the job to the third candidate, Mrs Susan Best, who starts work the following week. At the beginning of her second week John Baker gives the new employee a written statement of her main terms and conditions of employment. Since engaging Mrs Best, he has decided to change her hours of work a little so that she finishes work each day at 3.30 p.m. rather than 3.00 p.m. This change is incorporated into the statement and he tells her of his decision when he gives the document to her. She is most unhappy about the change, saying that this will make it impossible for her to meet her five-year-old son from school. He says that he is sorry but argues that the change is necessary in the interests of branch efficiency.

Work through this case study and comment on the correctness in law of John Baker's actions, with regard to:

1 The advertisement.
2 The telephone enquiry.
3 The rejection of the fifty-five-year-old candidate.
4 Questioning about domestic circumstances.
5 John Baker's concern about trade union activists.
6 The change in Mrs Best's hours of work.

6 Involving the Individual in the Job

In the previous chapters we examined the process by which individuals are brought into the organisation. At this time attempts are made to select employees with the potential to perform jobs effectively. Whether or not employees live up to the expectations of those who selected them depends on management's success in motivating them to work effectively. In other words:

$$capability \times motivation = performance$$

Though this equation is oversimplified, it stresses the centrality of motivation to the employment relationship. Personnel specialists are charged with responsibility to find this 'philosopher's stone' or means of resolving management's problems, so far as employees are concerned. The next few chapters look at techniques aimed at increasing the effectiveness of workers. In this chapter we are concerned with the general nature of motivation to work and its relationship to techniques concerned with the management of people.

6.1 Motivation

Probably no subject has taxed the energy of management pundits more than motivation to work. Many famous theories now exist for the guidance of managers. Unfortunately they are often contradictory.

Exercise 1

Here is a list of factors which may affect your feelings about your job. Rank them in order of importance to you personally. Put 1 against the factor that is most important to you, 2 against the next and so on.

Rank

1 Security of employment
2 Promotion prospects
3 Salary or wage

4 Personal relationships at work
5 Life outside work
6 Physical working conditions
7 Interesting work
8 Challenging work
9 Opportunities to be creative at work
10 Status
11 Fringe benefits or 'perks'
12 Recognition of a job well done

Of course there is no right or wrong answer to this activity. Your answer will depend on such things as:

- the job that you do;
- your age;
- your experience of life and work;
- your hopes for the future.

A further complication is that your feelings about work may change from time to time. For example, while you are doing your job you may be concerned that it is challenging and interesting and gives you opportunities to be creative. When your next pay increase is due, you may be more concerned about the money you are paid.

Ask friends or colleagues to do the above exercise. The variety of their answers and the discussions which you have with them afterwards should further convince you of the complexity of this area.

Do employees work for love or money?

The research evidence is contradictory. Some research subjects stress the importance of pay. By contrast the majority of workers seem convinced that they would continue to work if they inherited a fortune or won the football pools. There is anecdotal evidence to support this from workers who have found themselves lucky enough to be able to make this choice. Clearly for them money is not the only source of motivation!

Before looking at the social scientists' explanations for this seemingly contradictory evidence, we should pause and think about the effect on the behaviour of managers. Many have their 'pet' theories about ways of encouraging employees to work harder. This affects the personnel management techniques chosen to this end.

If you believe that it is possible to increase productivity by making jobs more interesting, you are likely to use job redesign techniques to achieve this. By contrast, if you believe that an attractive working environment is vital to workers' motivation, you may spend much time selecting attractive potted plants and designing colour schemes.

Most managements have traditionally operated on a 'carrot and stick' theory of motivation, believing that provision of appropriate incentives, particularly money, encourages workers to expend the maximum effort. This is the theory behind many payment systems (see Chapter 13). Support for this thesis can be derived from the nature of our consumer society. Not surprisingly workers have materialistic values; those who perform dull jobs may have little else than money by which to be motivated!

Maslow's hierarchy of needs

This is the most famous classification of human needs based on the assumption that people have wants directed to specific goals. Maslow postulated five main categories of need arranged in a *hierarchy*, i.e. once a lower order need is satisfied, the individual becomes motivated by needs which exist at the next highest level of the hierarchy.

In Figure 6.1 we see that Maslow assumed that if people have enough to eat and drink their attention turns to the need for security – the tramp's dream of a roof over her/his head or the worker's concern to avoid redundancy. Once this is satisfied, attention turns to relationships with other people – the need to feel wanted and loved. At this stage workers are concerned with their membership of a work group and of an organisation. The higher-order needs for self-esteem or status and recognition in the eyes of the world, and finally for self-actualisation or the achievement of full potential, become motivators only when the lower-order needs have been satisfied.

Exercise 2

Do employees cease to be concerned about money once their basic needs have been met?

Fig. 6.1   Maslow's hierarchy of needs

A complication of Maslow's theory seems to be that money is a means of satisfying needs at most levels of the hierarchy. It would appear that employees are motivated by different aspects of jobs in different situations. Thus, on the same day, they may demand more money in a negotiating meeting and more satisfying work on the job. It seems that two or more levels of the hierarchy may operate at the same time.

Despite these criticisms, Maslow's hierarchy has value for managers and personnel specialists, suggesting that:

- the nature of the motivation to work is complex;
- there is no single overriding source of motivation;
- managers or personnel specialists cannot afford to 'rest on their laurels', having given workers a generous pay increase for example. Demands at a higher level in the hierarchy should be anticipated.

Herzberg's 'two factor' theory of motivation

In the view of the American organisational psychologist, the wants of employees can be divided into *satisfiers* or motivators and *dissatisfiers* or 'hygiene' factors. The first group are said to be effective motivators because they are a source of personal growth. They include:

- achievement;
- recognition;
- advancement;
- responsibility; and
- the work itself.

By contrast, as indicated by the terminology, the presence of 'hygiene' factors prevents dissatisfaction and poor performance. In other words, such aspects of job context must be present if the employee is to feel fairly treated. Hygiene factors include:

- wages or salaries;
- supervision;
- working conditions; and
- company policy and administration.

These factors do not act as motivators, but if they are not present or are felt by employees to be inadequate, they will act as a source of dissatisfaction.

Exercise 3

According to Herzberg, is money a source of motivation to work?

Like Maslow's hierarchy of needs, this theory has been accused of being overgeneralised and too simplified. Nevertheless it provides food for thought in its message that, no matter how satisfactory the context of the job, if the work itself is dull and meaningless, the employee will be apathetic.

6.2 Orientations to Work

Psychologists focus on the needs and wants of the individual employee at work. Sociologists, by contrast, analyse the degree to which wider social forces impinge on the work behaviour of employees. To understand workers' attitudes and values, we need to know what workers expect from and value in their work. The term 'orientation to work' is used to categorise employees' preferences about various features and rewards of work. In a famous study, John Goldthorpe (in J. H. Goldthorpe *et al.*, *The Affluent Worker: Industrial Attitudes and Behaviour*, Cambridge University Press, 1968) identified the prevalence of an 'instrumental' orientation to work among highly paid manual workers. These people tended to see work as a means to an end, a way of earning a living to support an affluent lifestyle outside work. For them work was not a central life interest.

Exercise 4

Goldthorpe's evidence suggests that the employees concerned were prepared to put up with dull, repetitive jobs, for example on car assembly lines, as long as the financial rewards were satisfactory. Does this contradict the findings of the organisational psychologists?

A further argument for Goldthorpe's findings lies in the nature of the employment relationship. This is predominantly an exchange of wages for effort. Thus it is hardly surprising if employees see work largely in calculative terms. Goldthorpe's affluent workers and many other like them receive little from their work other than financial rewards. An absence of positive or moral commitment is not remarkable.

Nevertheless sociologists have identified other orientations to work. For example some employees have a bureaucratic attachment to the organisations in which they work. These are mainly white-collar workers who have some expectation of upward movement through the organisation structure. For them career development is very important and work is a central life interest. Involvement in work is moral rather than simply calculative. Some employees are 'cosmopolitans' in that they see themselves not as employees of a particular organisation but as members of a professional or occupational group. That is, the major group with which they identify is outside the firm rather than inside it. For them to work is a central life interest but their orientation is to opportunities in the labour market generally rather than within the organisation in which they happen to be currently employed.

More recently attention has been given to the 'culture' of work organisations. This approach prompts us to see that employees' motivations and orientations to work are subject to influence by management. Work is a significant part of life experience for most people; they are more likely to perform effectively if management takes care to build purpose and promote appropriate values in the workplace.

Managers and personnel specialists can learn a great deal from the work of social scientists on motivation and orientations to work:

- The relationship between individuals and their work is complex. Managers and personnel specialists should not assume that any change of employment policy or practice will provoke the same response from all employees.
- Work is a central life interest for many people; behaviour at work can be significantly influenced by management.
- Employees' attitudes and priorities may change over time and in different circumstances. A key skill which you will need as a manager or personnel specialist is to put yourself in other people's shoes and see work through their eyes.
- Know yourself! Be aware of your own assumptions and 'pet' theories which influence your dealings with other people at work.

6.3 Designing Jobs to Encourage Efficiency and Commitment

Suppose that you need to decide on the content of a shop assistant's job in terms of its duties and responsibilities. Two objectives which you would have in making these decisions are:

- The requirements of the business for productivity and quality of service.
- The needs of the job holder for satisfying work.

Management has tended to give much greater priority to the first objective than to the second. The resultant lack of involvement of employees in decisions relating to them and their consequent lack of motivation has prompted a debate about the quality of working life. (Part of this debate is about the need for greater employee participation in managerial decision-making, see Chapter 14.)

Three effects of highly specialised and routine jobs on employees are:

- They do not satisfy needs for personal fulfilment and growth.
- Research undertaken in the USA indicates that those who perform machine-paced specialised assembly jobs suffer from particularly high levels of psychological strain and somatic complaints. Stress is not restricted to those who occupy managerial roles.
- They do not use employees' full abilities; they are frustrating and may encourage participation in unproductive acts ranging from shoddy work to literally throwing a spanner in the works; they can result in absenteeism, wildcat strikes and refusal to co-operate with management.

In times of full employment, dislike of these jobs leads to recruitment difficulties. When jobs are scarcer, management may experience unacceptably high levels of sickness and absence or difficulties in getting employees to accept technological change because of fears that it threatens the narrow range of skills on which they depend for living.

Efforts to create a more positive commitment by employees by redesigning their jobs have affected only a small proportion of the workforce. This shows how deep-rooted are employers' assumptions about the link between specialised, narrow tasks and high productivity.

What are the options in redesigning jobs?

Imagine that you are a personnel specialist in a large supermarket chain. Many problems which can be categorised as poor motivation to work have been experienced with checkout-operators. Three options for redesigning this job are:

- You could include one or more other tasks at the same level of difficulty within the operator's job. For example, if another assistant packs customers' shopping while the checkout-operator enters prices into the till, you could give one person responsibility for both tasks. This addition of related tasks is known as 'job enlargement'.
- Another option is *job rotation*, whereby all assistants are moved between various routine tasks in the store such as shelf-filling, checkout-operating and, where relevant, serving customers on specialist counters.
- The third option needs more radical redesign of the job to add elements involving more responsibility in decision-making. This probably would involve adding elements of the job of first-line supervisors for signing cheques, exchanging faulty goods and dealing with customer complaints. It also might involve the work group becoming more self-managing over time. The term used to describe this is 'job enrichment'.

Elements of the first two options would be found in many supermarkets since they are much more congruent with the philosophy of 'don't do as you think, do as you're told'. They have been criticised as merely 'adding one

Mickey Mouse job to another'. There is evidence that where workers favour enlargement or rotation, fatigue and boredom have been reduced. However, there is little evidence of productivity improvements and once the new tasks become familiar the motivational effect often wears off. Sometimes employees have expressed dislike of job rotation because it breaks up established work groups and thus reduces opportunities for the development of social relationships at work.

Job enrichment

By contrast, job enrichment is said to create opportunities for increased performance and satisfaction. Job enrichment generally has three elements:

- Reduced repetitiveness of work.
- Incorporation of some of the activities of related jobs into the enriched jobs. In the case of manual jobs this often involves responsibility for reordering of stock, inspection and maintenance.
- Delegation of decision-making to employees. Again in the case of manual workers this may involve responsibility for scheduling and planning their own work.

Autonomous group working

This is an extension of job enrichment in which members of a work group are given responsibility for immediate production planning and for task allocation arrangements. These groups work without direct supervision.

Exercise 5

What is the difference between autonomous group working and the other three job redesign techniques (job enlargement, job rotation and job enrichment) so far discussed in this chapter?

There has been limited application of this technique in Britain. Most of the experiments in this form of job redesign and employee participation occurred in the 1970s in Scandinavia.

The main reasons for introducing job enrichment and autonomous group working in the 1970s were management concerns about:

- the 'quality of working life' in industrialised economies;
- the difficulty of recruiting and retaining workers in repetitive, specialised jobs, especially where unemployment was low;
- attendant problems of absenteeism and poor timekeeping;

In general terms, therefore, management was responding to the rising expectations and aspirations of a higher paid and better educated workforce.

However, these techniques did present some problems to management:

- Workers and their representatives sometimes felt that pay increases should result from their contribution of a wider range of skills to the organisation.
- Initial investment costs could be substantial, for example where new manufacturing techniques were introduced.
- The evidence suggests that there could be an initial drop in productivity as people adjust to new jobs; training costs were substantial.

When levels of unemployment rose in Britain in the 1980s, the popularity of the techniques described in this section declined. Concerns about the 'quality of working life' were replaced by anxieties about the scarcity of jobs. Recruitment and retention difficulties and the associated managerial problems became a thing of the past. Nevertheless, managerial concerns to increase workforce commitment have continued. A more strategic approach to the direct involvement of employees in their work is discussed in the next section. More general issues about the management of change – an increasing focus of attention in many organisations – is covered in Chapter 10.

6.4 Direct Participation as a Means of Encouraging Employee Commitment

Job enrichment and autonomous group working give opportunities for employees to contribute to decisions about work they perform. It is a form of direct employee participation in organisational decision-making (see Chapter 14, p. 192).

Imagine that you are an employee of Byteman Computer Services. The company has 1,000 employees in four locations in the UK. Employees are unionised. There is bargaining at company level between management and trade unions. A joint consultative committee draws employee representatives from all four sites. There are no other mechanisms for employee participation in managerial decision-making. Such systems of indirect participation, if seen as fair and effective by employees, might increase your general satisfaction with your terms and conditions of employment. Likewise, if through your representatives on the joint consultative committee you receive information on company plans and the current situation, you might feel more positive towards your employment by Byteman. However, research shows that such efforts to introduce participation at the highest levels alone run the risk that only at election times do employees feel involved in organisational affairs.

This is the argument for direct participation. Such experiments have been small-scale in the UK. Long-established methods of collective bargaining and consultation have been more prevalent.

Methods of direct participation

These include:

- quality circles and other quality initiatives;
- teamworking initiatives;
- suggestion schemes;
- approaches to employees' empowerment.

Quality circles

These have been imported into the UK as part of the attempt to make our industry more competitive by learning from the Japanese. Supervisors and work groups are provided with training in quality control and other problem-solving techniques. They are encouraged then to attempt to identify and solve work-related problems using specialist advice where necessary.

Suppose that you are the quality manager of Dynamic Machines, a large UK manufacturer of aero-engines. You have secured the agreement of the general manager to the launch of a trial quality circle. Now you are ready to choose a department in which to locate the circle. Three criteria which you should use in making the choice are:

- Management, supervisors and employees in the department must be enthusiastic about participating in the trial. Middle managers can be particularly critical as evidence suggests that they are the group most likely to feel threatened by these schemes. If their support is not fostered at an early stage, it is all too possible for passive or even active sabotage of the programme to occur.
- Industrial relations in the department must be good and trade union representatives should be willing to participate in the circle.
- Departmental management must be known to be willing and able to listen carefully and responsively to employee proposals.

It may be that we can identify some key similarities between Britain and Japan which account for the success of quality circles in some British companies. These are:

- rising aspirations and increased education of workers;
- the need to reduce the specialised and routine nature of many production and clerical jobs;
- the need to increase the commitment of many employees both to the organisation and to the jobs they perform within it.

Nevertheless many differences exist between the employment relationship in Japan and in the UK which should prompt managers and personnel specialists to pause for thought before launching quality circles or any other aspect of Japanese personnel management.

There is some evidence that the decline in the popularity of quality circles recently has been caused by:

- The failure of management to keep up the momentum, by regenerating the agenda for change and emphasising the achievement of quality circles.
- Disillusionment of staff as a result of the failure to implement proposals or to give good reasons for these not being taken up.
- The lack of really effective training for quality circle members as well as leaders, equipping them to tackle identified problems. This can be taken as a signal that management do not take seriously the efforts they ask of employees and are seeking only to obtain employee commitment with minimum interference.

One conclusion from some of the failures of quality circles is to see them as one of the fads and fashions in managerial attempts to involve employees. A more enthusiastic view is that companies have simply moved on, having learned from quality circles, to more ambitious and integrated employee involvement programmes. Some of these are covered below.

Teamworking initiatives
Again these innovations are largely inspired by Japanese examples. They are an attempt to increase innovation and quality of output through a focus on teams. In some ways the ideas involved bear some resemblance to the Scandinavian experiments with autonomous work groups covered briefly in Section 6.3 above. However, these more recent initiatives are much more shaped by management than by considerations for quality of working life or individual development. Teamworking is seen as a vehicle for greater task flexibility and co-operation, as well as for extending the drive for quality. Teamworking need not be about organisational structures – for example, changing from sequential to cellular manufacturing. Rather, it involves the explicit recognition by management that a team begins with individuals whose contributions are recognised and valued and who are motivated to work together to achieve clear, understood and challenging goals for which they are accountable.

Exercise 6

From your knowledge of employee involvement initiatives so far, list two possible pitfalls of teamworking initiatives.

Total quality management (TQM)
These programmes are more wide-ranging than quality circles. They derive from a growing belief that commercial success comes not simply from reducing costs but also from high and reliable quality. This is believed to be

achieved through a bringing together of stable and mutual relationships between suppliers and customers. There is also high emphasis on the need for the commitment and customer awareness of employees all the way through the organisation. This includes 'internal customers in the company who will use a department's output'.

Exercise 7

Give an example of the 'internal' customers of a personnel service.

The stated aim of TQM programmes is to create a culture of 'continuous improvement'.

In this way, TQM tends to subsume quality circles or teamworking arrangements into a more integrated approach. However, its main focus is on the customer. It therefore tends to be marketing or image-led rather than being driven primarily by the need to involve employees in their work and in the organisation. That is, it emphasises performance far more than the quality circles or teamworking initiatives and is less concerned with employee satisfaction or development. Nevertheless, effective TQM initiatives can increase employee commitment.

Suggestion schemes
Only rarely have suggestion schemes been effective in involving employees in organisational decision-making. This is because traditionally employees have not been involved in either the design or operation of these schemes and feel that the decision-making process about the acceptance or rejection of their suggestions is remote from them. Frequently such decisions are made by a committee of managers with no obligation to tell the initiators of suggestions the reason for their decision. The committee may take time in communicating the results of its deliberations. Further, managers and supervisors often feel that suggestions made by those for whom they are responsible are implicitly critical of their performance. Conflict can also arise over the size of the monetary or other reward for the submission of a successful suggestion.

Criteria for the establishment of a successful suggestion scheme are:

- Commitment of all levels of management.
- Involvement and support of recognised trade unions.
- Involvement of employees during the evaluation of their suggestions.
- Active support of departmental management, supervisory and specialist support staff in the operation of the scheme. It should be clear that the emergence of suggestions is not a criticism of their competence.
- An effective administrator for the scheme – probably a personnel specialist, who services the committee, monitors the scheme, organises training and generally performs a co-ordinating role.

Where a more strategic approach to the management of change is adopted, there is likely to be recognition that the encouragement of innovation is vital. Such a strategic aim, if well communicated and accepted throughout the organisation, may increase the effectiveness of a suggestion scheme.

Empowerment initiatives

Many organisations are now talking about employee 'empowerment'. Is this yet another fad aimed at increasing employee commitment or is it something which will have a long-lasting impact on the way that we run our organisation? When we use the term we need to be clear what we mean. One definition is:

> People exercising personal responsibility and using their own judgements in the interests of the organisation and its customers.

In some organisations this has been accompanied by a plethora of American razzmatazz, the impact of which may be somewhat problematic.

Exercise 8

Why may this be the case?

Emerging experience of empowerment suggests that organisations should make clear their expectations of 'empowered' employees. For example, staff can be given – or, probably better, be involved in drawing up – guidelines defining management's expectations of their behaviour. For example, one organisation asks its staff to 'never turn a blind eye to anything you think is wrong or silly'. In other words, politeness and cheerfulness are expected in dealings both with customers and with other staff. As with other examples of employee involvement, supervisors and managers may feel very threatened by being asked to hand over power and authority to the staff whom they previously supervised. Indeed, managerial jobs may well be threatened by these initiatives, which are often part of the general trend to the flattening of organisational hierarchy. Although employee empowerment initiatives differ, almost all of them have changed the role of the supervisor. There is less emphasis on allocating tasks to other workers and checking on targets and rotas, and more on the supervisor's role as facilitator and coach, encouraging individual employees or teams to set up and measure their own systems of producing products or supplying services.

In summary, managerial and supervisory behaviour seems critical to the success of employee involvement initiatives. Helpful behaviours include:

- ensuring openness;
- promoting co-operation;
- delegating authority;

- developing people;
- communicating effectively;
- encouraging innovation.

Exercise 9

Which of the following statements are true and which are false?

1 Money is the only effective motivator of employees. *True or false?*
2 Managers and supervisors should not assume that any change of employment policy or practice will provoke the same response from all employees. *True or false?*
3 Job rotation, job enlargement and job enrichment are all methods of work restructuring. *True or false?*
4 Quality circles are a long-established method of direct employee participation, which originated in the UK. *True or false?*
5 There are many effective suggestion schemes in UK companies. *True or false?*

7 Appraising Performance

7.1 What is Performance Appraisal?

'Getting the best out of people' is a crude expression of management's key target so far as employees are concerned. In the last chapter we examined the general issue of employee motivation. Performance appraisal, the subject of this chapter, rests on the assumption that if employees' performance is scrutinised and feedback is given, the motivation to work more effectively should increase. Problems of employee motivation where this is not done or done badly can be expressed as 'the good people don't know what they should be doing or how well they are doing' and 'nobody finds out the bad people'. In this chapter we look at ways of righting such situations using performance appraisal.

The dictionary definition of the verb *to appraise* is 'to fix a price for' or 'to value an object or thing'. When we use the term 'performance appraisal' we imply that we are concerned with the process of valuing the employee's worth to the organisation, with a view to increasing it.

7.2 Purpose of Performance Appraisal

Management's objectives in performance appraisal include:

- To help improve current performance.
- To set objectives for individual performance.
- To assess training and development needs.
- To agree plan for employees' future development.
- To assess future potential for promotion.
- To give employees feedback on their performance.
- To counsel employees on career opportunities.
- To rate the employees' performance for salary review purposes.
- To encourage managers to think carefully about the performance of their staff in general and factors influencing it, including their own style and behaviour.

Who is appraised?

Managerial, professional and technical staff traditionally have been more likely to be appraised than holders of routine clerical and manual jobs. One reason for this is the association between appraisal and training and career development. However, significant numbers of organisations now have appraisal systems for clerical and manual employees. There are signs that organisational changes such as those to harmonise employment conditions for all non-managerial grades are encouraging the development of appraisal systems for these groups.

7.3 **Designing an Appraisal System**

Suppose that you are managing director of XYZ Systems Ltd. Your main competitor, ABC Systems Ltd, employs roughly the same number and skill-mix of employees as you. You wish to begin to use a performance appraisal system. ABC has such a system. Should you attempt to cajole your counterpart in ABC to let you have this system?

Aside from the unreality of this, in that your main rival is unlikely to let you have anything which might make you more competitive, the answer is probably 'no'. It is generally unwise to attempt to transfer systems concerned with the management of people from one organisation to another, however tempting this may appear. Appraisal systems, like other aspects of personnel management, must suit the company culture. Even though ABC is your main competitor it may differ in tradition, methods of dealing with employees, structure and organisation of work and so on.

If you believe that an appraisal system can contribute to the efficient running of XYZ you would be better advised to 'grow your own'. To do this it is useful to use the experience of others. A summary of trends in performance appraisal shows:

- increasing criticism of appraisal systems which attempt to measure personality characteristics such as intelligence, loyalty, commitment or drive;
- increased emphasis on more objective, job-related criteria and objectives – a 'results-oriented approach';
- more involvement of employees in their own appraisal;
- more concentration on improving performance in the current job rather than assessing future potential.

We shall examine each of these in turn.

Personality-based appraisal systems

Do you believe that managers are able to make judgements about their subordinates on such dimensions as intelligence, initiative or loyalty? The answer must be 'With difficulty!' To illustrate this point let use the example of a manager who is asked to rate the intelligence of a subordinate:

- Firstly, it is necessary to understand the nature of intelligence.
- Secondly, the manager must be competent to judge the degree to which it exists in other people.
- Thirdly, is it reasonable to assume that all staff exhibit all their intelligence at work? For example, if you give an intelligent adult a task to do which would only test the intelligence of a ten-year-old, is it fair to judge intelligence by her or his job performance?
- Fourthly, there is the requirement to assess all subordinates in the same way against the manager's definition of intelligence.
- Fifthly, the manager is likely to find it difficult to justify feedback given to the subordinate based on personality trait rating.

In addition, studies have shown that, whatever the chosen personality characteristic appraisal was likely to reveal, women and members of other minority groups emerge as having less of it than their white male counterparts. The existence of anti-discrimination legislation thus makes it unwise to use appraisal systems which have the effect of treating employees of one sex or race less favourably than other people in decisions which relate to promotion (see Chapter 12, p. 152). In appraisal, as in selection, the roots of prejudice tend to be very close to the surface.

Competence-oriented appraisal systems

Exercise 1

How could you design an appraisal system where managerial judgement is more likely to be valid than in the personality-based techniques described in the previous section?

Using job analysis (see p. 29), behaviours which constitute actual job performance are defined. Levels of performance for each behaviour are described. For example, if judgement and initiative are required, relevant performance standards must be defined; raters then assess job holders from observation of past work performance. A major limitation of these systems is the difficulty of determining which performance levels equate to observed behaviours of the appraisee. However, they are useful in the definition of development needs.

The increasingly competency-based approach to training is also having an impact on appraisal systems. (For a definition of competence, see Chapter 8, p. 102.) This approach is requiring organisations to be more specific about the knowledge, skills and attributes which enable optimum performance. For example, if negotiating skills are a key element in the effective performance of a sales job, then this form of appraisal necessitates the definition of the specific behaviours required of the jobholder. Such a definition might be:

> Plans and executes negotiations selecting from a variety of strategies or tactics to reach optimum results.

In this way, the gap between required competencies and the individual's current performance can be highlighted and development needs identified.

Results-oriented appraisal systems or performance reviews

It follows that fair judgements of performance must be:

- capable of more objective judgement by appraisers;
- genuinely related to job performance.

This justifies an emphasis on job-related performance criteria, particularly for managerial, supervisory, professional and technical employees.

Exercise 2

Identify a common link between these jobs which is of critical importance to the operation of a results-oriented performance appraisal system.

These methods concentrate on specific outcomes achieved as a result of job performance. Many experienced practitioners argue that performance reviews are more effective motivators if they involve the setting of specific job-related objectives. Six or so key performance measures can be selected at the appraisal interview as relevant target areas for the employee for the next year. These can then be turned into specific objectives.

For example, a key performance measure for a training specialist might be: 'the design and implementation of management development programmes'. An objective for a particular trainer might be 'to investigate the detailed training needs of line managers in accountancy and finance, to design a short course (not more than five days' duration) and to run three such courses each for 12 line managers within the next six months'.

Three advantages of this objective setting procedure for use in performance reviews are:

- It should be relevant to the personal needs of employees. Therefore their commitment should be greater.
- It should be relevant to the requirements of the job and of the organisation.
- It encourages both appraiser and appraised to look carefully at what has actually been achieved in the immediate past as well as what realistically may be expected over the year ahead.

Review of performance is based on the extent to which objectives have been met as measured by predetermined success criteria. Increasingly objectives are jointly agreed between subordinate and manager; this is thought to:

- increase commitment to achieve goals;
- commit managerial support;
- help to ensure that the necessary resources are made available.

Progress towards objectives should be monitored regularly.

Objectives-based performance review methods rest on assumptions of what can be achieved during a given time-span (usually one year) and to a given standard. Superficially this appears to be simple. However, detailed job analysis is necessary to clarify the tasks involved and the priorities which they should be afforded. Much effort is needed to agree clear, reasonable performance standards. Difficulties in establishing agreed criteria against which to measure performance have caused some such schemes to founder.

Exercise 3

From the discussion of performance appraisal methods in this chapter, list three ways of developing criteria against which employees' performance can be rated.

The use of rating scales in reviewing performance

Key criteria of performance thus established become yardsticks against which managers can be asked to rate subordinates. Often rating scales are used for this purpose.

Imagine you are an employee of a company where this rating scale is used for the assessment of performance:

1 Excellent.
2 Very good.
3 Adequate.
4 Below the required standard.

This scale has only one category for ineffective performance. Managers are usually required to communicate their evaluation of performance to subordinates. Imagine your disillusionment if you were labelled as 'inadequate' or 'below standard' in this way. Possibly you would live up to your reputation! Management is more likely to encourage employees to improve by jointly agreeing how they can be helped to improve, for example by further training and development.

The focus on the need to manage poor performance has sharpened recently. It should be dealt with when it arises and not left to an annual performance review. Managers should be trained to deal with this difficult problem.

Another problem of rating scales is that managers' definitions of 'excellent', 'very good' and so on may differ. Stereotyping (see Chapter 3, pp. 40–1) also is likely to affect managerial judgement of performance. Only trained appraisers using common yardsticks should use rating scales.

Employee involvement in appraisal

Appraisal systems are now more 'open' than they used to be. That is, there is a greater likelihood that employees will be shown either all or a part of their appraisal reports. This should increase employees' motivation to improve their job performance. Employees often are encouraged to contribute to the review process by the use of interview preparation forms or self-assessment procedures.

Many managers find 'open' appraisal threatening. This is because there is pressure on the appraiser to make the appraisal as complete and constructive as possible. Bland phrases and generalisations are likely to be challenged by employees together with the more obvious inaccuracies which indicate the manager's ignorance of the real nature of the employee's job.

The trend towards more openness has been accompanied by greater emphasis on results-oriented approaches. The joint problem-solving and developmental approach to performance review makes it easier to justify assessment of performance based on the key results areas of the job rather than on more nebulous, and less obviously relevant, personality traits.

Current performance v. future potential

Many managers do not see assessment of potential as a prime purpose of appraisal, being more concerned with current performance. Some companies now encourage people to make sideways moves to increase their experience, knowledge and skills before or instead of upward progression.

Potential reviews

Separate systematic reviews of potential are useful for those for whom career or management development is contemplated. Many managers find the assessment of potential difficult since their experience of the individual is limited to observations of performance in their current job. For this reason a 'grandfather' figure – a more senior manager – is often used to avoid some of the prejudices of the immediate manager. Another way of assessing potential is to use an assessment development centre (see Chapters 3 and 10, pp. 46–8 and 129–3).

There is a growing tendency to record career aspirations when performance is reviewed together with the assessor's comments. Formal career counselling is undertaken sometimes, for example using external consultants or workshops. The latter encourage individuals to set themselves career and life objectives and to plan ways of achieving these.

7.4 **Performance-Related Pay**

Recently there has been considerable debate about the effectiveness of linking performance with pay as a means of motivating employees. This issue is covered in Chapter 13, pp. 181.

7.5 **Who Will Appraise?**

So far in this chapter we have implied that appraisal is commonly undertaken by the immediate supervisor. This is most often the case. Sometimes, as mentioned in the previous section, a more senior manager is used in an overseeing role. More open appraisal implies a shift in the control of appraisal from the appraiser to the appraisee. Some companies use self-appraisal schemes where the employee takes the lead. This may be useful where employees' work is frequently unsupervised and elements of it are not easily assessable; for example, professional employees. In similar circumstances, peer group appraisal can be used, where each employee nominates one or two colleagues whom she/he trusts to evaluate her/his performance. Some organisations are also showing an interest in subordinates' assessment of their managers' performance. However, in most organisations, managers prefer to retain control of appraisal.

7.6 **The Appraisal Interview**

The appraisal interview is seen by most organisations as the key feature which will determine the success or failure of the performance appraisal system. Most appraisal schemes include the provision for interviews. The appraisal is one of the most difficult forms of interview which managers undertake because:

- Difficult issues such as inadequate performance and the weakness of the individual employee must be explored.
- Managers must display a wide range of interpersonal skills.
- It is difficult for managers to observe anyone else in the role of interviewer except when they have been appraised.

Some characteristics of effective appraisal interviews are:

- A support and problem solving approach by the interviewer makes it more likely that the employee will accept the results of the appraisal and make changes as a result of the feedback.

- Emphasis on job performance rather than on the employee's personality is more likely to generate a positive climate.
- The setting of specific goals which the employee will seek to meet seems to have a more powerful effect on subsequent performance than a general discussion about the goals.
- There should be a minimum of criticism since this builds up defensiveness and reduces the possible learning from the interview for both parties.
- Emphasis on the employee's participation in the interview as opposed to its domination by the manager.

7.7 **Training for Appraisal**

One of the main reasons for the failure of appraisal systems is the lack of managerial skills in handling the review interview. With the more frequent use of a joint problem-solving approach to appraisal, the training of managers in relevant skills becomes even more vital. Not only are interview skills important but also an understanding of the objectives of appraisal.

7.8 **Other Problems of Appraisal**

A now classic research study (Kay Rowe, 'An appraisal of Appraisals', *Journal of Management Studies*, vol. 1, no. 1, March 1964) revealed that:

- managers are often reluctant to appraise subordinates;
- where they do, their written comments are often glib, generalised and evasive.

Four reasons can be suggested for this:

- Managers often find appraisal schemes cumbersome and suspect that little action will be taken on the results.
- Often managers lack training in appraisal.
- In life we are often reluctant to tell others how we feel about them. Why should we behave any differently at work?
- It is notoriously difficult to formulate standards for employee performance.

Such research findings have led some people to see performance appraisal as a 'ritual of employment' without real benefit to either management or employees. Indeed, there is some evidence that both employees and managers approach appraisal fearfully. The employee expects to hear what is wrong with his or her performance, while the manager expects to have to sell the evaluation to a reluctant and possibly hostile member of staff.

To gain further information on these potential problems, you may find it useful to talk to someone who has participated in appraisal in the last year either as an appraiser or as an appraisee. (If you have had such an experience, use this.) Think about the advantages and disadvantages of appraisal.

Whilst it is important to be clear about the pitfalls of appraisal, there are also grounds for optimism. There is considerable evidence that careful design and implementation can yield good results.

What works as an appraisal system differs widely. Much depends on the nature of the organisation, the appraisal system and the skills of those involved. My list is meant to trigger further thought.

Advantages

- In an appraisal interview boss and subordinate have a formal opportunity for a candid exchange of views, provided that the relationship between them and the nature of the appraisal scheme encourage this.
- Good performance appraisal systems encourage line managers to think systematically about career and management development for their subordinates.
- Performance appraisal can provide very useful data for the analysis of training needs and the design of training programmes.

Disadvantages

- The relationship between boss and subordinate is frequently fragile. It can be harmed by the necessity for the manager to formulate in words, written or spoken, what he really feels about his subordinate. In the words of one appraisee after an appraisal interview, 'I went in bruised and came out bleeding.'
- Even after training, some managers have difficulty with appraisal interviews.
- Many appraisal systems involve too much paperwork. This hinders rather than helps.

7.9 Conditions Necessary for Successful Appraisal Schemes

Despite all the criticisms, the evidence is that the popularity of appraisals has not declined. Over 80 per cent of organisations have appraisal systems. Recently, there are signs that greater priority is being given to the development of such systems.

So are there any general lessons to be learnt before introducing an appraisal system? Careful analysis of the organisation's particular circumstances is vital before embarking on this difficult path. Here are ten suggestions:

- Get top management support.
- Clarify management's objectives for performance appraisal.
- Plan and prepare carefully.
- Beware glossy consultancy packages or some other company's scheme.
- Give oral introductory presentations to managers, trade union representatives and employees and prepare explanatory pamphlets for all those involved.
- Train appraisers.
- Make sure that the scheme is effectively implemented.
- Ensure that promises made in appraisal interviews, for example for further training, are carried out.
- Avoid close linkage with pay.
- Closely monitor the operation of the scheme.

Lastly, keep it simple! If a vast bureaucracy can be avoided, avoid it. Some companies have found that the key to successful appraisals lies in the appraisal interview. In a review of performance using key results areas only, a written record of those and of the associated objectives for the year ahead, together with any training needs, are vital.

7.10 A Cautionary Tale

George has been test department manager in an engineering company for the last ten years. He sees the personnel department as a source of incessant gimmickry, particularly on performance appraisal. Systems come and systems go and all complicate his relationship with his subordinates. He fails to complete his appraisal forms when he can get away with it. At present the personnel manager has the ear of the production director and George has been given an edict to undertake appraisal for all trainees, technicians, engineers and supervisors. The current appraisal system contains the following elements:

- agreement of key objectives for the year ahead between appraiser and appraisee;
- personality trait assessment of such characteristics as decision-making ability, leadership ability, alertness and mental capability;
- assessment of potential on a rating scale – promotable in the near future/ possibly promotable/not promotable;
- training and development needs.

George obediently completes the forms and sends them back to the personnel department thinking it a useless exercise but at least that will be that for another year. Then to his annoyance a young personnel officer, whom George considers still 'wet behind the ears', telephones to inform George that the exercise is incomplete. The system now requires interviews to be conducted to communicate the results of appraisal to employees. George agrees to do this, suspecting that it is futile to argue. He is not happy with some of his assessments of personality in particular and has rated 50 per cent of those appraised as not promotable. This won't go down too well, he knows, but the firm has been reducing its labour force and promotion does consist of waiting for dead men's shoes. Presumably the personnel department, with its fancy knowledge of human behaviour, knows what it's doing!

He calls in each of his subordinates, reads the form to them and, not very enthusiastically, waits for a response.

Exercise 4

1 List three failings by the personnel department in this case.
2 How effective do you think George's appraisal interviews would be?

8 Training for Current Jobs

8.1 What is Training?

From childhood we learn to cope with living. Is this training, or is it
education? These terms are often used as if they were synonymous. They are
not, and an understanding of the differences between them is important to
an understanding of the training process in business organisations. Both are
processes which help people to learn, but they differ in orientation and
objectives. It is probably simplest to define training as oriented towards the
needs of the organisation while education is oriented to the needs of the
individual. These differences can be summarised as shown in Table 8.1.

You will see from Table 8.1 that, while there are many contrasts between
them, the line between training and education is sometimes very blurred.

Table 8.1 **Differences between education and training**

Characteristics of the learning process	Education	Training
Objectives	More abstract objectives geared to the needs of the individual and to society generally	Specific behaviour objectives to make workers more effective in their jobs
Timescale	Generally a long-term process	Can be very short-term especially when concerned with the acquisition of specific skills
Content	Widely drawn content	Often fairly narrow content specific to the employee's work situation

This is easy to see if we examine the content of qualification courses designed to develop managers. Some aspects of such programmes can be described as training since they enable intending or practising managers to develop specific skills, such as interviewing or computer programming, of direct relevance to current or future jobs; other aspects are more broadly educational such as the analysis of the perspectives of the parties in industrial relations or of the social context of work organisations. Such courses should contain elements of both education and training if employees are to be fully competent to contribute to the achievement of corporate objectives.

8.2 Objectives of Training

Two of the most commonly stated objectives of the training process in a work organisation are:

- To assist workers to perform at the optimum level in current jobs.
- To develop employees for future jobs.

An often unstated aim is to strengthen the organisation's 'culture' by developing a broad understanding of 'the way that we do things here'.

8.3 Training Policy

To ensure that the organisation's workforce is effective, the training function must be acquainted with or, preferably, involved in the strategic planning process. Training policies must be supportive of corporate policies and goals.

Fred's Food Processing Company, a manufacturer of frozen foods, plans to acquire a chain of frozen food shops over the next two years. The company's training function needs to be involved in the implementation of this decision, so that, when the retail business is acquired, there is a trained labour force to run it. Fred intends to recruit an entirely new workforce for the retail operation. Here is Fred's training policy.

Fred's Food Processing Company

Statement of Training Policy
The aim of this policy is to ensure that all employees are assisted to develop themselves in order that they may make the best possible contribution to the achievement of company objectives.

In the training area it is our policy to:

1 Draw up a training plan with reference to company objectives.
2 Involve managers in the identification of training objectives for their units.

3 Base training on a thorough analysis of needs.
4 Provide employees with potential with opportunities for further training and development.
5 Have a specialist training department charged with responsibility for the development and implementation of training plans.
6 Provide induction training for all employees.
7 Provide day release for first qualification training for all staff between the ages of 16 and 25.
8 Provide training courses and other training facilities to satisfy needs identified by managers or specialist training staff.
9 All training will be funded from the training budget and must be authorised by the head of the training department.

Exercise 1

What element in this policy statement is inconsistent with Fred's plans to move into retailing?

8.4 A Systematic Approach to Training

Training can contribute to the effective use of the organisation's resources, but only if approached systematically. Imagine that you are the owner of a shop. You recruit a school leaver as a trainee shop assistant. Before starting to train the young person you would need to answer the following questions:

- What are my new employee's training needs?
- How can I meet these needs?
- How can I conduct a training programme to ensure that he/she acquires the knowledge and skills to help me in the most efficient manner?
- How can I check the effectiveness of the training programme?

The rest of this chapter attempts to answer these questions. The phases of the training process are shown in Figure 8.1 (The figure includes the links between training and company policy to emphasise the necessity for this integration.)

8.5 Stage 1: The Identification of Training Needs

'I don't know why I've been sent on this course. I don't see how it can help in my job.' Such a statement from a participant on a training course indicates that a thorough analysis of training needs has not preceded the decision that training is necessary. The importance of clearly defining needs before embarking on a training programme cannot be over-emphasised.

A training need can be defined as the gap between the requirements for skills and knowledge inherent in the job and those possessed by the current

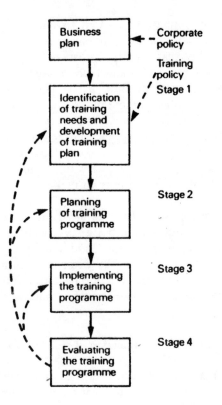

Fig 8.1 Training process

job holder. It is vital that this gap is adequately analysed to establish exactly what training is required (see Figure 8.2).

It is misleading to imply that training needs analysis should take place only at the level of the job. A thorough analysis starts with an attempt to assess total organisational training needs in the context of:

- management's plans for the future of the organisation;
- the current organisation structure;
- current expectations about the use of employees.

Fig 8.2 Training needs analysis

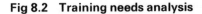

An example will emphasise the need to undertake such an organisational analysis. Bob Brown owns a bakery. The business has been in existence for over fifty years and has prospered. Capital has accumulated. The firm has a good reputation and there is potential for expansion. The management team consists of Bob, as managing director, and a sales manager. Bob is a trained baker and spends most of his time supervising production. The sales manager supervises the delivery workers, checking van loads in the morning, and returns and cash at the end of the day. From time to time Bob has looked at retail outlets and other possible bakery premises with a view to expansion. However, he seems to lack both the time and the energy to make his dreams of expansion a reality.

In this case there appears to be a real need for a change in organisation. We have very scanty information, but a superficial analysis would suggest that the jobs of Bob, in particular, and the sales manager should be redefined to allow them to plan the company's future; they should be released from many of the demands of day-to-day supervision. Until such redefinition of jobs has taken place training would be futile.

Organisational analysis for identification of training needs

An analysis of organisational characteristics and problems is necessary if training is to be adequately linked to business plans. The sort of information required is:

- existing and new product range;
- planned technological developments;
- planned changes to organisation structure;
- planned changes in work methods;
- current and likely future financial position.

It will be necessary also to use the staffing information generated as a result of Stage 1 of the human resource planning process (see Chapter 2, pp. 12–20). This includes:

- Characteristics of current employees, by age, sex, grade, etc.
- Data on the utilisation of employees.
- Analysis of labour turnover.
- Information about tasks currently being undertaken.
- Analysis of reports such as those on accidents or training.

In practice many training officers or consultants who embark on such a task find that much of the data employed is incomplete, over-generalised or of doubtful value.

Exercise 2

Are job descriptions always an accurate picture of the jobs undertaken by employees? List two ways in which they may be deficient.

It will be necessary to analyse available data and to supplement it by interviews with employees, managers and personnel specialists, and by direct observation of work.

All this information should be compiled into a report which can form the basis of the training plan.

Training plans

The training plan represents the translation of training needs into action.

Suppose that Fred's Food Processing Company loses a number of unfair dismissal cases. Investigation of the facts behind these dismissals reveals that one of the problems was the inadequate handling of problem employees by supervisors, which was compounded by their lack of understanding of employees' legal rights in this area. An entry in the company training plan to cover this might read:

Training need	*Estimated benefit*	*Action*	*Response-ibility*	*Time scale*	*Budget*
Handling of disciplinary cases by first-line supervisors	Fewer industrial tribunal cases and the company will be likely to win those which arise	Plan and run two-day training course for all first-line supervisors	Training department	Complete within six months	£6,000

The process of training needs analysis at organisational level is summarised in Figure 8.3.

Training needs analysis at individual level

Before training programmes can be organised for individual employees, it is necessary to analyse their jobs for training purposes.

Job analysis

In Chapter 3 we examined briefly the process of job analysis in recruitment and selection. Such analysis is relevant for training purposes. However, the emphasis here is on those aspects of the job which make it difficult to learn.

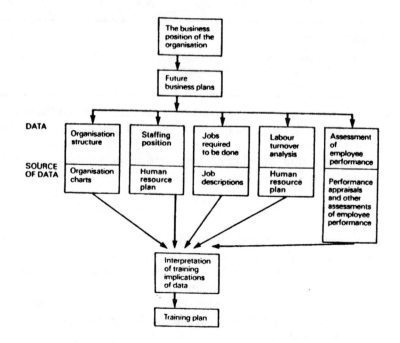

Fig 8.3   Training needs at organisation level

It is important to specify what procedures, techniques and skills the trainee must be proficient at by the end of a programme of training. This can be done by means of a job specification.

In order to ensure that training is appropriately orientated to the improvement of job performance, there is increasing emphasis on the definition of competencies required for effective job performance. A definition of a competence is:

> The observable combination of knowledge, skills and attributes that enables optimum job performance.

Competencies are not fixed for all time but must change to meet new business needs. Also it is important not to lose sight of the essential competencies that people already possess, since many of these must be maintained and carried into the future. Effective organisations build on their strengths, developing additional competencies in anticipation of future demands on staff. Competence to meet today's demands will not be sufficient to achieve success tomorrow.

In many ways competence definitions resemble personnel specifications used for recruitment and selection. Look back to the discussion of personnel specifications in Chapter 3, pp. 33–5 and 102.

Exercise 3

What do you notice about the differences between the definition of a competence given above and some of the headings in a specification of the characteristics of the ideal candidate for recruitment and selection purposes? Give an example.

Some of the characteristics of candidates defined in personnel specifications are not amenable to training. Only in the totalitarian world of Big Brother might an employee be 'trained' to have domestic circumstances and interests ideal for the requirements of the job. Thus most specifications used in training needs analysis have two basic headings of 'knowledge' and 'skills'. Individual employees' knowledge and skills can then be compared with these and training programmes designed accordingly.

The training specification is a detailed statement of the trainee's learning needs based on a comparison between the criteria defined in the personnel specification for selection purposes and the trainee's present level of performance.

Assessment of individual training needs is one of the outputs of the performance appraisal process (see Chapter 7). Alternative methods of undertaking such an assessment are:

- interviews with individual employees and/or with their managers;
- assessment and development centres (see Chapter 3 and 10); and
- psychological testing (see Chapter 3).

8.6 Stage 2: The Planning of Training Programmes

Earlier in this chapter you were asked to imagine that you were a shop-owner who had recently recruited a school leaver for training. Suppose that you have just completed an analysis of the young person's training needs and are ready to plan a training programme. Questions which you would need to ask now are:

- What are the overall objectives of the training programme?
- Where and when should training take place?
- What should be the content of the training programme?
- What learning methods should be used?
- Who should undertake the training?
- Who should administer it?

Specification of training objectives

Ideally the objectives of a training programme should be expressed in terms of the behaviour of competencies expected of the trainee when training is complete.

Look at the extract from the training plan for Fred's Food Processing Company on p. 101. Two possible objectives for the training programme which will have to be organised for the supervisors are that by the end of the training programme supervisors should be able to:

- demonstrate a working knowledge of the law on discipline and dismissal;
- demonstrate improved skills in the handling of disciplinary interviews.

The objectives of training programmes should fit trainees' needs. Note that the first objective here is related to supervisors' needs for knowledge and the second to the skills which they require in order to interact effectively with those they supervise.

The competency-based approach to training

As indicated earlier in this chapter, recently there has been an increasing emphasis on the definition of competencies required for effective job performance as a basis for the design of training programmes. In developing competencies trainers must be able to define:

- the input or qualities which are needed for effective job performance;
- the processes – the tasks and procedures – which employees need to be able to carry out;
- the outcomes which emerge from effective job performance – the result which employees are expected to achieve.

Using some or all of the these approaches, many organisations have now defined the competency requirements for each function and level of job. An example for the broad competence of managing people at each level of line management within an organisation is given in Figure 8.4 This approach provides a useful basis for:

- the profiling of jobs;
- the mapping of development opportunities;
- the design of development programmes.

Systematic approaches to the definition of competencies are particularly useful in that they make it easier for all managers to take part in the planning of training activities. A logical, comprehensive and consistent competence model assists in the identification of individual and organisational development needs. It provides a simple system for mapping training resources and development interventions to identify training needs. In this sense it makes the link between achieving business results and investing in the development of individuals. However, there are disadvantages to competency-based approaches in that they can be:

- too rigid and inflexible – not adequately taking account of the changing context within which businesses currently operate;
- over-bureaucratic and rule-bound;

Fig 8.4   The competence of managing people

Recruit	Contribute to identification and selection of personnel	Recruit and select personnel	Obtain an adequate supply of competent people
Develop	Contribute to the development of teams, individuals and self to enhance performance	Develop teams, individuals and self to enhance performance	Initiate, implement and evaluate programmes to develop people
Allocate	Contribute to the planning, organisation and evaluation of work	Plan, allocate and evaluate work carried out by teams, individuals and self	
Build relationships	Create, maintain and enhance productive working relationships	Create, maintain and enhance effective working relationships	Create and promote opportunities to maintain and enhance effective working relationships

- tending to reduce jobs into their parts rather than looking at them as wholes;
- under-estimating the extent to which different people achieve the same outcomes in different ways;
- over-specifying goals for training in ways which may hamper participants' own definition of their goals – which, of itself, is a source of learning.

Since these issues are of greatest concern when we examine approaches to management development, they are covered in more depth in Chapter 10 – see pp. 124–5.

Timing of training programmes

The main considerations are:

- the need to minimise disruption to the trainee's work group;
- the trainee's view of the most appropriate time for training;
- the optimum integration between job demands and the content of the training programme – it is not much use to send trainees on courses when there will not be any immediate opportunity to use newly acquired skills or knowledge;
- the availability of trainers, training rooms and other necessary resources;
- the need to work within budgetary constraints.

Location of training programmes

Exercise 4

List three places where the shop-owner's assistant can be trained.

Off-the job training at the workplace
Most large organisations have a training centre or training room. The advantage of such 'in-house' provision is that it can encourage identification with the organisation and thus the integration between work and training. Also, if all trainees are fellow employees, cross-fertilisation of ideas and the breaking down of departmental barriers can occur. Possible disadvantages include the exertion of pressure on trainees to return to their jobs if crises arise, and the lack of opportunity to mix with employees of other organisations.

On-the-job training at the workplace
'Sitting by Nellie' has long been favoured as a means of passing job knowledge and skills to new employees. Learning can be put into practice straight away. However, the success of this approach depends very much on the quality of 'Nellie', whose bad habits the trainee may acquire, or who may be unable to pass on job knowledge. Ways of overcoming these potential problems include:

- Ensuring that 'Nellie' performs the job exactly in line with management's requirements.
- Training 'Nellie' to be an effective teacher and coach (see Chapter 10, p. 135).

This will not overcome problems of work environment. The hustle and bustle of a busy office may not be conducive to training a typist to be an effective word processor operator.

External courses
Sometimes it is not economic to design 'in-house' programmes to meet trainees' needs. In addition, development programmes for managers and specialist staff, especially those which lead to formal qualifications, frequently have an educational orientation. Such provision is normally available only externally. The advantages of external courses are:

- the tuition may be better than can be provided within the organisation;
- trainees may feel freer to question and experiment;
- mixing with people from other organisations may facilitate learning. For example managers may learn that there are other options in the resolution of customer service problems by contact with their counterparts in other institutions.

The use of trainers

External trainers or consultants can be used to run training programmes, or the organisation can use suitable employees, usually training specialists. The relevant considerations here are:

- whether the training department or others available as trainers in the organisation have sufficient expertise and time available to undertake the training programme;
- what financial resources are available;
- whether it is desirable to encourage trainees to learn about the relevant policies and practices of other organisations; external trainers are often able to help here.

When external trainers or consultants are used, it is vital to brief them properly with relevant details of the organisation, the training needs analysis on which the programme is to be based, the backgrounds and expectations of the trainees and the training traditions of the organisation.

Increasingly companies are recognising the benefit of encouraging managers to develop training skills. This can be an efficient means of increasing the training resource; as importantly, it encourages managers and their staff to work closely together in the resolution of problems and to learn from their experience.

Administration of training

It does not follow that you can be sure of successful training if you hire the right trainer. Effective administration of the training process is also vital. For example, an apparently minor problem such as the non-appearance of coffee at the pre-arranged time during a training session is likely to hinder both the ability of the trainer to organise the learning process and trainees' concentration and hence their learning. Good training administrators ensure that:

- clear joining instructions are sent to participants well before the start of the programme;
- trainees understand the objectives of the programme;
- training is uninterrupted and necessary services (training materials, meals, etc.) are available.

Content of training programmes

The basis of our understanding of this subject lies in an area of psychology known as learning theory. Unfortunately, while the learning theorists have provided us with some pointers to the conditions under which training best takes place, they have been unable to find a solution for every case where training is necessary. Different people learn in different ways. Here is some guidance from learning theory which is relevant to the design of training programmes.

- Trainees should be able to clearly define their personal goals and targets.
- Elements of new knowledge required by trainees must be identified and presented in a way which aids learning.
- Learning is assisted if it can be related to the trainee's previous experience. Trainers should be familiar with the background of trainees and should try to 'speak their language'.
- Learning often occurs through experience. Trainees should be given the opportunity to use previous experience and to practise newly acquired skills and knowledge.
- There should be the opportunity, where relevant, to observe the skilled performance of others.
- 'Learning how to learn' is a skill which trainees should be helped to acquire. Thus trainers should be prepared to provide access to assistance with literacy and numeracy as well as generally to facilitate the learning process.
- Trainees' rates and methods of learning vary greatly. Older people, for example, differ from younger people in this respect.
- Some trainees reach a standstill or plateau in their learning from time to time. Trainers must try to understand the reasons for this to help trainees to make further progress.
- One of the most important influences on trainees' progress is their level of motivation. We looked at motivation theory in Chapter 6. Trainers should be aware of factors likely to affect trainees' motivation.
- Feedback on progress supportively delivered should be an integral part of the training process.
- Trainees can provide each other with feedback and mutual support.

Increasingly it is recognised that the trainer is by no means always the most effective manager of the learning process. Three principles of learner-centred approaches to training are:

- Trainees are responsible for their own learning;
- Trainees have the right to analyse their own learning needs;
- Trainees have the right to design their own training programmes.

If you adopt this approach to training you see the role of the trainer as facilitator and counsellor rather than as teacher. (For examples of this approach to management development, see Chapter 10, pp. 134–6.)

Training methods

Training methods are many and various:

- lectures;
- one-to-one instruction;

- conferences;
- workshops;
- case studies;
- roleplay;
- discussions;
- experiential learning;
- sensitivity training;
- action learning;
- brainstorming;
- coaching;
- projects;
- distance learning or self-study;
- open learning.

These categories are not mutually exclusive. For example, experimental learning workshops can be run.

We lack space here to examine the relative merits of each method; however some general comments are relevant. Already in this chapter we have mentioned two categorisations of training methods:

- by location of training; and
- by relationship between trainer and trainee.

Exercise 5

List three types of training which are examples of the first categorisation and two examples of the second.

Trainers must select methods which are suitable to the needs of the trainees and to the resources available. It is useful for this to be done in conjunction with trainees after making sure that they understand the aims and objectives of training. 'Variety is the spice of life' in training, and a number of methods can usefully be combined. For example, trainers frequently are subject to pressure from line managers to shorten training programmes in the interests of short-term productivity. Trainers can accommodate such pressures sometimes by encouraging trainees to use well-designed self-study texts. Attendance on a training programme can be used for learning in areas where participative methods must be used.

Open and distance learning
Where training is delivered mainly through formal courses certain practical barriers to learning are likely to occur:

- the limited availability of specific courses in some geographical areas;
- fixed starting dates, location and times of attendance;
- inappropriate learning methods or group composition;

- inconvenience and cost of attending a fixed location;
- unwillingness or inability of some employers to sponsor training.

Such limitations have led to a growth in demand for open and distance learning. Such approaches are argued to be:

- centred on trainees' needs rather than on the limitations of educational institutions;
- problem-centred, incorporating a mix of learning methods, materials and support in order to meet the needs of individual trainees.

In this way trainees should be able to determine the place, pace and content of their learning. In practice there appear to be several problems with such approaches:

- Trainees' commitment may be insufficient to meet the demands of the courses.
- The link between the content of such materials and trainees' previous experience may not be readily apparent.
- Trainees may reach learning plateaux and find it difficult to progress.
- Trainees may lack the study skills to cope with the material.
- Support for trainees and feedback to them may be inadequate.

These potential disadvantages may be overcome wholly or in part if the trainee has a coach or mentor in the organisation who is capable of assisting with learning problems. This may be a trainer or a trained manager.

8.7 **Stage 3: Implementing Training Programmes**

You will have learnt by now that effective training programmes depend on thorough training needs analysis and good programme planning and design. However, if the delivery of the programme, is inadequate, this preparatory work will have been wasted.

Selection of appropriate trainees for training

Some points to bear in mind here are:

- *Size of the group*   Some participative methods such as role play cannot be conducted effectively with large numbers. Even with more teacher-centred methods large numbers may be unhelpful; trainees can fail to become actively involved in their own learning.
- *Mix of participants*   Work group members may be assisted to work together more effectively by a common training experience such as a team-building workshop. Conversely individuals may develop ideas about possible new ways of solving work problems from a training programme which gives the opportunity to meet people from other departments or organisations.

- *The process of selecting trainees should also involve their superiors*   Much useful learning from training programmes fails to be carried back into the workplace. If the trainee's supervisor is responsible for pre- and post-programme briefing, this is likely to occur.
- *Trainees should want to be trained*   Only those employees who wish to undergo training should do so. Sometimes trainers have to work with course participants who have been told that they must be trained. In these cases there is resistance to learning and little is achieved.

Conducting training programmes in accordance with objectives and design

We stressed the need to give care to the selection of trainers and training administrators when we examined the planning of training programmes. Effective communication with trainees is vital, as is the careful organisation of materials and other resources.

Giving trainees feedback on performance during the training programme

Informing trainees of their progress during training encourages appropriate behaviour to be continued and inappropriate behaviour to be dropped. It allows the trainer to discover whether trainees have learning problems and to help these to be overcome.

8.8 Stage 4: The Evaluation of Training Programmes

Evaluation methods

Post-programme evaluation
Most trainers will tell you that the best time to get a positive reaction to a training programme from trainees is at the end of the last day. This reaction may not be valid in that the trainees are often in a state of euphoria at this time with lots of ideas buzzing around in their heads. it may be appropriate to administer a questionnaire at the end of the course which is clearly linked with the training which has been undertaken. It can be linked to a pre-course questionnaire to check the degree to which the course has come up to trainees' expectations and has increased their knowledge.

Because of the problems of administering such questionnaires at the end of a course, some trainers send them to participants weeks or months afterwards. This too has its disadvantages in that the response rate tends to be low. However, the greatest validity problem of post-course reaction questionnaires completed by trainees is that, to be effective, evaluation must measure whether training objectives have been achieved; that is, whether the trainee's job performance has improved. Asking for trainees' reactions to a course or even attempting to measure improvements in their knowledge does not assess whether they are more effective employees as a result of training.

Other training evaluation methods

Training is rarely evaluated other than via trainees' reactions. However, it can be evaluated with reference to:

- the behaviour of the individual employee on the job;
- managers' assessment of individual job performance;
- organisational performance in areas where training has been undertaken;
- the degree to which the whole organisation has benefited from training and development.

What is certain is that the further away you get from trainees' reactions to training the more difficult evaluation becomes. This is because other factors may be responsible for the changes detected.

Exercise 6

Fred's Food Processing Company sends all its supervisors on the training programme outlined in the extract from the training plan on p. 101. The following year, claims of unfair dismissal fall by 50 per cent and the company wins all the cases which go to industrial tribunal. Can it be claimed that this is the result of the training programme?

Evaluating changes in trainees' job behaviour

Managers can be consulted and trainees and trainers can meet in workshops or with individual managers to discuss the effects of training. It is best if this occurs some months after the completion of training so that the full effects can be evaluated. This can act as useful reinforcement for the trainee and can assist trainers to make decisions about modifications to training programmes.

Another useful mechanism is for trainees to be encouraged to compile action plans at the end of a training programme. The success of the training programme can be evaluated by the degree to which the plan is achieved.

Evaluation by trainers of their contribution

It is important that trainers systematically review the extent to which they assisted trainees to meet the objectives of a training programme.

Evaluation at organisational level

Relevant indicators include:

- labour turnover rates;
- accident rates;
- waste of materials;
- absenteeism;
- productivity.

Only thorough investigation is likely to reveal whether the improvements in these areas can be attributed to training. Some organisations use a training committee of senior managers to supervise such an assessment.

Feedback of evaluation results

To complete the systematic approach to training outlined at the beginning of this chapter, it is vital to feed back the results of evaluation to all those involved in the training process.

In summary, the evaluation of training initiatives:

- Enables the effectiveness of investment in training to be appraised.
- Provides feedback about trainees' performance which can be used in subsequent training.
- Improves future training programmes.

8.9 Role of the Training Specialist

In Chapter 1 we categorised the roles of personnel specialist as:

- audit;
- executive;
- facilitator;
- consultancy;
- service.

An example of an activity undertaken by a training specialist under each of these headings is:

Audit: Checking that job descriptions are accurate prior to embarking on a training needs analysis.
Executive: Running a training course.
Facilitator: Assisting trainees to identify their learning needs and objectives.
Consultancy: Advising a manager on the degree to which training can resolve a problem of inadequate employee performance.
Service: Providing management with regular reports on training activities which have taken place in the organisation.

9 Developing Organisations for the Future

If employing organisations are to respond effectively to the changes – political, economic, social and technological – within their environment, they must develop themselves and their people to be able to respond to this turbulence. Personnel practitioners have a key role to perform in these processes.

Table 9.1 summarises the requirement for organisations to focus both on the development of their own competence and on that of their people.

In this chapter we focus on organisational change and development. Chapter 10 provides the complementary focus on individual development in organisations.

9.1 Organisation Development

Organisation development involves the systematic and long-term application of behavioural science knowledge and theory as a means of improving organisational effectiveness. Through the attendant processes organisations should be better prepared to respond to change by adapting goals, structures, culture, style, etc. Organisation development does not focus only on the formal organisation structure. Rather it focuses on the whole organisation – informal as well as formal. Organisation development practitioners put much effort into 'surfacing' data about attitudes, perceptions, values and behaviours arising from informal as well as

Table 9.1 **Competent organisations require competent people**

Organisational competence	Individual competence
When the organisation has a clear mission or common purpose	Concern for quality and commitment to business performance
Action	Demonstration of appropriate personal qualities and skills

formal relationships within organisations. This focus tends to carry with it an assumption that organisations either are or can become places which reflect and pursue goals and objectives which are in the interests of and have the support of all individual members.

Exercise 1

Is this realistic?

A recent emphasis in the organisation development and management of change literature has been on the process of organisational learning. Many organisations now aspire to become learning organisations. This approach is not simply about training individuals. It can only happen as a result of learning at all levels and through all systems and processes within an organisation. In summary:

> A learning company is an organisation that facilitates the learning of all its members and continuously transforms itself. (Mike Pedler, John Burgoyne and Tom Boydell, *The Learning Company: A Strategy for Sustainable Development*, McGraw-Hill, 1991)

For example, where management is striving to put the learning organisation idea into practice, you would not only expect to see lots of people working hard on their own and others' development. You should also see finance staff and other functional specialists trying to assist learning about financial matters and encouraging all staff to take appropriate responsibility for the financial resources allocated to their department or unit.

Exercise 2

What do you think are the implications of the learning company idea for the roles and relationships of personnel specialists?

Organisation development also now gives much more attention to the political aspects of organisations. Strategies for change take much more account of power and influence. Sometimes this is achieved by defining those individuals and groups who have a stake in a particular issue or problem. Attention is then paid to their perceptions and ways in which these might be changed. The possibility of consensus between stakeholders is not taken for granted. Rather, effective organisation development techniques assume that conflict is likely but seek to deal with it in a productive way.

9.2 **Where Should Organisation Development Take Place?**

Organisation development interventions occur at many levels, although there is some evidence that top-down changes are more likely to be successful. The units within the change may be managed are also many:

- between organisations;
- within the whole organisation;
- between groups/teams/departments;
- within groups/teams/departments;
- within small groups at the level of the individual.

Table 9.2 gives examples of work done by organisation development specialists at each level.

Table 9.2   **Examples of organisational development activities**

Levels of work	Examples of organisation development work
Inter-organisational	• Reviews of relationships between buyers and suppliers • Development and implementation of merger proposals
Intra-organisation	• Development of change management strategies including whole organisation diagnosis
Inter-group	• Workshops/activities to develop understanding and relationships between key organisational groups, e.g. doctors and managers • Team to team work between functional advisory teams, e.g. Personnel, Finance and Marketing • Clarification of roles between external consultancies and internal specialists, e.g. development of IT strategies
(Group) team	• Team development – Boards, executive teams, senior management teams, functional teams, departmental teams – often linked with work on organisational/ departmental principles and values and development of change management strategies
Small group	• Development of managers as developers (of own staff) • Assistance to those involved in establishment of quality management processes • Development of internal consultants
Individuals	• One-to-one support of/mentoring of top managers and other key staff • Advice to individuals on development opportunities • Diagnosis (in depth) of development needs and development counselling • Design and development of development centres/workshops • Development programmes where there is a clear organisational (as well as individual) need

9.3 The Role of Personnel Specialists in Organisation Development

Exercise 3

Look back to the definitions of personnel roles and responsibilities in Chapter 1. Which of these roles would the personnel specialist be most likely to be performing when involved in organisation activities?

In this chapter we have emphasised that organisations are subject to and ideally need to manage constant change. For most, the status quo is not an option. Failure to seize new market opportunities or in other ways to fail to react to external pressures, for example from central government or its agencies, is likely to have adverse consequences. It is a truism that change can only be achieved through people and therefore personnel specialists are frequently becoming involved in the management of change. You may be asked to fulfil the role of internal consultant or to hire external consultants. Internal consultants have the advantage of being immersed in the organisation and its problems and being known to all the key players. But this familiarity may breed contempt, or, perhaps more significantly, it may mean that you are too inclined to share the value systems and perceptions of other organisational members. This may make you less likely to question existing practices and assumptions. Outsiders, by contrast, may have a freshness and naivety which shakes the status quo and provokes innovation.

Personnel techniques may themselves be very helpful aids to organisational change. For example a performance appraisal system is likely to place new requirements on the behaviours of managers to their staff and vice versa. By being explicit about these behaviours and their linkage with the organisation's expectations of its managers and employees, you will be assisting the management of change just as significantly as you would if you assisted a team development workshop or hired an external consultant in this capacity.

9.4 Organisation Development Tools and Techniques

Types of interventions chosen as appropriate to the needs of any particular situation and the people involved may range from very directive and, indeed, prescriptive to much lower profile. Thus, successful organisation development practitioners ideally must be able to operate in a variety of roles:

- listening to clients;
- acting as a prompt to change and/or speeding up the rate at which change takes place;

- confronting discrepancies between what clients say or think they do and what they actually do;
- diagnosing problems and prescribing appropriate remedies.

Exercise 4

Look back to the description of organisation development on page 115. Which of the roles listed above is the organisation development practitioner or consultant *least* likely to perform when working effectively within an organisation?

9.5 Changing Our Pictures of Effective Organisations

Too often our images of organisations are of machine-like predictable bureaucracies. More fluid, responsive, developmental organisations are needed which rely less on clear definitions of organisational boundaries and roles and more on networks committed to continual change.

This requires us to find new images or new ways of organising. However, we are easily trapped by our previous experiences, perceptions and assumptions. We create our own view of the world and of the organisations within which we work. If we are to change our organisations and our ways of operating within them, we must accept that our previous assumptions about managing are based on only partial insight. Organisation development practitioners (often in their roles of speeding up change and confronting assumptions) will need to surface clients' assumptions about hierarchy, structure and rules and their propensity to assume that change can only be achieved by reorganisation or by the rethinking of structures. Such principles of organisation are probably very suitable for delivering services or manufacturing products where the external environment is relatively stable and predictable. However, such bureaucratic organisations with their reliance on stable and predictable structures and operating rules tend to thwart change.

How can we describe organisational forms more responsive to the constantly changing world in which we live? How do these differ from more traditional ways of organising? We can use metaphors to assist people to reframe their understanding of the opportunities afforded to their organisation by its continually changing environment. For example, you could see your organisation as a living organism – perhaps an amoeba – which constantly changes shape in response to the demands of its environment. Such an approach leads to a rejection of an over-reliance on organisational charts and formal structures as a means of controlling the work process.

Exercise 5

What are the implications of an image of the organisation as a living organism for;

(a) recruitment and selection practices?
(b) payment systems?

Increasingly, writers and practitioners are beginning to see organisations as much more like fluid networks of interaction than bureaucratic structures. For example, some organisations are beginning to develop partnerships with their suppliers, involving a frequent cross-fertilisation of ideas and regular exchange of information. Perhaps the most striking example of network development is to be found in the film industry, where film studios that hold exclusive long-term contracts with actors and directors, have a staff of full-time composers and script-writers and own and operate fully equipped productive studios are a thing of the past. Now the studios act like brokers who negotiate a set of contracts for film production. Organisations like these are constantly trying to find and create the new initiatives and processes which will contribute to their success. It is kind of 'adhocracy', finding and developing its form as it goes along.

Assisting with the development of more responsive and flexible organisations

In assisting managers to develop new 'mind sets' about their organisations, personnel and other organisation development specialists must develop processes which:

- clarify the barriers to current organisational effectiveness;
- begin to develop a shared vision within the organisation (and possibly with suppliers or other potential or actual partners) of the future;
- develop and progress action plans for the management of the necessary changes.

A helpful first step in formulating a realistic and shared action agenda is to take stock of those factors which are currently blocking and those which are assisting change. Such a 'force field analysis' can be used to increase mutual understanding of the current situation. This analysis may be undertaken by interviewing the key players and then analysing their views for sharing and clarification in a workshop or meeting. Often the analysis takes the form of a table of pushing and blocking forces (Table 9.3).

Having taken stock of perceptions of the status quo, it is important to begin to build a shared vision of the future. A helpful process here is sometimes called 'future basing'. This requires participants to pretend that they are working in a specific year in the future. Assumptions about major political, economic, technological and social influences, both national and local, on the organisation at that time are explored. Participants then

Table 9.3　**Force field analysis**

Pushing forces influencing effective change	Restraining forces blocking effective change
Current State	Desired State

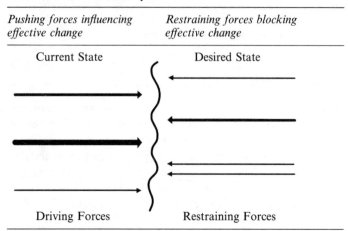

Driving Forces	Restraining Forces

address questions about their organisation's success or failure to achieve its objectives at that time. These could include:

- How are we doing in the delivery of our services to our customers? What's going well? What's not going so well?
- What have we, as a management group, done together and separately to get to this position?
- What capabilities have we demonstrated? What are our failings?

This process supports the development of the strategic agenda to move the organisation towards the emerging picture of the future.

Having examined the current position and developed a view of the future, the bit in the middle then needs consideration – the transition which needs managing. One way of handling this may be to establish a group responsible for managing the changes defined as a result of work to establish a future vision. A key task for such a group is to develop a shared understanding of the reality of the current position of all stakeholders in the changes. Who supports and who opposes the changes being planned? Tactics can then be developed to increase the commitment to the change of those stakeholders whose more active support is needed. Inviting such people to events where ways to manage change are being explored is more likely to succeed than merely communicating decisions and future plans. It is important to design learning opportunities not only to maximise formal learning for individuals but also to afford opportunities for more informal sharing of experiences. This emphasises the vital link between organisation and individual development referred to in the introduction to this chapter.

9.6 The Essence of Learning Cultures for Developing Organisations

If organisations are to become more effective in managing change in an increasingly unpredictable world, they will need cultures (or ways of doing things) which rely more heavily on learning than in the past. For example, there will need to be a recognition that:

- learning is part of managing;
- learning and change are one and the same thing;
- both managers and staff must own their own learning;
- organisations need people who are capable of assisting others and themselves to learn.

Human resource specialists have a key role to play in the development of learning cultures. In the next chapter we explore their role in individual learning and development.

10 Developing People for the Future

Here our focus is on the preparation of individuals to thrive in the rapidly changing circumstances of today's organisations. The most effective development processes yield benefits *both* for the individual *and* for the organisation.

In this chapter we examine individual processes for employees in general but particularly for those in managerial roles or with managerial potential. Specific attention is also given to the equal opportunities issues involved in development as they relate to women, ethnic minorities and disabled staff.

Management development is covered in the greatest depth for two reasons: firstly, because almost all organisations attempt to develop potential managers, and secondly, because the principles involved here can be applied to other staff. By the end of the chapter you should be able to apply a systematic approach to the development of employees in general.

10.1 What is Development?

The term 'development' implies improvement, becoming more accomplished and more effective. Development occurs not just because an employee seeks new knowledge and skills through education and training processes but because the individual also achieves increased self-awareness and understanding by watching and listening to others, reflecting on this and on their own practice, and challenging their own and others' assumptions. In other words, development happens when people live their lives in ways which enable them to learn and adapt.

Exercise 1

Why is this important in today's organisation?

Development, therefore, can be aimed at the improvement of capabilities within the current job or the acquisition of new capabilities to operate in a different arena. As organisational change becomes ever more rapid, employees need to continuously improve their capabilities to make an effective contribution to the organisation. In the next section we explore the characteristics of development processes which encourage both better performance in current roles and support competence in new spheres of activity.

10.2 What is Good Development?

Good development occurs when:

- There is benefit both to the individual and to the organisation.
- Learners are in charge of the process and developers support them.
- Learners are supported and challenged in their development by their managers and colleagues.
- Its focus is both learners as people (as well as employees) and the world within which learners and their organisations operate.
- There is an implicit recognition that both learners and their organisations are on journeys and therefore the past and the present are helpful sources of understanding about possible futures.
- It supports people through difficult issues and phases of their lives both at work and outside.
- It encourages learning from experience by reflection, questioning, encouragement of appropriate risk-taking and feedback.

Exercise 2

Why is the third characteristic of good development (a focus on learners as people and on the world within which they and their organisations operate) in the above list important?

10.3 Management Development

Common sense, character, background and job experience have been thought to be the most important determinants of an effective manager. Recently the increasing complexity of business and of managerial work, together with rising levels of expectation and education among young managers, have led to demands for greater professionalism. There is widespread recognition of the connection between economic growth and effective management. With some notable exceptions, Britain's managers have lacked the development, education and training opportunities of their counterparts in competitor countries. Over the past 25 years, however, there has been a tremendous growth in both undergraduate and postgraduate management courses; in-company development programmes have become more prevalent; business schools have developed and major companies have made graduate recruitment and that of other staff felt to be worthy of long-term development routine.

The state has encouraged management development, in particular through the Management Charter Initiative (MCI), which began in 1988 in response to concerns over the quality of management. In 1989 it drew up a management code which exhorted organisations to improve leadership and management skills and to encourage managers and supervisors to gain relevant qualifications. It has published standards or competencies for managers and supervisors. There is a direct link between MCI and the National Vocational Qualifications initiative in that the MCI standards can be used as the basis for an NVQ in management up to level five.

Exercise 3

Remembering our discussion in Chapter 8, define a competency and list two possible problems with a competency-based approach to management development.

One criticism of the MCI approach is that it bureaucratises learning, leading to a focus on rules, procedures and assessment at the expense of learning. More fundamentally it can be argued that the competency movement tends to break managerial work into artificial component parts whilst managers experience their work as a whole. They don't divide it into nice tidy boxes labelled operations or people management. Research suggests that managers don't work in an orderly and well-planned way. Rather their activities are more spontaneous and piecemeal. Typically they undertake many small tasks in a day and much is achieved by verbal communication. The reality is that management is a messy and complex process rather than an orderly one. Indeed, a key role of managers is to create disorder so that change can be achieved. Personal style is a key component of leadership and management. Different people achieve the same outcomes in different ways.

In summary:

- Managers need not only to be *efficient* – to do things right – but also to be *effective* – to do the right thing.
- If our organisations are to be effective then we need people who have vision and wisdom, people who know themselves, their values and so on.
- We need principles and values as the starting point for learning, rather than narrow behaviours.

- If managers are to be effective learners, they need not only to be able to learn facts and skills, but also to understand who they are, what roles they have, how these fit within their organisations and to have clarified and developed their personal values.
- Learning is then more effective if people themselves define their goals within a broader understanding of their personal principals and values and those of the organisation within which they work.

Nevertheless a competency-based approach to management development is being found to be helpful within many organisations. This seems to be particularly the case when personnel practitioners take care to make sure that the MCI standards are customised to fit the local culture, values, policies and procedures. A balance needs to be struck between very precise or indeed rigid definition of required characteristics for effective managerial performance and a very rudimentary appreciation of those capabilities. Over-specification may thwart change whilst vagueness will not assist management development to be a focused process which supports organisational functioning and development.

10.4 **The Focus of Management Development**

Suggestions about the most effective ways to develop managers vary greatly. It is superficially simple to implement a 'package' for the off-the-job training of potential managers. It is less easy to develop techniques which meet the needs of a particular organisation.

Exercise 4

Why do you think this is?

Nevertheless it has now been widely accepted that management development should be geared to the particular organisational circumstances of the manager's job. Requirements for effective management vary greatly from organisation to organisation depending on market circumstances, organisational size, history and so on.

10.5 **A Systematic Approach to Management Development**

Suppose that you have responsibility for management development in your organisation. Think back to Chapter 2, 'Planning for people' and to Chapter 8, on training; the questions which you would need to ask yourself to develop a systematic process for the selection and development of people for potential for managerial positions within three years are:

- What managerial jobs will we need to fill in three years' time?
- What will be the competencies of the individuals suitable to fill these positions?
- How can we select people for development to these positions?
- What development do these people need?
- What programmes should we design and implement to meet these needs?
- How can we evaluate the effectiveness of these programmes?

The rest of the discussion in this chapter attempts to answer these questions.

The link with human resource planning

As the first question implies, we need to estimate the demand for managers in future and the likely supply. Estimating demand is more difficult than some years ago. Organisations and their structures are less stable than some decades ago. Therefore, it is more difficult to predict in detail the kinds of managerial jobs which will be needed in future and from this the numbers and types of managers required. However, where organisations are committed to growing their own managers, it will be necessary to make some assumptions about the number of those with potential who should be developed as tomorrow's managers. Examining the likely supply of managers from within the organisation is somewhat simpler. Information which you would need to forecast the supply in three years' time includes:

- Number in managerial jobs now – by grade, age, job, etc.
- Retirement over the next three years.
- Labour turnover over the next three years.
- Movement into other jobs within the organisation as a result of promotion, demotion or other job changes.

On-going career development programmes for those with managerial potential also will affect the future supply of managers.

Exercise 5

Having estimated the demand for and likely supply of managers in three years' time, list the next three stages of the human resource planning process.

Decisions by organisations to 'grow their own' future managers often occurs because:

- The characteristics of managerial effectiveness often seem to depend on the particular nature of the organisation. Employees who understand 'the way things are done around here' are often felt to be a safer bet than outsiders.
- The opportunity of promotion may act as a spur to hard work.

Other factors may be the cost and uncertainty of the recruitment and selection process. Information from performance appraisal should act as a basis for judgements of employees. Early identification of potential gives time for systematic development prior to promotion.

Conversely, senior managers, in particular, are often recruited externally because an injection of 'new blood' can guard against stagnation or complacency.

Choice of a strategy for management selection and development should be made after careful consideration of organisational circumstances.

10.6 **Managerial Succession Planning**

Despite the difficulties of planning in the rapidly changing external environment of most organisations, succession planning remains a high priority for most personnel practitioners. However, conventional definitions of this process such as:

identify particular individuals as possible successors to specific posts

are too narrow a limit for the current reality of most organisations.

It is probably more appropriate to adopt a broader definition such as:

the strategic processes and actions aimed at ensuring a supply of suitable successors for key jobs and future roles.

This definition enlarges succession planning beyond identifying people for specific jobs to the processes by which the optimum quality and quantity of people become available for key managerial roles in the future. In this sense the line between succession planning and succession management is becoming increasingly blurred to include such personnel practices as:

- planning individual career paths;
- career counselling; and
- accelerated promotion schemes.

In more and more organisations practice in these areas is informed not only by the interests of the organisation but also by those of the individual. For example, it is becoming more common for management to accept that employees should no longer be expected to comply automatically with company wishes for job assignments.

In summary:

- Succession planning and succession management is beginning to focus more on individuals and less on jobs.
- The definition of broad managerial competencies to meet the demand of likely future roles is seen as essential for effective succession planning.
- Succession planning and succession management processes have a much greater focus on individual aspirations and life circumstances than was previously the case.

10.7 Analysis of Development Needs

In Chapter 8 we looked generally at the process of establishing training needs both at organisational and individual level. When considering development for either current or future managers, it is important to compare their current capabilities with the competency requirements of the job. In other words, development needs must be assessed in the light of the demands of the particular organisation and, where practicable, the particular job. Development programmes generally are not particularly effective where they are based on generalised assumptions of need.

Exercise 6

Who should take the lead in the assessment of development needs – the line manager, the potential participant in management development or the developer?

10.8 Selecting for Management Development

After reminding yourself of our discussion of the disadvantages of the selection interview in Chapter 3, you should be able to list some of the likely problems of using an interview as the sole method of selecting employees for management. These include:

- Selection interviews may be only as reliable as sticking pins in a list as a method of selecting the best candidate.
- Interviewers may be affected by stereotypes or other types of bias. In selecting a successor a manager may select 'in his own image'.
- As a result, interviewers may ask faulty questions or fail to listen adequately to candidates' answers.

Because of these problems it is advisable to use other methods to identify tomorrow's managers for development. The most common are:

- performance appraisal;
- development centres.

Performance appraisal

The advantages of using performance appraisal data for the assessment of development needs are:

- Employees can be given feedback on their performance as part of development counselling.
- Manager and employee together can take stock of the latter's development needs and career aspirations.
- This is a relatively cheap method of assessing development needs, compared, for example, with development centres.

However, you should be aware of the pitfalls of too great a reliance on this process for the identification of those people who should receive significant development investment. Immediate line managers may lack a broad perspective on the organisation both currently and for its possible futures. As a result they may find it difficult to discuss future roles and longer-term development needs with staff. Also they are likely only to be familiar with performance in the current job. This may be an inadequate indicator of the ability to do other jobs.

Development centres

Before reading this section you should refer back to the discussion of assessment centres in Chapter 3. Development centres use the same or very similar methods to assessment centres but their purpose is different. They are events in which managers identify their development needs for themselves – through activities and reviews with more senior managers and sometimes with external consultants or developers. The products of development centres are individual development plans. Centres can be used to identify needs related to current jobs or to long-term career aspirations.

Sometimes organisations run development centres to select participants for major development initiatives. In this case what occurs may be much more similar to an assessment centre. However, in my experience care must be taken to maintain a developmental ethos, for example by ensuring that candidates receive full feedback on their performance and are given the opportunity to fully think it through with the assistance of an appropriately skilled helper – be they a senior manager, personnel or development specialist or external consultant. Ideally, unsuccessful candidates should be assisted to define and implement appropriate development plans. The outcome of a development centre, therefore, should be that *all* candidates get a better understanding of the qualities needed to be a successful manager in their organisation. They should learn about their strengths and weaknesses and become better equipped to make more informed job and career development choices.

10.9 **Other Ways of Creating Individual Development Plans**

Development centres probably are the most rigorous way of generating individual development plans. However, both for managers and other staff there are other methods.

Career development workshops

The scope of these can vary from a focus on the next job to the creation of a lifeplan. They usually comprise a range of activities which enable participants to take stock of their lives and careers to date and to think through their aspirations for the future. Counselling is usually provided either as an integral part or an optional supplement.

Individual career counselling

Both internal and external resources can be used to provide a personal counselling, support or coaching service for managers. This can be very useful in encouraging the production of high-quality development plans.

Exercise 7

List two disadvantages of this sort of service for managers.

Psychometric tests and feedback

This is an increasingly popular method of identifying development needs. In effect it is a more limited version of career counselling services. However, you will require experts who are licensed to administer the tests, and who can both interpret the results and handle the feedback sensitively. This can mean using external consultants. (For a fuller discussion of psychometric tests you should refer back to Chapter 3, where their use in selection is covered.)

10.10 **Designing Management Development Programmes**

There are large numbers of management development techniques, but, as we said earlier, these must be appropriate to individual and organisational circumstances.

You might find it useful to talk to some managers about how they learned to do their jobs. The items which people mention most frequently include:

- doing the job;
- doing other jobs;
- courses at the place of work or elsewhere, including pre- and post-experience qualification programmes;
- life experience;
- television, video, radio and newspapers;
- friends, relatives or other influential people in life;
- thinking, reflection and self-assessment.

From this list you can see that management development can be driven by the orientations and perceptions of the teacher or by the individual in that it builds on her/his work and life experience.

Teacher-centred approaches

Most managers have experienced taught management programmes. The distinction between education and training made in Chapter 8 is relevant here. Managers need specific skills and knowledge to be effective. Training courses are designed to teach selling techniques, particular areas of legislation, negotiating techniques, effective speaking and so on. If well designed and run, these are useful, especially if they give the opportunity for participants to exchange views and experiences with others in similar positions.

Management education specialists argue that managers or potential managers must be flexible and adaptable to meet the changing circumstances of organisations. Courses therefore place high emphasis on the understanding of environmental context as a basis for enhanced ability to resolve problems and meet new situations. A variety of diploma and higher degree courses have been developed to this end by many universities and other institutions. Their quality varies greatly and the intending user should scrutinise a programme carefully prior to enrolment.

Learner-centred approaches

While good management teachers will assist managers to build positively on their experience, programme content and teaching methods are largely prescribed. This may adversely affect the extent to which participants are able to transfer their learning to work situations. There are other approaches to management education and development where learners take more responsibility for the diagnosis of their own development needs and the design of appropriate methods of meeting these. In Chapter 8, we outlined the main characteristics of learner-centred approaches to training.

Exercise 8

List three of these characteristics.

Learner-centred approaches to management development are now well established. They encourage managers to take responsibility for their own development and learn from their experience. Here we examine two of them – action learning and self-managed learning.

Action learning

This approach is based on the work of Reg Revans who, after an industrial career, became a professor of management. He quickly became disenchanted with management education, saying quite simply, 'Courses won't work'. We must give management education back to the managers and let them learn with and from each other during real work. Thus, action learning programmes have two common elements:

- Participating managers work on complex and important problems to which the final answer is not known but to which a series of acceptable next moves might be suggested.
- These managers meet together regularly and on equal terms in 'sets' to report to each other and to discuss problems and progress.

Programmes vary in their structure but participants spend either all or part of their working time on the diagnosis of a complex and important business problem. The important difference between this and other management development or research projects is that participation in action learning means that managers must 'own' the problem and must be able to implement their solutions. Revans favours the exchange of participants between organisations, so that a manager experienced in one organisational context is placed in a strange environment with a complex problem. In this way there is a freshness of approach and a likelihood that organisational conventions will be broken.

A vital element of action learning programmes is 'sets' of four to six participants. These meet regularly and are assisted by a set adviser. The function of the set is to help participants resolve the business problem which each owns. The set adviser, who may be a teacher, trainer, consultant, personnel specialist or manager, helps set members in a mutual process of giving and receiving help and generally assists with the action learning process.

Exercise 9

Which of the roles played by personnel specialists, described at the end of Chapter 1, does this description of the functions of the set adviser most closely resemble?

Action learning differs greatly from more conventional management education programmes with a defined syllabus, where participants are more dependent on teachers:

- An assumption of action learning is that managers learn by managing, whereas more conventional management education programmes aim to teach managers to manage.
- Participants on action learning programmes 'own' a real business problem and are responsible for implementing a solution.
- The role of staff on action learning programmes is to provide the conditions in which managers can learn by resolving practical problems. By contrast, teachers on more conventional programmes are concerned with the transfer of knowledge and skills to participants within the limits of a predetermined syllabus.

Self-managed learning

There are many similarities between this approach and action learning; participants in both programmes are responsible for the management of their own learning and there is no predetermined curriculum. Self-managed learning programmes also use 'sets' as a support and progress mechanism. Set advisers again assist the set to manage the development process. However, in self-managed learning programmes, managers analyse their own development needs and choose the associated learning methods in conjunction with fellow set members and other people associated with the programme. The resultant individual programme of study need not be centred on a business problem as in action learning. Rather, managers identify their personal learning objectives in the light of current and likely future life and work circumstances and goals. The task of the participant engaged in such a programme is to fulfil the requirement of their personally defined development programme. This may involve a variety of learning methods, such as attendance at formal training courses or educational programmes, projects at work or in other organisations, role plays, guided reading or attempts to improve performance directly on the job with structured feedback from peers, subordinates or superiors. Learners are responsible for evaluating and assessing their own learning in conjunction with fellow participants or set members and the set adviser.

The increasing popularity of learner-centred approaches

There is an increasing concern amongst senior managers that management development should not only be directly related to corporate goals and business needs but that it should also be supportive of the career and personal aspirations of individual managers. Continuous development by individuals is a necessity for business survival in an increasingly complex organisational environment. For these reasons there is a greater tendency than previously to design management development activities in response to the direct needs of managers and their day-to-day work. A summary of the reasons for the increasing emphasis on learner-centred approaches to management development follows:

- There is a greater recognition that people learn in different ways and of the implication of this for the effectiveness of management development initiatives. Learner-centred approaches to management development encourage individuals to identify their preferred learning styles and to design personal development programmes accordingly.
- It is now recognised that many apparently useful management development courses have had little impact on job performance. A better integration between learning and work is essential.
- There is an enhanced understanding of the importance of boss–subordinate (and other workplace relationships) to the development process. It is easier to ensure an integration of learner-centred approaches to development within this network than is the case for more traditional course-based development.
- Organisational culture itself is changing as senior management recognises that in today's less stable and predictable environmental circumstances they can take less responsibility for the direction of individual managers' careers; nothing is certain, not even the survival of the organisation; individuals must take greater responsibility for their own development and encourage their subordinates to do the same.

The implications of learner-centred approaches for the role of the manager

In organisations that place a high value on training and development activities, managers become indirectly involved in training through the appraisal system. Where individual managers are encouraged to take greater responsibility for their own development, the manager becomes an essential contributor to the learning process. There are a number of structured ways in which managers can take on this role. Two are explored here:

- the manager as coach;
- the manager as mentor.

The manager as coach

Coaching rests on the assumption that someone who performs a job is qualified to assist a more junior employee to develop the capability to undertake a task or project more effectively. This 'helping' process involves both discussion and guided activity to encourage the learner to acquire new knowledge, skills and competencies. Thus, the coaching process has two elements:

- improved task performance;
- learning and development from undertaking the task.

To be an effective coach the manager must assist the subordinate to identify personal learning needs and agree how the undertaking of a particular task will assist these to be met. The coach should hold regular sessions with the learner to review progress and give further counselling and guidance.

A major advantage of coaching as part of a management development programme, which may also include courses and other more formal learning experiences, is that a close relationship between superior and subordinate should ease problems of integrating new learning with the requirements of present or future jobs.

A word of caution must be sounded! Not all managers are effective coaches. Training in relevant skills is vital, as are certain personal qualities.

To give you a feel for the nature of the coaching relationship, you may find it helpful to try to analyse your own development needs and take the list to your boss for discussion. Ask for help in attempting to prepare a personal development plan including the selection of a suitable task or project which may assist in meeting your learning needs. This is a useful exercise in itself. However, to attempt to build your knowledge of and skills in the coaching process, after the interview list the skills needed by your boss to help you. Your list is likely to include:

- Good communication skills.
- Willingness to listen and to learn.
- A participative style rather than a desire to impose solutions on you.
- Interest in you and in your development.

The manager as mentor

Mentoring, like coaching, is concerned with the personal development of the learner, but the process through which the helping relationship is undertaken is much less specific. The mentor assists the learner with the development of life goals and nurtures learning in pursuit of these. In this sense it formalises the help and encouragement which some people have been fortunate to receive early in their careers from their more senior counterparts. Just as not all managers are effective coaches nor are they effective mentors. The latter process is demanding intellectually, emotionally and spiritually. The effective coach focuses on 'Why?' This is more confronting for the learner but can lead to development breakthroughs at work and in life generally which have a significant long-term effect.

Where managers are trained to contribute to the learning process, they are most inclined to ensure that their staff are fully trained, not just once, not just for the job, or for the job as currently defined – but continuously prepared to contribute to corporate success. In developing themselves as essential contributors to the learning process, line managers too acquire insight and challenge. The organisation itself should benefit both directly from improved performance of both managers and their staff and indirectly from the encouragement of greater questioning of the appropriateness of corporate goals and of the ways in which they are pursued.

The implications of learner-centred approaches for the role of the trainer

In many ways changes in the role of the trainer mirror those in the role of the manager from a directive to a supportive or facilitative role. There will be less direct teaching and more facilitation of group events, individual counselling and coaching, provision of learning resources and consultancy support to line managers.

10.11 Evaluation of Management Development

It is probably more important to review the results of management development systematically than it is for other types of training activity. This is because the expenditure per employee of both time and money is likely to be greater.

Exercise 10

List three ways of evaluating the results of management development. Think back to our discussion of the evaluation of training in the last chapter, pp. 111–13, to help you to do this.

In deciding on your answers to this question you should have recalled the problems of evaluating the results of training discussed in the last chapter. Only by a continuous process of feedback can management development activities become closely aligned to organisational needs.

10.12 Career Development for Young People

After our examination of management development we will look briefly at planned development activities for young extrants to organisations. These are usually eighteen-year-old school leavers or graduates. Generally, approaches to their development are of two types:

- the 'Cook's tour' of the organisation;
- specific training in one job.

A case study

When I first graduated I went to work as a personnel management trainee at the headquarters of a large retailing and wholesaling organisation. The selection process was intensive and highly competitive, bearing considerable resemblance to an assessment centre in the techniques employed. I was keen to gain experience of personnel management. The personnel department was divided into sections dealing with recruitment and selection, industrial relations, salary administration, employee benefits and so on. Trainees were given a 'Cook's tour' of the department, spending three months on each section.

Initially we were enthusiastic about this, believing that it would afford the opportunity to acquire a good grounding in all the aspects of personnel work. I became disillusioned after weeks in the 'sickness section' dealing with the administration of the company's scheme under the supervision of a clerk the same age as myself whose experience of personnel management was limited to his present job. I spent my days doing manual calculations of sickness entitlements and benefits. I never saw an employee or a manager. My next move was to an industrial relations section. Here the work was more interesting and I was supervised by a graduate industrial relations officer who was keen to help me to learn. To cope with the job I needed considerable understanding both of industrial relations and of payment-by-results systems, since the task was to prepare negotiating briefs for management. I tried to gain appropriate knowledge by intensive reading of files of previous cases. This was not entirely satisfactory since my learning was very fragmented and needed consolidation.

The industrial relations officer was frequently out at factories assisting with negotiations, and his superior, the industrial relations manager, was openly hostile to me. He had opposed the appointment of graduate trainees, believing that we were a hindrance to the smooth running of the department. We had day-release one day each week to attend a local college course which led to the examinations of the Institute of Personnel Management. The course seemed to have little relevance to our work and we generally saw it as a day off work!

The five problems of career development using a 'Cook's tour' illustrated by this case study include:

- The high expectations of the trainees generated by the rigorous nature of the selection process were not fulfilled by the development programme.

- The employees charged with the day-to-day supervision of the trainees were inadequately integrated into the programme. Hence supervision was generally inadequate.
- The development programme was actively opposed by some members of the department.
- There was a failure to ensure that trainees had adequate skills and knowledge to cope with the tasks which they were given or readily available support and guidance when necessary.
- The college course was not integrated with work experience even in the broadest sense.

Only if these problems had been overcome would we have reaped the advantages of such a 'Cook's tour': that is, we would have learnt about the various types of personnel work and their relationships with each other and with the other parts of the business. A further advantage of such approaches to the development of young people is that they enable them to make better decisions about their career goals. In particular they allow general management trainees to decide on the function of management in which they wish to specialise.

Many young people move straight into a permanent job and receive development related to that job. The advantage of this approach is that it gives greater opportunities for the development of skills, by contrast to the 'tour' which may give trainees a wide but superficial knowledge of the organisation. Young people in junior management, technical or professional roles learn by coping with the demands of their own job rather than by watching others. In this situation a sympathetic boss with highly developed coaching skills is vital.

10.13 Equal Opportunities in Career Development

As we shall see in Chapter 11, positive action can be taken to train women or members of ethnic minority groups where it can be shown that they are under-represented in particular jobs. Fear of resentment from other workers has discouraged some employers from taking such initiatives. However, many organisations now are taking active steps to implement equal opportunity policies. As a result programmes to provide development opportunities for members of groups previously under-represented in certain occupations have been started.

Targets can be established for numbers of women, black people or the disabled to be in particular posts within a specified time. This is the human resource planning stage of the development programme. People with the potential to fill these positions must then be selected.

Exercise 11

Remembering our discussion of a systematic approach to training in the last chapter, and that of management development in this chapter, list the next two stages of an equal opportunities career development programme.

Employees selected for development in this way will have occupied relatively routine jobs for many years, which may not have made full use of their personal capabilities. Hence, equal opportunities programmes usefully include confidence-building activities and assertiveness training as well as very good facilities for counselling and guidance. The support of managers and other people involved in the programme is vital. Some organisations run training programmes in racism and sexism awareness for managers involved in making development and promotion decisions, to help to ensure that career development for members of minority groups becomes a reality as part of the implementation of equal opportunities policies.

10.14 Development of High Flyers

More attention is being given to identifying, developing and rewarding those deemed to have the potential to occupy senior management positions in future. Such people are asking for greater responsibility earlier in their careers. Many organisations are making great efforts to ensure their retention. Two ways of achieving this are:

- by decentralisation and divisionalisation which gives more people experience of running a business;
- the development of consultancy or secondment opportunities within or outside the business.

Flexible organisations need flexible managers

It is apparent that organisations need to be increasingly flexible to respond rapidly to fast-moving business conditions. Traditionally managers have been recruited on the basis of skills required to resolve immediate operational problems; little attention has been paid to the development of long-term strategy. The pace of change now suggests now suggests that the emphasis should be on the potential to acquire new skills in the future.

10.15 A Final Word on Development

Uncertainty and opportunity face management. Trainers and developers can make a very significant contribution if they seize the opportunity for change and are not afraid to try new approaches. We hope that in this chapter we have convinced you that systematic development not only of managers but also of other groups of employees is vital if such future challenges are to be met!

11 Looking after Employees: Welfare and Counselling Services

The development of welfare services in industrial organisations began in the UK in the late nineteenth century, when there was no welfare state and working conditions could be appalling. Some paternalistic employers, most of them Quakers, believed that they had a responsibility to look after their employees for both social and economic reasons. The question we attempt to answer in this chapter is whether it is still necessary for employers to provide welfare services.

The are many reasons for the provision of welfare services for employees by management:

- To ensure that employees' productive capacity is not handicapped by personal problems.
- To fill gaps in the provision of state welfare services for employed people.
- The social responsibilities of employers.
- The legal responsibilities of employers. The law requires employers to provide adequate lighting, fume extraction, air conditioning, facilities for washing, rest breaks and meals and so on. As we shall see in the next chapter, the law also, lays down statutory minima for the provision of certain rights. Maternity pay and maternity leave would fall into this category.
- The desire to be perceived as a good employer as an aid to recruitment.

It is difficult to prove a link between the provision of welfare services and productivity, but many managers would argue that encouraging employees to have a positive attachment both to their jobs and to the employing organisation is in the interests of economic efficiency.

State welfare services are geared mainly to the needs of those who do not work. An ageing population has put strains on these.

11.1 How Can We Define 'Welfare' in the Context of Modern Personnel Management?

The first comprehensive list of the range of personnel management activities to be compiled in Britain was published in 1943 (G. R. Moxon, *Functions of a Personnel Department*, Institute of Personnel Management, 1943). It listed welfare or employee services activities as:

- Administration of canteen policy.
- Sick club and benevolent and saving schemes.
- Long-service grants.
- Pension and superannuation funds or leaving grants.
- Granting of loans.
- Legal aid.
- Advice on individual problems.
- Assistance to employees in transport, housing, billeting, shopping and other problems.
- Provision of social and recreational facilities.

The comprehensive nature of this list was more an expression of hope for the future than of reality in most organisations in the immediate postwar period. Can it then be said to be some sort of indication of the welfare services provided by employers today?

Most large employers do provide specialist welfare services to employees of the sort listed above, though there has been some shift of emphasis from those where state services are now more comprehensive (housing, transport and recreational provision) towards greater provision or counselling and other personal advice service.

With technological change, more of the organisation's resources tend to be invested in plant and machinery. Hence payments to employees become a lesser proportion of overall operating costs, and so the provision of, for example, counselling services becomes relatively cheap. As the ratio of capital invested per employee increases, management may become more aware of the need for employees to be fully effective. Welfare services are both cheap and efficient to provide.

However, there are arguments against the provision by management of welfare services for employees today. These can be summarised as:

- State welfare provision is much more wide-ranging than before, and there is no need for employers to duplicate such services.
- 'Welfare' sounds like nineteenth-century paternalism and 'do-gooding'. It may even be a device for discouraging employees from joining trade unions.
- The provision of such services by employers can increase the gap between the 'haves' and 'have-nots' in our society, and as such is undesirable.

This is a summary of the counter-arguments to those mounted in favour of welfare provision by employers at the beginning of this chapter. There is no right or wrong answer. Much depend both on your values and on the circumstances of the employing organisation. Some employers have a policy of peaceful competition with trade unions. This usually involves employment policies which are generous by comparison with others. Such employers would tend to provide a full and attractive range of employee welfare services.

11.2 Occupational Stress

Employers have come to recognise the effects of stress on job performance. Stress is an individual reaction to aspects of life. A certain amount of stress can be a good thing. Active management of stress, both at work and outside, can pay dividends. The fact that many of us do not cope well with our problems is evidenced by the total cost of stress to industry – estimated at between 3 and 3.5 per cent of GNP (gross national product) – 10 times more than all industrial disputes.

Research has suggested that everyone is susceptible to stress. Particularly affected are those who have little control over the circumstances in which they work, such as fire-fighters, air traffic controllers, ambulance personnel, police and assembly-line workers. It has also been argued that women and ethnic minorities are particularly liable to suffer from stress; many organisational cultures are still very dominated by white men. Sexual and racial harassment occurs more frequently than many managers would like to believe. Greater recognition of specific work-related situations which may be particularly stressful – relocation, technological and other organisational changes and redundancy, to name but three – is leading many employers to take further steps to ensure that welfare and other employee support services are oriented towards the prevention of stress-related problems and provision of help to employees who experience an inability to cope.

11.3 Personal Services for Employees: Counselling

Most organisations seem to provide employees with counselling and advice services. Think of times when your employer has provided you with advice or counselling. If you are not working at present, ask someone who is working to provide you with the examples. Your examples are likely to fall under these headings:

- Career development.
- Legal advice.
- Housing.
- Bereavement.
- Sickness.
- Divorce/marital problems.
- Retirement.
- Redundancy.
- Working relationships.

You may have had difficulty with this if your organisation does not provide such services formally. Managers of personnel specialists may be called on to help employees in this way but they cannot be called professional counsellors. Fewer professional counsellors work in the employment field in the UK as compared with the United States.

Who should undertake employee counselling?

The relationship between manager and subordinate often will not be amenable to the development of a counselling relationship. The manager may be concerned with personal status and thus unwilling or unable to adopt the subordinate's perspective. Also, there may be a tendency on the part of the manager to be protective of information which might be useful to the employee, such as the latter's *real* prospects of promotion. The employee, too, is likely to find it difficult to seek counselling from the manager. For example, disclosure of domestic problems may hamper promotion prospects.

Specialist personnel staff often take on a counselling role. They may experience fewer problems than line managers. Nevertheless the problems of trust and fear of confidentiality so far as employees are concerned will arise. For this reason, some organisations use specialist independent services staffed by professional counsellors. Even where this is done it is certain that both managers and personnel specialists will take on the role of counsellor from time to time. In order to carry this out effectively they must be trained.

We have stressed the need for professional individual counselling services, but sometimes non-professional helpers may play a very useful role. For example, in career planning, employees can assist each other to identify career and life goals and to plan ways of achieving these. In this way mutual support is possible. This has been found particularly helpful for female employees and members of ethnic minority groups who often fail to achieve their full potential through lack of confidence and skills and a tendency by employers and others to undervalue their abilities. Some employers encourage such counselling as part of equal opportunities programmes.

The skills of counselling

It seems that effective counsellors:

- encourage trust from their clients;
- relate empathetically to their clients;
- are people rather than task-centred;
- encourage clients to clarify the situation and to search for their own solutions rather than depending on others;
- supply relevant information but refrain from giving advice.

For which employees may personal welfare services be necessary?

Young employees

Trainees, and employees who have recently completed full-time education, may need special support during the first weeks and months of their employment. Frequently this is provided by those responsible for operating training programmes. Where young people have had to leave home to take a job, employers sometimes provide help with housing.

Those nearing retirement

Many employers have encouraged workers nearing retirement age to retire early as part of a policy to reduce the size of the labour force. For these people and those due to retire at the normal date, it is now common practice to provide retirement counselling and/or pre-retirement courses. Topics which could form part of a pre-retirement course include:

- Investment.
- Keeping healthy.
- Activities outside the home.
- State benefits for retired people.
- Taxation.

Some organisations also provide assistance to retired employees who suffer financial hardship or have personal problems.

Redundant employees

Redundancy usually comes as a shock to employees. Hence many employers provide similar support to that provided to those nearing retirement. Four other topics, in addition to those listed above, which may be covered in a course for employees about to become redundant are:

- Career counselling.
- Job-search skills.
- Starting your own business.
- Government training schemes.

Frequently, at a time of redundancy, attention is focused on those who will have to leave, both in terms of the financial compensation for loss of jobs to be awarded and other support services available. Those who will continue as employees should not be forgotten. Often they will have uncertainties about the future of the organisation and their own future within it. Management may need to be particularly vigilant to allay such uncertainties.

The bereaved and the sick

Both employees whose close relatives die and those who experience long periods of absence from work because of personal sickness will have financial problems. Personal welfare services can provide advice and assistance.

Increasingly employers are providing support for those suffering from stress-related illness. In these cases it is important to make provision for members of the employees' family to be able to make the approach to a counselling service, since they are often best placed to identify the danger signals, such as increased drinking or irritability.

11.4 Group Services for Employees

Some employee services are provided for groups rather than for individuals. Into this category fall:

- canteen services;
- sports and recreational facilities;
- facilities for the purchase of goods, in particular those produced or sold by the organisation.
- occupational health facilities.

Canteen facilities

Only the smallest organisations tend not to provide any catering facilities for employees. The reasons for this include:

- Their cost can be offset against corporation tax and therefore they are relatively cheap to provide.
- They help the image of the organisation as a good employer.
- The provision of adequate catering facilities on the premises may reduce the attraction of nearby restaurants and pubs. As a result employees will be less likely to take over-long lunch-breaks!

Canteen facilities can be the most controversial aspect of employee services. As a result many organisations have canteen committees – a specialist form of joint consultation. The presence of employee representatives should ensure that the 'consumer' is represented in decision-making about the provision of services, and that as a result employees will feel that the correct way to voice dissatisfaction is through their representatives. In this way management hope that any grievances can be dealt with systematically.

The practice of using outside catering contractors has increased. Professionalism, bulk buying and economies of scale in other aspects of catering provision frequently result in such contractors being able to run the canteen cheaper than can the employer. However, employees will still complain to the employer if the service is inadequate.

Sports and social facilities

Welfare services for employees originated at the end of the nineteenth century, when provision of state services in this general area was sparser than today. Many paternalistic employers opened sports and social clubs for employees and their families. Today, not only has provision by local authorities and private organisations increased, but the recreational and social habits of the population have changed. Many employees like to spend their leisure time away from premises provided by the employer. Some employers have kept their facilities but have made them more open to the public at large. Increased concern about the effects of occupational stress has encouraged some employers to rethink policies on the provision of recreational facilities. For example, it is becoming more common for employers to provide fitness centres themselves or to make arrangements for employees to have access to such facilities.

Facilities for the purchase of goods

Some companies run 'staff shops' where goods purchased by the employer or associated employers can be purchased at a discount and provide facilities for personal services, such as banking or hairdressing.

Occupational health facilities

Each year, about 350 million working days are lost because of sickness and industrial injuries. In most years this is over thirty times the working days lost through strikes. It makes economic sense for employers to provide occupational health services for employees. In Europe such services are usually a legal requirement.

The aims of an occupational health service are:

- To assist in the establishment and maintenance of the highest possible physical and mental health of employees.
- To ensure that employees' health allows them to cope with their jobs.
- To project employees from any health hazard which may arise from their jobs.

The interpretation of such aims will differ from one organisation to another. Where the nature of the work is inherently hazardous more attention is given to the provision of occupational health services.

Many employers see occupational health provision as an educational or preventive service and therefore may include medical screening and counselling on smoking, alcohol and diet. The increased attention being given to work-related stress is emphasising the importance of these services.

11.5 Childcare Facilities

During the period of relatively full employment in the 1980s, many employers were concerned to attract female employees. Hence, many opened or extended childcare facilities; others provided women with childcare allowances. As the recession began to bite in the late 1980s some of the impetus behind these arrangements declined.

11.6 Status Considerations

In the UK it has been customary to stratify employee services provision and fringe benefits according to the status of employees. This is a reflection of our class structure. Recently many employers have moved towards single status for all employees, though often this excludes senior management, who retain rights to 'top-hat' pension schemes, separate car parks and other symbols of position.

Differences in the provision of employee benefits and facilities have been a source of discontent. Yet moves to 'single staff status' may also be a cause of grievance for higher-grade employees who resent the loss of status differentials. Change in this area needs careful handling by management.

11.7 The Future of Employee Services

Trends likely to affect the provision of employee services over the next five years are:

- Employers are likely to feel an increased responsibility to fill gaps in state provision for their employees. If the UK adopts the European Social Chapter, then this is particularly likely to be the case.
- The continued 'de-layering' of organisations, together with the emphasis on improving competitiveness, is likely to mean that many organisations will continue to shed staff. Hence, the emphasis on redundancy compensation and outplacement counselling is likely to continue.
- As organisations become more capital-intensive, i.e. as the amount of financial investment per employee increases, so it becomes relatively cheaper to provide a full range of employee services.
- Competitive pressures to slim down organisations also tend to increase the hours worked by managerial staff in particular. This and other performance pressures will continue to make occupational stress a focus of attention.

Exercise 1

Which of the following statements about the provision of welfare services to employees are true and which are false?

1 All organisations provide a range of welfare services for their employees. *True or False?*

2 When managers undertake career or redundancy counselling they should persuade employees to accept the solution which is in the interests of the employing organisation. *True or false?*

3 Even though they are not professionally trained, employees can counsel each other on career development. *True or false?*

4 Employers often provide pre-retirement courses for employees. *True or false?*

5 Good sports and social facilities encourage loyalty to the organisation by its employees. *True or false?*

12 The Law and the Rights of the Individual Employee

12.1 Checklist of Individual Employment Rights

When someone applies for a job, they are protected from:

- race and sex discrimination;
- the need to declare 'spent' offences;
- discrimination as either members or non-members of a trade union
- discrimination against a disability.

On starting work, employees are entitled to:

- protection against dismissal or other unfavourable treatment on grounds of race, sex or trade union activity;
- equal pay (both men and women);
- paid time off for antenatal care;
- paid time off for trade union duties*;
- paid time off for safety representative duties;
- time off for trade union activities*;
- time off for public duties*;
- statutory sick pay;
- written statement of terms of the contract;
- itemised pay statement;
- monetary compensation if employer becomes insolvent;
- be consulted in the event of redundancies.
  *only those working 16 hours or more per week

One of the complexities of employment law is that the length of service required before workers acquire particular legal rights varies quite considerably. The following checklist summarises the current position.

With service, employees accrue additional rights, as follows:

After 4 weeks:

- a minimum period of notice;
- guarantee payments and protection from dismissal, if the employer cannot provide work;

- monetary compensation and protection from dismissal, if the employer suspends workers on certain medical grounds.

After 26 weeks:

- statutory maternity pay.

After 2 years:

- written statement of reasons for dismissal;
- protection from unfair dismissal (provided the employer has twenty or more workers);
- redundancy compensation;
- paid time off to look for work in case of redundancy;
- to return to work after pregnancy or period of confinement.

Most of the rights here apply to full-time workers, part-time workers who work more than 16 hours per week, and part-timers who work more than 8 hours per week and have at least 5 years' continuous service.

However, as we indicated in Chapter 5, the impact of European law, as interpreted by the European Court of Justice, is making the distinction in the UK between full and part-timers increasingly difficult to apply. As we have seen, those who work less than 16 hours per week for 5 years are excluded from a range of employment rights, while those who work less than 8 hours per week have no protection at all in employment law.

In pursuit of this issue the Equal Opportunities Commission sought and won a judicial review in the House of Lords which declared that the differing levels of service requirements are incompatible with Article 119 of the Treaty of Rome and of EC Directives on equal pay and treatment: a recognition that these requirements indirectly discriminate against the predominantly female part-time workforce.

Another key factor in determining employment rights is the difference between an employee and someone who is self-employed. Some employers have seen advantages in encouraging employees to become self-employed. The distinction is a critical one since it determines liability for income tax and National Insurance contributions, a person's entitlement to statutory sick pay from the company together with rights to employment protection.

Whether or not a person is an employee or an independent contractor, is determined by the relationship between the two parties to the contract. Therefore an employer who sees advantage in this arrangement needs to recognise that a firm agreement to this effect with an 'employee' may have to stand scrutiny from the courts who will examine whether the circumstances of the relationship can be defined as one between independent contractors. There is also an issue you may wish to consider about the way in which this approach can undermine ideas like company employees being in the same team.

In this chapter we focus on the major legal rights of employees other than those associated with the termination of the contract of employment.

12.2 Anti-Discrimination Legislation and Employee Rights

Promotion opportunities

In the same way as they must not discriminate against applicants for employment, employers must give equal opportunities for transfer and promotion.

In 1979 nearly half of the 900 platform staff employed by Bradford Metro, the public bus company in Bradford, West Yorkshire, were of Asian origin. Many of them had 10 to 15 years' service. There were no Asian inspectors and only one Afro-Caribbean inspector out of 50 people employed in this capacity. An investigation by the Commission for Racial Equality (CRE) revealed that the district manager instructed interviewers to be cautious in appointing Asian inspectors. Reasons given for this included fear of opposition from white busmen and of problems with the travelling public. As a result higher standards of performance, including those required in a written test, were demanded of Asian applicants.

Exercise 1

Remembering the discussion of the law on discrimination in Chapter 5, comment on the legality of Bradford Metro's promotion procedures. What action should have been taken to remedy the situation?

Training

Legislation protects employees who believe themselves to have been denied equal opportunities for training. In addition the Sex Discrimination Act and the Race Relations Act include positive discrimination provisions, where during the previous year there were no (or comparatively few) persons of one sex or race doing a particular type of work. In such circumstances the provision of special training programmes is permissible. This is the only legal provision for positive discrimination in the UK at present. Once members of minority groups have received training, they must be selected for jobs on merit alone.

Benefits, facilities and services

Employers must give equal access to fringe benefits to all their employees. Thus it would be illegal for a bank to offer low-cost mortgages to male employees only.

Genuine occupational qualifications

Exercise 2

A newspaper publisher wishes to promote a journalist to the position of Middle East correspondent. Would it be illegal to consider only men for the job?

12.3 The Equality Commissions

The Equal Opportunities Commission (EOC) and the Commission for Racial Equality (CRE) are charged with the identification and elimination of obstacles to equality of opportunity. Their members and employees operate independently of the government, though they are paid by the state. They must keep relevant legislation under review and where necessary suggest amendments. There is also a responsibility to promote research and educational activities. The commissions can draw up codes of practice giving practical guidance on the elimination of discrimination. Such codes are not legally binding, but are admissible in evidence before an industrial tribunal or court (see Chapter 5, p. 59).

Both commissions can conduct formal investigations, either on their own initiative or at the request of the Secretary of State for Employment. There have been a number of such investigations into employment practices. Where evidence of unlawful discrimination is found, non-discrimination notices can be issued to prevent further discrimination.

12.4 Equal Pay

Like the Sex Discrimination Act, the Equal Pay Act deals with discrimination at work.

Broadly, the Equal Pay Act deals with wages and other terms and conditions of employment; as we have seen, the Sex Discrimination Act covers the terms of an offer of employment and is concerned with the elimination of discrimination in recruitment, training, promotion and other aspects of the employment relationship.

The Equal Pay Act gives men and women the right to equal treatment in individual contracts of employment.

Exercise 3

Does the Equal Pay Act apply to all employees?

Claims under the Equal Pay Act

Here we shall discuss the law as if it were dealing with a woman's claim for equal pay.

It is up to the applicant for equal pay to select the male worker with whom she wishes to compare herself in order to make a claim. He must be employed by the same or an associated employer and normally he must work at the same place as her; she and he must be employed under the same terms and conditions of employment. It is possible to make a comparison with a male predecessor but only if he occupied the job in the recent past.

Having found a man with whom to compare herself, the employee must be able to show that she is employed:

- on 'like work' to that of the a man; *or*
- in a job which, though different from that of a man, has been rated as equivalent under a job evaluation scheme *or*
- under the Equal Pay Act (Amendment) Regulations, on work of equal value to a man's in terms of the demands on her under such headings as effort, skill and decision-making; in such cases there need not be a job evaluation scheme, or where there is, she can claim that it has discriminatory results.

'Like work'

'Like work' is defined by the Act as being of 'the same or broadly similar nature' to the man's work. The courts have said that tribunals need not undertake a minute examination of the differences between the work done by the women and that done by the man. For example, a cook who prepared meals for an executive dining-room compared her work with that of an assistant chef in the works canteen. Differences in the hours worked and in the volume and nature of the meals prepared, were felt to be insufficient justification for unequal pay. That is, they were not of 'practical importance'.

The points which tribunals consider, to determine whether differences are of practical importance, are:

- the nature of the differences;
- whether they occur in practice;
- how often they occur;
- whether the differences are sufficiently significant to justify differences in terms and conditions of employment.

Some tribunals have used as a yardstick whether two men would be paid differently if they did the jobs in question.

Work 'rated as equivalent'

For the applicant to have access to equal pay by this route, the organisation in which she works must have a job evaluation scheme. Surveys suggest that, while the majority of large employers use such techniques, many small companies do not. For the employer to use the defence that the woman's work has been classified as unequal to that of her male comparator through the application of a job evaluation study, the latter must be shown to be valid. Non-analytical methods (see Chapter 13, pp. 168–9) are unlikely to be valid.

'Equal pay for work of equal value'
Because the UK is a member of the European Economic Community, its legislation can be challenged in the European Court of Justice. In 1982 this court ruled that because the Equal Pay Act does not entitle a woman to claim equal pay for work of equal value unless her employer uses a job evaluation scheme, UK legislation failed to comply with EEC law. As a result the Equal Pay Act has been amended. A woman who cannot achieve equal pay by either of the routes described above may achieve it if a tribunal considers that her job is of 'equal value' to that of the man with whom she compares herself. This route can be used where there is no job evaluation scheme or where the woman wishes to challenge an existing job evaluation scheme as discriminatory. Comparisons may be made between jobs covered by different evaluation schemes or pay structures. Independent experts approved by ACAS are used by tribunals to determine whether the two jobs are of equal value.

Genuine material differences
Even where the tribunal agrees that two jobs are 'broadly similar', 'rated as equivalent under a job evaluation scheme' or of 'equal value', the employer can avoid equal pay by proving that there is a 'genuine material difference' between them. For example, if the woman has less experience than the man or is younger than him and these are relevant factors in determining pay, then it would be reasonable in law to pay less to the woman than to the man. For equal value claims the employee must show that the difference in pay is due to sex discrimination.

12.5 **Maternity Rights Legislation**

Exercise 4

List three legal rights of female employees during pregnancy and early motherhood.

Maternity leave

Due to the influence of European legislation, i.e. the Pregnant Workers' Directive, UK maternity rights have now been enlarged quite considerably.

All women, irrespective of their length of service or hours of work, are entitled to 14 weeks' maternity leave. They also have the right to return to work in the same or similar job with equally favourable conditions. A woman with 2 years' service by the eleventh week before her expected week of childbirth has a right to 29 weeks of maternity leave provided she gives to her employer:

- At least 21 days' written notice of her intention to take maternity leave.
- The expected week of childbirth.
- When she intends to return to work. If earlier than the end of maternity leave period, she must give the employer seven days' notice.
- Her intention to exercise her right to the 29 weeks' maternity leave period, if entitled.
- At least 21 days' notice of her intention to return to work.

Women may choose when to start their maternity leave, as long as it is before the eleventh week of the expected week of confinement. (The latest it may begin is the date of the actual birth.) There is a compulsory period of maternity leave for two weeks after the date of birth.

Exercise 5

Before pregnancy, Jane worked as secretary to the personnel manager of British Industrial Chemicals. On her return from maternity leave she is offered a job as secretary to the computer manager. She does not like the latter and refuses to accept the job. What is her position in law?

Statutory maternity pay (SMP)

The government is gradually shifting the responsibility of SMP to employers. The maternity payment rules that were introduced by the Trade Union Reform and Employment Rights Act 1993 cover the SMP a woman is entitled to receive.

To qualify for maternity pay a woman must have been continuously employed by her employer for 26 weeks at the fifteenth week before the expected week of her confinement.

She is also entitled to the same benefits she would have received from her employer had she not been pregnant.

Maternity and dismissal

The dismissal of a woman is automatically unfair, regardless of her length of service, or hours worked, if it is due to her inability to work because of pregnancy. This also applies to situations of redundancy or unfair selection for redundancy.

Paid time off for antenatal care

Reasonable time off is available to pregnant women for antenatal care. The employer may ask for proof both of the pregnancy and of the date and time of appointments.

12.6 Other Rights to Time Off from Work

Three other reasons which entitle employees to time off from work other than for antenatal care are:

- Paid time off for trade union duties.
- Time off for trade union activities.
- time off for public duties.

Time off to look for another job in cases of redundancy is covered in Chapter 15.

Time off for trade union duties

Trade union representatives have the right to paid time off for duties connected with industrial relations in the organisation in which they work. This includes:

- collective bargaining with management;
- communicating with members about such negotiations;
- consulting full-time officers;
- dealing with members' grievances and disciplinary cases;
- attending relevant training courses.

Safety representatives also have rights to paid time off to perform their functions.

Time off for trade union activities

Members of trade unions recognised by the employer for collective bargaining purposes have the right to unpaid time off to take part in the activities of the union. These activities include:

- attending a conference as a union delegate;
- attending union meetings;
- voting in union elections.

There is no right to time off for anything connected with industrial action. Some clarification of these legal provisions can be found in the ACAS code of practice, *Time Off for Trade Union Duties and Activities*.

Time off for public duties

Employees are entitled to reasonable time off without pay to perform the following duties:

- justice of the peace;
- member of the local authority;
- member of any statutory tribunal;
- member of a health authority;
- member of the governing body of an educational establishment maintained by a local educational authority;
- member of a water authority;
- jury service;
- member of the voluntary reserve forces.

12.7 Discrimination against Disabled Persons

The employment provisions, in the Disability Discrimination Act, 1995, protect disabled people and people who have been disabled. Disability is defined as 'a physical or mental impairment which has a substantial and long-term adverse effect on a person's ability to carry out day to day activities.' Employers are required to provide equal opportunities in employment terms to those who come within this definition. This includes recruitment and selection, training, promotion and other opportunities and benefits which an employer provides. It is important to understand that the Act places an obligation on employers to take reasonable measures to ensure that disabled persons are able to receive equality of treatment, for example by altering a disabled person's working hours to make travelling to and from work easier, by modifying or acquiring appropriate equipment, or by allocating a different place of work, if access to the designated working area is difficult for the disabled person.

12.8 Sick Pay and Medical Suspension

Employers are responsible for the payment of statutory sick pay (SSP) for the first eight weeks of sickness. Such payments are related to earnings. However, many employees have contractual rights to sick pay over and above those laid down in this legislation. The regulations governing SSP are complex. If you are concerned with this area of employment you should ensure that you are fully conversant with the details.

Suspension from work on medical grounds

Workers whose health has been put at risk by exposure to hazardous materials must be taken off their normal jobs and may be suspended from work on full pay for up to six months. Management can offer suitable alternative work which may be or may not be within the terms of the employees' contracts. (The legal definition of 'suitable alternative work' is discussed on pp. 212–13 in relation to redundancy.)

There are detailed regulations covering this area of employment law. However, it should be recognised that the number of workers covered by them is very small. You should check whether employees for whom you have responsibility are covered.

Exercise 6

You are a manager in a nuclear power station. Workers for whom you have responsibility wear film badges which indicate their level of exposure to radiation. The badges show that the limit has been exceeded. What should you do?

12.9 Payment to Workers When There is No Work to Do

Management has no right to suspend employees, cut their minimum rate of pay, introduce short-time working or lay them off unless this is provided for in their contracts of employment. However, many agreements with trade unions do provide for guaranteed minimum earnings during a period of lay-off. In addition workers are entitled in law to minimum 'guarantee payments' for days when no work is provided. These statutory payments are very small. Frequently collective agreements provide for higher payments in these circumstances.

12.10 The Working Time Directive

This Directive was adopted by qualified majority voting by the European Community in 1993 and must be implemented by Member States in November 1996. The Directive sets out maximum weekly working times, provisions for daily and weekly rest periods, work breaks, night work and patterns of work. From November 1996 all public sector workers are covered by the provisions which are directly enforceable. Private sector employers are not bound by the Directive until the Government's regulations come into force. Member States can derogate, i.e. exclude employees, by Regulations or collective agreements, in a number of instances, for example, where continuity of service is needed, such as with workers in hospitals, or in the gas and electricity industries. At the time of writing there is uncertainty about the implementation of the Directive in the UK, although government will have to introduce regulations to comply. It is estimated that 6.5 million workers in the UK will benefit from the Directive's provision which Member States cannot derogate – three weeks paid annual holiday.

12.11 Transfer of Undertakings

On going to press this is the most contentious area of individual employment rights. Again it illustrates the impact of European legislation on UK employment law and the intensely complex legal uncertainties which can develop from judicial interpretations in both UK courts and the European Court of Justice, and there have been a string of decisions which have interpreted the meaning of the legislation. At the root of the problem is the difference in intention between the UK's Transfer of Undertakings Regulations, 1981 and the EC Business Transfers (Acquired Rights) Directive of 1977 which it sought to define. The UK's Regulations held that where an undertaking is transferred from one employer to another the contracts of employment and employment rights of employees are similarly transferred to the new employer.

The differing interpretations of the law have arisen over what is meant by 'an undertaking'. Do the Regulations apply to non-commercial organisations such as the Civil Service, local government and the National Health Service (NHS)? The Trade Union Reform and Employment Rights Act 1993 made it clear that they do and what is meant by 'assets'.

Initially each new case has tended to make the situation a little less clear, although it is evident that the European Directive, and its interpretation by the European Court of Justice and UK courts, appears to accept a broad view of the need to protect employment rights against a wide definition of what is meant by 'a transfer of undertakings'.

This means that if after all or part of a business is contracted out and it still does the same thing, or uses the same methods and requires the same employees, then it is covered by the Transfer Regulations. Any dismissals in connection with the transfer will then be automatically unfair.

In practical terms this means that if your organisation is taking over another or contracting for services you would be wise to seek legal advice.

12.12 The Limits of Employment Law

You may have gained the impression that the employment relationship is greatly influenced by legislation. Certainly since 1963, when employees got rights to minimum period of notice, there has been a vast increase in the importance of this area of labour law. However, much of the relationship between management and employees is untouched by legislation.

Did you know?

The UK and Denmark are the only EEC countries which have no general legislation on hours of work. In the UK only some occupational groups, such as drivers, are protected in this way. Most European countries have a legal minimum number of days of holiday.

In the UK there is no legislation fixing the length of holidays, nor is there a national minimum wage. Indeed government in the early 1990s has been concerned to abolish wages councils, bodies which historically have set minimum rates for various groups of vulnerable workers.

It is thought by some people that a national minimum wage will lead to increased unemployment, while the removal of wages councils is seen as a stimulus to create more jobs. Both of these are debatable points for which we do not have space here.

Exercise 7

Do you remember Fred's Food Processing Company in Chapter 8? There we learned that Fred was opening a chain of frozen food shops. That was two years ago. Now he has six shops in a number of towns in the Midlands. He has recruited staff for the shops and for the distribution side of the business.

You are asked to examine the legal implications of some of his current problems with employees.

1 A female checkout operator in one of the shops, who has six months' service, claims equal pay with a male storekeeper in the manufacturing company. There is no job evaluation scheme and Fred has separate bargaining arrangements with the unions for his retail business and his manufacturing company.

2 Fred's secretary is expecting a baby. She has three years' service with the company and says that she wishes to take maternity leave. She is not married. Fred says that she cannot return to work as his secretary since he disapproves of her behaviour, and anyway it is unreasonable to expect him to hold the job open. He cannot manage with a temporary replacement.

3 One of the shop stewards in the manufacturing company notifies Fred that he will be attending an advanced shop steward training course. Fred says that the steward knows quite enough already and that he never gets a full day's work out of him!

4 One of the frozen food shop supervisors tells him that she has been elected as a parent governor at her daughter's school. She will need one day off work a term to fulfil this responsibility. He says that this is monstrous! How is he supposed to cope without the regular attendance of key employees? On reflection he agrees that she can have the time off without pay.

---

13 Fair Pay and Employee Benefits at Work

The assumption behind most reward systems is that pay is a key motivator. In Chapter 6 we concluded that, while there are motivators other than money, pay is a major factor in the employment relationship. It is management's task to find the package of inducements which prompts maximum employee productivity.

By the end of this chapter you should be able to:

- discuss the factors which affect the level of wages and salaries;
- define 'job evaluation' and discuss some of the major methods;
- appreciate the range of payment systems which management uses to encourage employee productivity;
- list some of the most common fringe benefits and discuss their effectiveness in encouraging employee commitment.

To be effective, reward systems must fit particular organisational circumstances and be reviewed regularly.

A well-designed payment system is one of the most effective ways an employer can communicate a view of an employee's worth. A poorly designed system will soon show itself in high labour turnover and low morale.

Factors to consider which affect the design of a pay system include:

- size and structure of the organisation;
- type of employment/business;
- composition of the workforce;
- presence of trade unions;
- legal limits.

13.1 Factors Affecting Salary and Wage Levels

These include:

- the importance of the individual or the job to the organisation;
- the productivity of the individual or group;

- the profitability of the organisation;
- the supply of and demand for particular skills in the labour market as a whole;
- general movements in pay levels.

Summarising, pay levels reflect the rate for labour in the external 'market', internal organisational factors mainly associated with the establishment and maintenance of pay differentials, and individual factors associated with performance and commitment as demonstrated, for example, by length of service. The level of pay can be seen as the result of interaction between management's desire to obtain maximum employee productivity at minimum cost and employee's wishes for the highest possible reward for the least effort.

In the crudest terms the contract of employment can be seen as a wage–effort bargain – see Figure 13.1. In other words, wages are exchanged for effort. Management's perception of the wage–effort bargain will vary according to the type of organisation, its management style and the sorts of people employed. Wage and salary administration policies therefore differ widely.

Fig 13.1   The wage–effort bargain

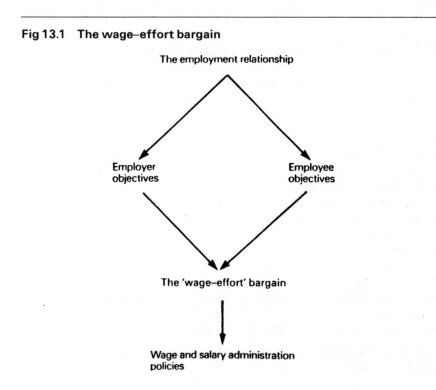

The employment relationship

Employer objectives

Employee objectives

The 'wage–effort' bargain

Wage and salary administration policies

13.2 **The Wage–Effort Bargain**

When an individual joins an organisation as a paid employee, a contract of employment is made. The employer expects a particular quantity and quality of performance in pursuit of organisational objectives; the employee expects to be fairly rewarded. The rewards may be:

- money;
- status;
- a sense of achievement, etc.

The complexity of the relationship lies in the fact that not all employees expect similar rewards. Also, management is usually not too specific about the effort required from the employee. This arises from the desire to use labour flexibly so that new requirements can be placed on employees as working processes or organisational structure change.

Exercise 1

Look at the job description for your current job. (If you are not working at present, look at that of a friend.) How does your employer ensure that you can be used in a flexible manner while laying on you specific job responsibilities?

13.3 **Wage and Salary Administration Policies**

The objectives for management in devising remuneration policies are many, reflecting the complexity of this area of personnel management. They include:

- to attract sufficient suitable employees;
- to encourage effective employees to remain in the organisation's employment;
- to obtain optimal performance from employees;
- to encourage employees to improve their performance;
- to have sufficient flexibility to reward high performers and deal with poor performers;
- to operate within the framework of current employment legislation and national economic policy where relevant;
- to operate at minimum cost;
- to ensure that jobs of equivalent value to the organisation are rewarded equally;
- to ensure that employees feel fairly rewarded for the jobs they do.

These are broad policy objectives likely to be supported by most managers. Their conversion into practice will depend on the relative priorities accorded

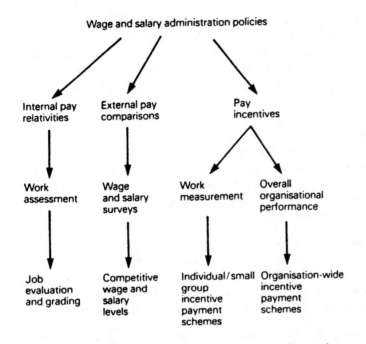

Fig 13.2   Wage and salary administration policies and practices

to them in light of organisational circumstances. For example, a company struggling for survival will place greater emphasis on operating at minimum cost and paying the lowest possible wages, rather than on the attraction and retention of employees who feel fairly rewarded for their efforts.

According to its policy objectives, management is likely to be concerned with three issues in the establishment of fair pay:

- wage or salary relativities – to ensure that what is paid is fair by comparison with payments received by other employees within the organisation;
- to ensure that the pay is fair in comparison with other employers;
- methods of payment which encourage effective performance and commitment by individuals of work groups.

This can be expressed diagrammatically – see Figure 13.2.

13.4 Job Evaluation and the Design of Pay Structures

Bernard Shaw in *Everybody's Political What's What* challenged the possibility of being able to 'assess in pounds, shillings and pence the difference between the social service of an archbishop and a turf bookmaker or to fix a wage for poets laureate and sausage makers'. Job evaluation attempts to establish the relative value of jobs to the employing organisation in which they are situated. In the UK there has been no attempt to undertake a national exercise of the type required to meet Shaw's challenge.

What is job evaluation?

● *Job evaluation is not an exact science – it relies on subjective judgement.*
In measuring the relative value of jobs, job evaluation requires the subjective, though systematic, exercise of judgement in identifying and assessing differences between jobs. It only works effectively if those involved believe it to be fair.

● *Job evaluation is not a method of determining rates of pay.*
Job evaluation precedes pay determination. After the relative value of jobs to the organisation has been established, they are usually grouped into grades or categories. Pay is attached to these. Where trade unions are recognised for collective bargaining purposes, this is done by negotiation.

● *Job evaluation is not concerned with the performance of the individual employee.*
Rather it is concerned with the demands of the job. Whether the individual carries out the job adequately should be immaterial. Good performance may be rewarded by merit payments but job evaluation is concerned with the value of the job relative to other jobs and not with the relative value of the employee as compared with other employees.

Exercise 2

Is it easy to make the distinction between the requirements of the job and the performance of the job holder?

In sum, job evaluation attempts to answer three questions critical to the management of people:

● What is the relative value of a job to the organisation?
● How can this value be determined?
● How can this be done in a way which is accepted as fair by most employees?

Job evaluation can be effective as a means of answering these questions only if it is part of what might be termed a 'total system of remuneration and motivation'.

Four other personnel management techniques which we have discussed so far in this book and which also should be part of this system are:

- work restructuring techniques;
- performance appraisal;
- career development;
- employee services.

The process of job evaluation

No matter which of the many available methods is used, the process of job evaluation must contain certain basic steps. Figure 13.3 emphasises the importance of obtaining much information about jobs before attempting to evaluate their relative value. We have already discussed job analysis and the writing of job descriptions. To encourage employees to believe in the fairness of the results of job evaluation, care must be taken at this stage to involve them or their representatives. This task should not be given to untrained employees or to line managers.

Three ways in which jobs can be analysed for job evaluation purposes so as to encourage employee involvement are:

- Employees can be asked to complete questionnaires on the demands of their jobs. These can be accompanied by a job description and signed by both the job holder and the line manager to indicate that the information presented is accurate.

Fig 13.3   The process of job evaluation

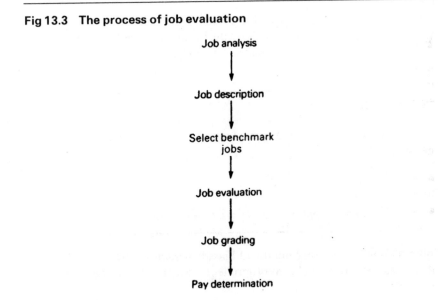

Job analysis

↓

Job description

↓

Select benchmark jobs

↓

Job evaluation

↓

Job grading

↓

Pay determination

- Job holders can be interviewed by a job analyst who then compiles the information on the demands of the job for signature as above.
- Job holders can be observed at work by job analysts who again compile information for job evaluation purposes. This method may be suitable only for manual jobs where activities are directly observable.

Job evaluation is most often used in medium or large organisations. In such cases it is most convenient to select a sample (10 to 30) of 'benchmark' jobs at this stage as a basis for the establishment of the job evaluation system. Benchmark jobs should be:

- well known to evaluators;
- representative of the level and type of jobs to be evaluated;
- not the subject of a current dispute between management and employees.

Now job evaluation, using one of the methods discussed below, can take place.

This will result in the establishment of a rank order of jobs in the organisation from the lowest to the highest job evaluated. After this the jobs in the hierarchy are grouped into grades. Only then is the pay for grades established either by negotiation or by managerial judgement.

Methods of job evaluation

There are two main ways of evaluating jobs – analytical and non-analytical. Analytical methods break jobs down into their constituent parts for assessment purposes; non-analytical methods evaluate jobs as wholes.

Non-analytical methods
Job ranking
This is the simplest method of job evaluation. Each job is assessed as a whole in relation to the others. Jobs thus evaluated are listed in terms of their importance. There is no analysis other than the opinion and decision of the evaluators.

Exercise 3

Suppose we use job ranking to assess four jobs. The rank order we establish is:
Electrician.
Cook.
Kitchen assistant.
Cleaner.
What will be a problem of putting this result in practice?

Job ranking can be a very blunt and biased evaluation tool. Its results may be questioned. It may be appropriate to the needs of the very small company, however.

Paired comparisons
This is a form of job ranking but with an element of scoring with measures whether a job is more important than, less important than or as important as another job, so producing a final league table of jobs. Again this non-analytical method tends to be used in small companies, though it can be applied in larger ones using benchmark jobs.

The paired comparison method of job evaluation is quick and cheap to use, and easy to understand. On the other hand, it is crude and insufficiently analytic to be likely to be very convincing to employees.

Job classification
This is not a form of job evaluation as such, but really a categorisation of jobs within broadly defined grades. It is used in the Civil Service and in teaching. Once the number of grades to be used has been determined a general job description for each grade is prepared. Here is an example from a well-known classification system:

Level 3
Tasks calling for independent arrangement of work and exercise of some initiative, where supervision is needed. Detailed familiarity with one or more branches of established procedures required.

This grade description is rather broad; quite different responsibilities could be grouped within it. Yet in certain circumstances it may be too rigid, leading to the exclusion of jobs on seemingly trivial grounds. Some companies have moved towards more analytical methods because these problems have made it difficult to encompass rapid changes in technology and the attendant more complex job descriptions. On the other hand, job classification systems are simple and cheap to administer.

Analytical methods
Here jobs are assessed and numerical values given under a number of separate headings such as decision-making, working conditions and knowledge required. In this way, by comparing total numerical values, assessors can gauge how much more difficult and responsible one job is than another; very different jobs can be compared.

Points rating
Points rating enables evaluators to give a points score to each job. There is no standardised points system available for all organisations and many use more than one system.

Stages of designing and implementing a points rating scheme:

1 Establish a representative committee. It is very common for schemes to be designed and implemented by joint management–union working groups as part of the process of attempting to ensure that the results of job evaluation are perceived as fair.

2 Analyse a significant sample of jobs and write job descriptions. Benchmark jobs should be selected according to the criteria listed on p. 168.

3 Select and define those criteria considered most critical in determining differences between jobs. This is difficult. Too many factors will make the scheme over-complex and may lead to elements of certain jobs being counted twice, so that the objectivity of the scheme may be cast in doubt. Too few factors may make it difficult to cover the full range of jobs effectively. It may be helpful to look at schemes used in the same industry or for similar occupation groups when designing a scheme. Great care must be taken to define each factor so that it can be applied to each job covered by the scheme.

4 Weight factors and convert to points. Commonly, certain factors have a higher number of points allocated than others, reflecting the relative importance an organisation attaches to a particular factor. Here is a list of factors which the joint management–union working group in Colin's Cars, a manufacturer of sports cars, has decided should be used to evaluate all the non-manual jobs in the company:

- education;
- experience;
- specialised knowledge;
- complexity of task;
- communication – contacts and relationships;
- management of people;
- supervision received;
- physical environment.

The next task of the group is to attach weights to the factors.

Exercise 4

Imagine that you are a member of the working group at Colin's Cars. Rank these factors in order of importance. Then using 100 points allocate the number of points to each factor which you think it is worth. You must use all the points.

After weights have been allocated, each factor definition will have to be subdivided into degrees, and these, like the factors, will have to be defined. Here are the factor and subfactor definitions for 'specialised knowledge' in the points rating scheme being designed for use in Colin's Cars:

Specialised knowledge (weighting 8 per cent)
This factor appraises the requirement for specialised knowledge or techniques which it is essential for a job holder to have.

Level:

1 No specialised knowledge required.
2 Some specialised knowledge or understanding of techniques and terminology to a working standard.
3 A higher level of specialised knowledge or understanding of techniques and terminology to a working standard.
4 A good 'in-depth' level of specialised knowledge or understanding of techniques and terminology such that some guidance and interpretation may be given to others.
5 Specialist knowledge and techniques associated with the job are required to be very well understood in great depth and detail so that available information can not only be well understood and interpreted but also translated into instructions for the guidance of others.

In points rating schemes it is common for a total of 500 points to be used. Thus a maximum of 40 points would be allocated to 'specialised knowledge' in this example.

Exercise 5

Suppose the working group decides to allocate points evenly across the levels of this factor. How many points would be given to a job which was felt to fit level 3 in terms of the specialised knowledge required of the job holder?

5 Test-run a selection of jobs. The benchmark jobs are evaluated using the newly designed scheme.

6 Compare with the established hierarchy of jobs. It cannot be stressed too often that job evaluation schemes only work effectively if the results are acceptable to employees. It is necessary to assess the likelihood of the system producing acceptable results. To do this the points allocated to each job in the test run are plotted against rates presently paid to job holders – see Figure 13.4.

A line of 'best fit' can be drawn through the points indicating those jobs which are out of line. In this table jobs *A* and *B* are out of line and are known as 'red circle' and 'green circle' jobs respectively.

Exercise 6

What does the job evaluation scheme show about the pay currently associated with jobs *A* and *B*?

Usually organisations 'buy in' job evaluation schemes; the wages bill will increase at the time that the new scheme is introduced. Normally the pay of holders of red circle jobs is frozen until cost-of-living increases catch up with them. Holders of green circle jobs may be given pay increases.

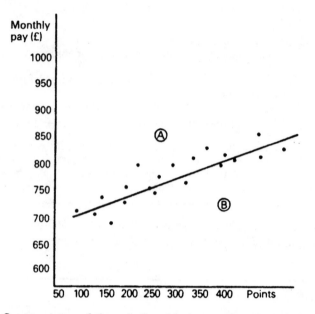

Fig 13.4   Scattergram of the relationship between points and existing pay levels

---

7 Adjust factor weights and points. There may not be such a good fit between points and pay as that indicated in Figure 13.4. In this case stages 5, 6 and 7 may have to be repeated until an acceptable result is obtained.

8 Evaluate all jobs. The remaining jobs should fall close to the line of best fit which has already been established. Red circle and green circle jobs will have to be dealt with as indicated above.

9 Divide the jobs into grades. The points scores provide a basis for determining the grades which will encompass groups of similar jobs. Careful thought must be given to both the break points between the grades and the numbers of grades.

Advantages and disadvantages of the points rating method of job evaluation
Advantages:

- It encourages careful analysis of job content.
- A rationale is provided as to why one job is graded higher than another.
- It seems to be more objective than non-analytical methods.
- It can be used to measure the value of new jobs and thus can accommodate technological change.
- It can cover a wide range of jobs.
- A points rating scheme can be devised to meet the characteristics of jobs in a particular organisation.

Disadvantages:

- It can give a spurious impression of mathematical accuracy. Like all job evaluation methods, it is subjective.
- It is time-consuming and therefore expensive, particularly if a large number of factors are used.
- In practice it is difficult to make a points rating system cover a very wide range of jobs – from managerial to manual, for example – because of the difficulty of weighting factors where one set of factors may be more relevant to one category of jobs than another.
- To be seen to be fair, management (and trade unions where relevant) may wish to give employees information about the system. This is likely to lead to problems, for example in justifying factor weightings.

In conclusion it should be said that points rating is probably the most popular method of job evaluation.

Job evaluation and the avoidance of unfair discrimination

Exercise 7

Are analytical or non-analytical methods of job evaluation more likely to be proof against challenges of unfair discrimination under the equal value legislation?

Employers committed to the development of job evaluation schemes free of sex bias should observe the following guidelines.

Use analytical rather than non-analytical schemes
A woman can make an equal pay claim where she is employed on work which is, 'in terms of the demands made on her (for instance, under such headings as effort, skill and decision)' of equal value to that of a man in the same employment. Analytical job evaluation schemes are potentially easier to defend against such claims.

Where analytical schemes are used, ensure that unfair discrimination does not creep back in at the checking stage
This may occur if the method of paired comparisons is used to check the results of a new points rating or other analytical job evaluation scheme.

Take care to choose factors for use in analytical schemes which are not unfairly biased against 'women's' jobs
Analytical job evaluation schemes can introduce factors which are likely to result in 'women's' jobs being placed unfairly at the bottom of the grading structure. For example, in a scheme covering manual jobs, the inclusion of

physical hazards and physical strength and the exclusion of dexterity and visual concentration probably will produce results biased on grounds of sex. All factors chosen should be fully representative of the range of work being evaluated.

Factor definitions should also be scrutinised for unfair sex bias
Definitions should be based on real job requirements. For example, length of experience would tend to favour 'men's' jobs, particularly if the definition is based on the average length of service of post-holders rather than the time needed to learn to do the job.

Exercise 8

On what basis are weights allocated to factors in points rating schemes?

Sex bias in factor weightings should be avoided
Allocating weights to factors is highly subjective; sex bias can easily influence designers of a scheme at this stage. Avoidance of this will be assisted by ensuring that neither very high nor very low weights are given to factors found exclusively in jobs performed predominantly either by men or by women.

'Women's' jobs should be included in the selection of benchmark jobs
This will help to ensure that factors selected as a result of the benchmarking process include those valid by the organisation which are a significant aspect of work undertaken by female employees.

Jobs performed by women should not be segregated into an alternative job evaluation scheme
Groups of jobs or 'job families' should be covered by the same scheme wherever practicable.

Female employees should be represented fairly on job evaluation panels
Such representatives must be aware of the traditional tendency in some organisations to devalue 'women's work'. The publicity given to 'equal pay for work of equal value' has drawn attention to women's rights in this area.

Job descriptions should be written to a common format and standard
Publication of guidance notes for writers of job descriptions and the involvement of employees in the drafting are two useful methods of avoiding sex bias.

Care must be taken to ensure that sex bias does not occur during the implementation of schemes
Here are some examples of the potential for discrimination at this stage:

- a tendency to place grade boundaries just above jobs predominantly performed by women and just below those undertaken by men;
- the 'red-circling' of 'men's' jobs so that their incumbents' pay is protected for some time after the implementation of job evaluation, while 'women's' jobs are not so favourably treated;
- the allocation of 'market supplements' for 'men's' jobs on top of pay based on job-evaluated grades.

Employees must be informed that if they feel that unfair discrimination has occurred they can appeal
Those who sit on appeals panels must be aware of the potential for sex bias in job evaluation.

Training for those involved in job evaluation must stress the potential for unfair sex discrimination
Training must include good practice guidelines and an opportunity for the exploration of the subtle processes by which value is ascribed to particular kinds of work and not to others. Particular attention should be given to the needs of those who chair job evaluation panels.

Mechanisms for the review of job evaluation schemes must be fair
Freedom from sex bias must be one of the criteria against which the effectiveness of schemes is assessed.

Checklist of general questions for management and personnel specialists contemplating the introduction of job evaluation

- Which method should we use?
- Should we use management consultants and if so in what capacity?
- Which categories of employees do we want the scheme to cover?
- Will more than one scheme be needed to cover all employees?
- Shall we involve trade unions or other employee representatives? If so, to what extent?
- What shall be the constitution of any working group needed to design and implement the scheme?
- Who can be used as job analysts and what training will they need?
- Who will be the job evaluators and what training will they need?
- What training will managers and union representatives, other than those directly involved, need?
- Who will do all this training?

- How much information about job evaluation should we communicate to employees?
- What mechanisms should we use to review the scheme to ensure that once it is implemented it works effectively?

More questions could be added to this list. From this section you will have understood that job evaluation can be complex and that great care must be taken in the design and implementation of schemes.

13.5 External Pay Comparisons

After the relative value of jobs to the organisation has been determined, we must find out what effect market rates are likely to have on the pay structure as a whole.

Exercise 9

Is there a market rate for a job?

Market rate surveys

It will be necessary to use market rate surveys to develop and maintain competitive salary and wage structures. Four sources of such information are:

- Company surveys. Sometimes companies form a 'club' for the exchange of this sort of information.
- General published surveys. These usually give information by industrial sector, size of organisation and job title. Sometimes information on employee benefits is also included.
- Specialised surveys. These are carried out by professional bodies, trade unions and employers' or trade associations.
- Analysis of job advertisements. This information is more problematic than the other sources since job descriptions may be 'glossy' to attract candidates, and salary data is often incomplete or inflated.

You should be aware of the inexact nature of this information. The skill is to extract a market rate for a job which is a reasonable compromise between all available data. In making such judgements the following questions will be helpful:

- Does the survey show a single rate or a range for a particular job?
- When was it carried out? Has it been updated since?

- Is the sample sufficiently large to be representative of the organisation, jobs, locations and so on which you require?
- Are the pay data comparable, i.e. are overtime, shift pay and other additions to normal earnings clearly indicated?
- Is information available on employee benefits?
- Are job descriptions available and not just job titles?
- For what purpose is the information produced – as a service, or to exchange information? Are there other purposes, for example consultants attempting to attract clients?
- Is the information clear and easy to understand?
- Is the survey value for money?

13.6 Salary and Wage Administration

Internal pay relatives can be established by job evaluation and then related to the external market for labour by the use of wage and salary surveys. Final pay levels will then be established either by managerial judgement or by negotiation with recognised trade unions. So far as manual jobs are concerned, this may be the end of the story, since there is likely to be a rate for the job regardless of length of service or performance. For non-manual workers it is more likely that, for each grade of job, there will be an associated salary range with a minimum and a maximum rate of pay. It is assumed that all jobs within the grade or band are of roughly equivalent value to the organisation, but that the salary of individuals in the same job grade may vary.

Progression through grades may be entirely on the basis of managerial judgement of 'merit' or automatically with length of service. Trade unions have tended to prefer the latter method since it restricts the prerogative of management to show favouritism. Very often there is an overlap between the salary range associated with one grade and that of adjacent grades. The rationale is that an employee with much experience in a job at one level is worth more to the organisation than a new recruit to a job in the grade above.

A further design feature of salary structures to which management should give attention is the width of the grade bands. Broad bands emphasise the performance of the individual within the grade whereas narrow bands place more importance on the level of the job and on promotion from one category to another. In many organisations narrow grade bands are more common for junior staff, recognising that there are limited variations in performance at this level. For more senior staff broad bands are felt to be needed for the recognition of individual responsibility. Sometimes there is a provision to pay exceptional staff more than the top of the salary scale of the grade in which their job falls.

13.7 **Pay Incentives**

Job evaluation is used frequently to give a structure for basic pay. However, other pay elements are often added to this. One of the most common, for production employees in particular, has tended to be incentive payments directly related to the effort expended by the individual or the work group.

Piecework

Sometimes the term 'piecework' is used to describe incentive payments systems.

Exercise 10

Attempt a definition of 'piecework'.

The main category of workers who even today are paid on a pure piecework basis is homeworkers, mainly women, who work in their own homes often on very routine tasks such as envelope addressing or garment making. Rates of pay for this work are lamentably low. Employees paid only on the basis of output have no basic earnings by which to support their everyday living requirements.

Payment by results

Here the incentive element normally comprises no more than 25 per cent of the pay packet and this proportion is tending to decline as a proportion of total earnings. The main reason for this is that much manual work has become subject to technological change, and has become more machine-paced. As a result the individual employee has a decreasing ability to affect the amount of production. In these circumstances payment by results becomes less appropriate.

The mechanics of payment by results systems

Work study or management services specialists play a prominent role in the operation of most payment by results systems. These rest on the concept of a 'standard time' – the time necessary for an appropriately qualified operator to complete a clearly defined task at an acceptable level of quality. Time standards are established through the systematic application of work measurement techniques. It is not necessary for the personnel specialist or line manager to understand them in detail since frequently specialists in this area will be available for help.

Effective use of payment by results

Payment by results systems are used primarily in production situations where:

- work cycles are generally short and repetitive;
- output can be measured in terms of units produced;
- work has a high labour content and is not predominantly machine-paced;
- high-quality production is not essential;
- jobs are relatively stable;
- sufficient back-up stocks are available to meet fluctuations in both demand and output.

Exercise 11

Why is the last feature important?

Other conditions for the successful introduction of payment by results systems are that:

- co-operation is forthcoming from employees who are not able to participate in the bonus scheme;
- high bonus earnings of individuals or groups will not stimulate pressure for parity from other employees;
- sufficient well-trained work study or management services specialists are employed.

Assumptions behind payments by results
Work-study-based payments by results systems, like job evaluation, are systematic rather than scientific techniques. They are based on the assessment of work study specialists and others of production times, and work as incentives only if all concerned believe them to be fair. They are designed on the assumption that the 'carrot' of more pay will encourage workers to greater output.

Exercise 12

From what you have learned so far in this book about motivation theory, do you think that the assumption is sound?

Research on the effect of incentives suggests the following problems may occur.

Bargaining over rates

Work study and management services techniques are subjective though systematic. As a result jobs are 'tightly' timed whilst others have 'loose' times. It is much more beneficial for the employee to have work for which the times are 'loose', since in these situations it is possible to make more money for less effort. As a result there is likely to be bargaining both over work allocation and over the times allotted to particular jobs.

Work group pressure to keep production down

Employees whose output is much higher than the norm of the group are often subject to pressure to reduce their productivity, since very high output by an individual can endanger bonus earnings in that management may come to believe that all are capable of more effort and may cut the rate paid accordingly.

Employees' dislike of fluctuating earnings

Employees attempt to create stabilising devices which may distort management's assessment of output.

Payments by results systems, then, can have disadvantageous effects on workplace employee relations.

Measured daywork systems

Often these are introduced to overcome the disadvantages of both payment by results and payment on the basis of time. Here pay is fixed at a higher level than management would normally pay to a time-rate worker, on the understanding that performance is maintained at a specific level. Bonus is paid for achieving this level of performance but pay does not fluctuate in the short term with actual performance. If an employee fails consistently to achieve the required standard even after further help and training, a wide range of sanctions are applied – withdrawal or reduction of bonus and ultimately dismissal.

Exercise 13

In payment by results systems, bonus is the reward for actual performance. For what is bonus paid in measured daywork systems?

Reasons why management may prefer measured daywork to payment by results include:

- the employee relations problems of payment by results systems are likely to be avoided while an incentive element is retained;
- there is a strong sanction against poor performance;

- there should be less resistance to changes in working methods since earnings will not be affected;
- employee co-operation and flexibility should be greater because bonus paid is the same on any job;
- there is greater control over wage costs;
- the system should be cheap to administer since bonus is standard and only the exceptions must be calculated;
- there is a positive incentive to training to maintain bonus earnings.

On the other hand measured daywork requires closer and better supervision than payment by results systems and a steady work flow and effective monitoring of the system. In addition some organisations which have changed from payment by results to measured daywork have experienced at least a short-term fall in productivity.

Performance-related payment schemes (PRP)

This is a method of payment where an employee receives increases in pay wholly or partly on the regular and systematic assessment of personal job performance, based on objectives set between a boss and his/her subordinate. Although such schemes were originally designed for managerial and administrative/clerical staff, technology has seen the introduction of a small number of schemes for manual workers.

The following arguments are used in support of PRP. It:

- focuses attention on what is to be achieved in terms of business objectives;
- improves motivation;
- links pay to the objectives of the business;
- rewards high performance or skill level;
- develops managers' skills in appraisal and objective-setting with individual employees.

However, there has been published research which suggests that PRP does not achieve the claims made for it. Thinking about the summaries of motivation theory in Chapter 6, what might these be?

Profit sharing and share ownership

These involve the distribution of either cash or shares from company profits in a pre-specified way to categories of employees.

In the past there has been a lack of interest in these approaches to payment in the UK. The reasons which have been suggested include:

- employees' difficulty in relating their individual efforts to the amount of bonus received;
- a low level of commitment by workers in the UK to the 'free enterprise society'.

However, even though government tax concessions seek to encourage it and profit sharing schemes are claimed to encourage employees to develop an identity with their company and its profitability, it is still not a popular method of reward.

As organisations become more capital- rather than labour-intensive and the pace of production and communications technology increases it becomes more difficult to design effective payment by results systems. Yet there will be a need for organisations to be more competitive. Therefore management will continue to search for financial incentives.

13.8 **Fair Benefits at Work**

So far we have examined methods of monetary remuneration. Before we leave this area of personnel management we must look at non-monetary or 'fringe' benefits.

You may find it helpful to talk to a personnel specialist in your organisation about the range of benefits other than pay which employees receive. Depending on the organisation in which you carried out this activity, your list may be very long indeed. Some of the items are probably services to employees such as sports and canteen facilities; we discussed these in Chapter 11. Others are likely to have related to the termination of employment and will be covered in Chapter 15.

Other benefits which are sometimes provided include:

- company cars;
- medical and life insurance;
- relocation allowances.

Exercise 14

How should management determine its policy on employee benefits?

13.9 **What of the Future?**

In chapter 11 we suggested there is a trend to harmonisation in terms and conditions of employment. Some writers predict this may also occur in payment and job evaluation systems as more and more employees are white-collar rather than blue-collar and as it becomes necessary to justify differences between men and women because of equal pay legislation. Petty and unjustified differences in rewards are likely to offend employees' sense of esteem and achievement. Equity between levels of tasks is vital to generate a sense of fair treatment in pay and benefits.

14 Managing the Employment Relationship

14.1 A Corporate Perspective on Employment Relations

In this chapter we explore the range of choices open to management in designing employee relations strategies.

In private-sector organisations the 'bottom line' is predominantly financial. In public-sector organisations financial objectives can be seen as a major means of achieving improvements in services to the public. In both cases, therefore, there is a concern to keep down employment costs while achieving the highest possible productivity. This often creates pressures which result in expedient short-term decision-making and the neglect of long-term strategy. This would not be acceptable in other areas of managerial decision-making. Why should employment relations be treated in this way?

In Chapter 8 we examined the training implications of the acquisition by Fred's Food Processing Company of a chain of frozen food shops. The majority of staff in the food processing plants belong to a trade union. Having acquired the shops Fred must consider what personnel and employee relations policies to adopt in this part of the company.

The issues to be considered include:

- how to encourage employee commitment in the frozen food shops;
- how to ensure the availability of appropriate managerial controls to achieve the necessary levels of productivity;
- whether the recognition of trade unions for collective bargaining purposes would be helpful in the light of the concerns about control and commitment identified above;
- if trade unionism is to be considered, with which union(s) Fred would prefer to deal, and for which employee groups (all staff or only non-managerial staff, for example);
- whether arrangements for employee consultation should be set up in the shops, and what, if any should be the involvement of trade union representatives in these;

- what mechanisms Fred should establish for communication with staff and what linkage, if any, should exist between these and bargaining or consultative arrangements.

The implications of corporate decision-making for the employment relationship are often examined after financial, production, service or marketing plans have been made. However, it is more useful to include personnel and employee relations as a facet of general organisational decision-making. Fred could have thought about the implications for employee relations of a decision to expand before he had decided that the best growth strategy was to acquire a chain of frozen food shops. If his food manufacturing company had a history of poor employee relations, he might have asked himself in what kind of expansion strategy he would be least likely to experience similar problems. The answer probably would be in smaller units and in the service rather than the manufacturing sector. These are areas of less contentious staff-management relations. This would not guarantee Fred industrial peace but it would suggest that this could be achieved with goodwill on both sides.

On the other hand, if relations between employees and management in Fred's food manufacturing company were good and productivity high, Fred might have decided that the least risky expansion strategy, from the employee relations point of view, would be to open another very similar factory. However, in reality, other aspects of the decision – finance and marketing in particular – are likely to be given greater significance than the employee relations dimension.

Exercise 1

Why is this?

Remember that employee relations and personnel policies are not independent of each other. If the company's expansion does not lead to promotion for those with managerial potential, there is likely to be reduced commitment and productivity from this group. Employment relations strategies must integrate employment policy and practice so as to further the pursuit of overall managerial goals.

It is not only expanding companies which should develop employee relations strategies. Organisations, whatever their market position, benefit from a periodic reappraisal of the employee relations position and decisions as to whether changes in policy and practice are necessary. It is now widely agreed that good staff–management relations require foresight, planning and commitment by top management. Only thus can consistent and effective relationships be maintained.

14.2 **Managerial Choice of Employment Strategies**

The strategies open to management are many and various. Increasingly it is recognised that employment strategies are central to the long-term survival of the organisation. The quality of the relationship with employees is at the heart of the features which characterise excellent organisations.

Underlying the choice of an employee relations strategy is a tendency for there to be stress *either* on control of employees; *or* on encouraging employee commitment.

Control is important to management because of the need to ensure that staff achieve tasks, and to justify the rewards associated with these. However, too stringent managerial controls may result in disruption to output. Management therefore needs employee commitment in order to contain recruitment and training costs, and to encourage initiative and overall contribution to organisational efficiency and effectiveness.

Ideally managers would like to be able to achieve both control over employees and their commitment to the immediate task and to the enterprise as a whole. Increasingly companies are developing employment strategies which combine high expectations of staff and of their contribution to the organisation with high levels of integrity in management's relations with these employees. This places significant demands on both the knowledge and skills of the personnel specialist. In the rest of this chapter we explore some of the techniques and skills which can be utilised in pursuit of these twin goals.

There are no general prescriptions for the creation of good employee relations. Therefore managers and personnel specialists can utilise their knowledge and skills successfully only if they are based on a broad appreciation of the nature of the employment relationship. It is necessary to exercise judgement in the analysis of particular factors which influence employee relations in the industry and workplace.

Knowledge

Examples of the areas of knowledge required for effectiveness in employee relations are:

- Senior management's expectations of other managers and personnel specialists in employee relations – both in the control of employees and in the encouragement of their commitment to their individual jobs and to the organisation itself.
- The nature of the demand for goods or services produced by the organisation and its impact on the employment of staff. For example, if demand is changing rapidly, there is likely to be a need for increased employee flexibility.
- Demand by other organisations for the sorts of people currently employed and the impact of this on their commitment and orientation.

- The procedures and systems to communicate and consult with employees.
- The nature of agreement between management and trade unions, where trade unions are recognised by the organisation, together with the structure and organisation of those trade unions.
- Employment legislation and its specific impact on relationships with employees in that organisation.
- State services in the area of employee relations such as conciliation and arbitration.

Skills

Those involved in employee relations need general people-handling skills. Some specific examples of these are:

- Communication skills.
- Skills in working with consultative committees and dealing with representatives where employees participate in managerial decision-making.
- Collective bargaining skills.
- Grievance and disciplinary interviewing skills.
- Counselling skills.

Neither of the above lists is definitive. An understanding of policy and senior management expectations in this area is vital. In large organisations it is necessary to co-ordinate employee relations practices.

However, even in small organisations it is advisable for all members of management to be fully aware of company policy and practice if good relations with staff are to be maintained.

A key role of personnel specialists is to assist managers to acquire those skills which will assist them to be effective in this area.

14.3 Perspectives on the Employment Relationship

A key skill which underlies all the others on the list in the previous section is that of seeing the situation from the other person's perspective. This gives you greater understanding of his or her position but should not seduce you into automatically agreeing with them! Unfortunately many of those involved in employee relations do not possess this skill; they are 'blinkered' by their own experiences and conditioning into believing that theirs is the only valid view.

Employee relations training courses can provide a vehicle within which managers can explore their perceptions of, attitudes to and behaviour in employee relations situations. In a 'safe' environment they can experiment with analysis from a different viewpoint.

Experience sometimes may be of help in the removal of a blinkered vision. Sometimes full-time trade union officers or senior employee representatives are recruited as personnel specialists. Such people should be able to put themselves in the shoes of union representatives or employees in general. However, as 'poacher turned gamekeeper' they may be trusted by neither management nor employees!

Managerial perspectives on the appropriateness of workplace trade unionism vary significantly. Some see conflict as unlikely to arise in the organisation if trade unions are not present and communications are good. Such people are likely to express a strong belief in the responsibility of management to manage.

Other managers see trade unions as playing a legitimate and welcome role in representing employees' interests. This is usually accompanied by an acceptance of collective bargaining and a recognition that conflict between management and employees is likely to arise but can be resolved if effective rules govern the relationship between management and unions.

In considering these different perspectives you should note that trade union membership in the UK has declined by almost 30 per cent over the last two decades.

It would be useful for you to discuss their perspectives with managers involved in employee relations. However, beware! The viewpoint of any individual may not fall neatly into either of these categories. Very often people reveal their perspectives by the words they use. For example, the term 'restrictive practice' is commonly used to describe methods used by workers to limit their flexibility and productivity by illegitimate methods.

Exercise 2

Suppose you were a member of a work group which wishes to protect its work by refusing to let members of other occupational groups encroach on its territory. What name would you give to a 'restrictive practice'?

14.4 Managing the Employment Relationship: The Options for Management

In this chapter we have emphasised that management has considerable choice in the processes and techniques by which it seeks to manage relations with its workforce. In the rest of the chapter we examine these options in more detail.

One way of analysing these is to express them diagrammatically in terms of the degree to which they encroach on the managerial prerogative – see Figure 14.1.

No share in management control

Here the managerial prerogative is absolute. Employees have no right to have their voice heard. Management adopting this approach to employee

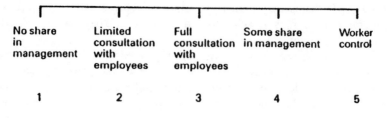

No share in management	Limited consultation with employees	Full consultation with employees	Some share in management	Worker control
1	2	3	4	5

Fig 14.1   Scale of employee involvement in managerial decision-making

relations may attach a great deal of importance to communications with staff. However, the aim of such activities is to improve understanding of company policy and practice rather than to seek employees' views on the appropriateness of these.

Limited consultation

The UK has a tradition of joint consultation in which management has consulted rather than negotiated with employees through committees established for this purpose. With reductions in the importance of collective relationships between managers and employees and more emphasis on relations between the manager and the individual employee, has come a greater emphasis on employee consultation. This is by no means always limited to consultation via trade union representatives, although the latter express unhappiness with any such arrangement. They criticise such approaches because they involve management frequently giving information to employees after decisions have been taken.

Very often any formal consultation with staff is on a narrow range of topics sometimes related broadly to employment conditions. Trade unions often criticise this as the 'tea and toilet rolls' approach.

Full consultation

This occurs through committees constituted in the same way as those described above, except that here employees or their representatives are given information on a very broad range of subjects by management. Production, marketing and financial plans as well as personnel matters are discussed. Yet, though mutually acceptable decisions are sought, employees are not able in any way to control managerial decision making.

Suppose that Fred has decided to set up a joint consultative committee for the food processing company which he owns. Imagine that you are Fred's personnel officer. Questions which you would need to answer before establishing the committee are:

1 *What are Fred's objectives in establishing the committee?*   Does he hope that in this way employees may come to understand better the organisation's objectives? Does he want to use the committee as a channel of information to employees? Does he hope to get suggestions from employees which will help him to run the business better? By answering this question you should be able to get some ideas for the terms of reference and constitution of the committee.

2 *What is to be the relationship between the committee and any other bodies?* Fred's Food Processing Company is unionised. What is the relationship to be between consultation and collective bargaining?

3 *What is to be the composition of the committee?*   A decision will need to be made as to whether the employee representation is to be restricted to union representatives. Thought will need to be given as to their numbers and the constituencies from which they are drawn. How many management representatives should there be and how should they be chosen? What about the representation of supervisors? Frequently these people are described as the 'lost people of management'. This can lead to their disaffection with the organisation and sometimes to their unionisation. Who should be the officers of the committee? This may be a role for the personnel officer.

4 *How are the elections for membership of the committee to be organised?* Who will organise them? When should they be held? What will be the procedures for nomination of candidates and for voting? Who shall be eligible to stand for election? Can all employees vote?

5 *What should be the detailed arrangements for the operation of the committee?*   When and where should it meet? Who will prepare the agenda and take the minutes?

6 *Shall the representatives have training to undertake their role?*   Ideally the answer should be 'yes'. Both management and employee representatives will need fully to understand the roles which they have taken on and will need skills both to be effective in committee meetings and to report back to their constituents.

From this we can conclude that, while joint consultation may have a bad reputation in some quarters because of the trivial nature of its subject matter, it can be a very useful communication mechanism if properly organised and used.

Some share in management

Some managers are happy to involve employees up to the second or third stage of the scale in Figure 14.1. In addition, drives to increase employee involvement and other forms of participation in decisions relating to the employee's own job are increasingly prevalent. However, fewer organisations are willing to give employees a real share in decisions about the management of day-to-day operations, whether at departmental level or for the organisation as a whole. There is also a reluctance to involve employees in decisions affecting the future of the business. This is based on fears of the loss of power to control the employment relationship.

Collective bargaining has been the traditional method by which unions have achieved some influence over managerial decision-making, but only in the limited area of terms and conditions of employment. The rules regulating the employment relationship which result are often classified into two types:

- procedural; and
- substantive.

Procedural rules are those governing the process of industrial relations, or which create a framework within which the parties – management and unions – can negotiate over substantive issues concerning actual terms and conditions of employment such as pay, holidays and fringe benefits. Types of procedure agreement include:

- disciplinary;
- grievance;
- negotiating;
- disputes;
- redundancy.

Some managers see trade unions as playing an important and legitimate role in representing employees' interests. However, this does not mean that they would agree that all matters affecting the employment relationship should be subject to negotiation. Research on this subject has shown that the vast majority of managers are not prepared to negotiate on:

- investment policies;
- pricing policies;
- product and market planning;

and other aspects of overall business planning.

On the other hand, where trade unions are recognised for collective bargaining purposes, managers frequently are prepared to negotiate on:

- working methods;
- payment methods;
- overtime allocation;
- manning levels;
- disciplinary issues;
- redundancy.

This is because the former items are very much associated with management's overall control of the enterprise, while the latter items are day-to-day operational matters which can be agreed with employee representatives without major challenge to the managerial prerogative.

Not all these rules are formal. In the UK traditionally there has been a high emphasis on 'custom and practice'. This has covered such things as:

- overtime;
- mobility of labour;
- manning levels.

However, now that there is much greater emphasis on the need for employee flexibility as a key means of retaining or improving the competitiveness of the organisation, efforts have been made to 'buy out' these informal rules where they added to the costs of labour. However, sometimes lower levels of management still 'turn a blind eye' to such practices, thinking it is worth neither the time nor potential conflict to eradicate them. Other techniques which give employees a share in managerial decision-making are:

- quality circles (see Chapter 6, p. 80);
- suggestion schemes (if a joint committee of management and employee representatives reviews suggestions and has final power to accept or reject them, see Chapter 6, pp. 82–3);
- worker-director schemes.

These latter are more widespread in Europe than in Britain. Worker representatives on a supervisory board can have the power to veto major investment decisions, mergers or take-overs. Those in favour of such schemes argue that in the long run they contribute to improved employee relations, since decision-making by the board will take account of the employee viewpoint. However, in the UK, management has generally been reluctant to abandon its prerogative unless forced to by legislation. Unions, too, have feared that board-level decision-making would conflict with collective bargaining and that worker-directors may have insufficient control to avoid endorsing unpopular decisions.

Workers also may acquire financial participation in managerial decision-making by profit- or equity-sharing schemes (see Chapter 1, pp. 181–2).

Worker control

Here employees totally control the organisation often through a worker co-operative. They hire managers to implement their decisions. Profits are shared by the employees. During periods of high unemployment worker co-operatives have been established by employees anxious to protect their livelihoods when their employing organisation has foundered. Many of these subsequently failed, probably because the hostile market conditions which had prompted the sale to staff persisted.

14.5 **Direct or Indirect Participation?**

In this chapter we have discussed ways in which employees may become involved in managerial decision-making in terms of the degree to which this encroaches on the right of management to manage. Another way of looking at this is:

- whether participation occurs through employee representatives (indirect participation), or
- whether employee involvement is concentrated on matters related to the worker's own job (direct participation).

Example of indirect participation are:

- joint consultation;
- collective bargaining;
- worker-director schemes.

Forms of direct participation are:

- quality circles;
- suggestion schemes;
- autonomous group working.

Participation should not be embarked upon lightly. The most important factors to bring it in effectively are the commitment of management and their ability to gain employees' commitment by their own efforts and example. The free flow of information up, down and across the organisation with the willingness to listen, evaluate and act at all levels is an essential ingredient of success.

14.6 **Employee Relations Roles in the Workplace**

In this section we consider the roles played by those concerned with the development of the employment relationship. In most organisations these are:

- various levels of management, including supervisors;
- employee representatives in the workplace;
- personnel and employee relations specialists.

Where collective bargaining is an important means of regulating the employment relationship, full-time trade union officers become involved as do employers' association officials in organisations which belong to such bodies.

Exercise 3

When should the implications of corporate decision-making for employee relations be examined – after or before financial, production, service or marketing plans have been made?

Managerial roles in employee relations

The roles and their skill requirements of those involved in the implementation of employee relations strategies largely depend on the extent to which management is prepared to involve employees in its decision-making. At the simplest level, management is a more straightforward process when workers have no share in organisational decision-making. So far as the management of people is concerned, the job of the manager is to tell employees what to do and to ensure that they do it.

Exercise 4

Is this strictly accurate?

Whilst planning, control and other managerial activities rest solely with management, this usually does not mean that attempts to gain the commitment of employees are neglected. It is important that managers' roles in employee consultation and communication are defined carefully. When workers do participate in managerial decision-making, managers must have the necessary information and skills to carry out organisation policy in this area. Senior management must ensure that they are vigilant in keeping first-line and middle managers fully informed such that they are effective in working with their own staff.

From this we see that employee relations strategies should not be formulated without careful analysis of the implications for managerial jobs. This should be followed by an assessment as to whether managers can cope with subsequent changes in their roles. In general such changes require managers to be more flexible. A more detailed analysis is likely to show the need for enhanced skills of:

- communication;
- oral and written presentation;
- interpersonal skills especially in dealing with groups.

In unionised workplaces procedure agreements define the formal roles of managers, who need skills in collective bargaining to execute them effectively. However, in many workplaces management and employee

No share in management	Limited consultation with employees	Full consultation with employees	Some share in management	Worker control
1	2	3	4	5
Management makes decisions and announces them to employees	Management gives some information to employees	Management discusses many decisions with employees	Management gives employees information and makes decisions jointly with them	Employees make decisions and tell managers to implement them

Fig 14.2 Implications of employee participation for managerial skills and style

representatives have off-the-record discussions during which problems are aired and solutions tested, prior to a more formalised negotiation.

One of the complications of industrial relations is that different levels and functions of management have different perspectives on, and roles in, this area. Senior management often does not play a front-line role. For example, a brief for bargaining with trade union representatives is often given a middle or junior management or personnel specialists. It will be designed so that it does not threaten fundamental corporate principles and preserves the power of directors and senior management.

Sometimes, when negotiations break down, the bargaining position of the negotiators may be overridden by their more senior colleagues.

Exercise 5

What are the dangers of this?

The role of personnel specialists

Personnel specialists act as advisers to management in the implementation of employee relations strategies. The skills necessary for effectiveness vary with choice of employee relations strategy. For example, some procedure agreements specify a role for the personnel function in workplace employee relations. The involvement of specialists should increase with the level of conflict because of the need for co-ordination and specialist knowledge, for example of job analysis, job evaluation and employees' legal rights. Personnel specialists should be concerned with the establishment and maintenance of a good procedural framework for workplace employee relations which fits management's policy objectives in this area.

A note of caution should be sounded here. Sometimes personnel specialists cast themselves or are cast into the role of policer of this procedural framework. Where organisations are increasingly concerned to create an impetus for change, procedures agreed with trade unions can become a mechanism which protects the status quo. Personnel specialists should ensure that they do not protect such agreements for their own sake but only when they are supportive of business objectives.

Conflict can arise between line managers and personnel specialists with regard to methods of resolving conflict with trade unions.

Exercise 6

The computer staff in a bank go on strike over a regrading claim. They have never been on strike before. What do you think their departmental manager will want to do to resolve the issue? Are members of the personnel department likely to agree?

Personnel specialists should have a longer-term strategic perspective on the employment relationship. Line managers' most immediate concern will be the need to maintain the processes they manage. There is evidence that if employees come to see strikes or other forms of industrial action as the only way of getting concessions from management, they may use this weapon more and more frequently. Also personnel specialists should be aware of the possible 'knock-on' effect of local managerial decisions on other parts of the business.

In situations where management have chosen an employee relations strategy which is predominantly consultative in focus, personnel specialists have an important role in designing and implementing appropriate committees and other processes for employee communication. They must also ensure that line managers use such processes effectively and propose changes where necessary.

Personnel specialists sometimes feel that they occupy positions of 'piggy in the middle' both in terms of the different managerial interest groups and as the interface with employee representatives, who see the personnel department as the first port of call when there is a problem.

The role of employee representatives

In unionised workplaces the most commonly used term for an employee representative is 'shop steward'. Such people have frequently been cast as the villains of industrial relations, particularly by those who see trade unions as introducing conflict into otherwise harmonious working situations. However, there is much more evidence that most managers who deal with shop stewards do not so regard them.

A shop steward or trade union representative in the workplace normally:

- is an employee of the organisation;
- is not paid by the trade union;
- spends part of the working time on trade union duties;
- is responsible for the representation of members' interests during the initial stages of negotiations with management;
- is often persuaded to take the job because nobody else wants it – though union rules do require election to office.

Three aspects of the role are:

- recruitment of members and ensuring that they remain in membership;
- representing members' interests to management;
- giving information on trade union activities and facilities to members.

In most workplaces, trade union representatives no longer collect trade union dues. 'Check-off' agreements with management frequently exist so that dues are directly deducted from pay. While this facility increases the efficiency of workplace union organisation, it has the potential disadvantage of reducing the need for frequent contact between members and representatives.

Like that of the personnel specialist, the role of the shop steward lies at an interface between management and employees. This can place contradictory pressures on the representative. In our example from banking in this chapter, the computer staff would expect the representative to get their jobs regraded, while personnel specialists would hope that he or she could persuade employees that their grading was correct.

In non-unionised workplaces or where management places emphasis on consultation as well as negotiation, employee representatives may exist independent of union organisations. Their ability to operate effectively will depend to a large extent on the facilities and information available. However, the provision of these will depend on managerial policies, thus reducing the independence of representatives.

14.7 The Lessons for Personnel Specialists on the Management of the Employment Relationship

These can be summarised as:

- the need to recognise your own perspective on this area of management, and that of other parties;
- an ability to recognise the need for employee relations strategies compatible with the needs of the business, which other members understand and to which they are committed;

- the necessity to ensure that all managers are competent to implement the organisation's policies so that the employment relationship is managed efficiently and effectively;
- the ability to communicate the nature of the personnel role in employee relations and to encourage managers to use specialist help when this would further the achievement of organisational goals or the resolution of problems.

15 Terminating Employment

15.1 Dismissal: An Introduction

It is vital that managers handle problem employees very carefully, so that accusations of unfair dismissal are unlikely to be upheld if the employee's contract is subsequently terminated. In this section we shall examine the constructive handling of employees in cases where disciplinary action is necessary as well as the law relating to dismissal.

The legal processes for dealing with dismissal cases are identical to those which are used to deal with employee complaints about employers' behaviour with regard to other aspects of the contract of employment.

To stimulate your thinking about discipline and dismissal, we have drawn up some questions for you to attempt to answer here. At the end of the section you will find some similar questions. If the chapter succeeds in increasing your knowledge of this subject you should find it easier to answer the second set.

Exercise 1

Comment on the degree to which the following statements are correct.

1 Employees must be given at least one warning before they can be fairly dismissed.
2 All employees can bring claims of unfair dismissal against their employer if they are dismissed.
3 An employee only has the right to be represented at a disciplinary interview when the final warning stage has been reached.
4 An employee who has been found guilty of a shop-lifting offence may be dismissed.
5 Employees have so many legal rights now that it is very difficult to dismiss them.
6 A rent collector, employed by a local authority, who 'borrows' his rent money may be dismissed.

To answer these questions you needed to be:

- familiar with relevant aspects of employment law;
- knowledgeable about disciplinary procedures in the workplace;
- aware of the way that similar cases have been dealt with.

Personnel specialists usually play a co-ordinating and advisory role here.

15.2 Defining 'Discipline'

The *Concise Oxford Dictionary* defines the verb 'to discipline' as 'to bring under control' or 'to train to obedience and order'. In the context of this definition it is important to note that the ACAS Code of Practice on Discipline emphasises that the primary purpose of disciplining employees should be directed towards obtaining improvement in their conduct and work performance, rather than dismissing them.

The general ground-rules for managing discipline are set out in the Code, *Disciplinary Practice and Procedures in Employment*. Practical guidance on how to handle discipline is provided in the ACAS handbook, *Discipline at Work*. Wise employers have incorporated these principles into their own procedures and practices. Although infringements of the Code are not of themselves actionable offences these may be taken into account by an Industrial Tribunal when determining a claim against an employer. Consideration will also be given to the circumstances. For instance very small companies are not expected to follow the same procedures as large companies. In each case the test of reasonableness will apply.

15.3 Disciplinary Procedures

The main provisions of the ACAS Code set out a reasonable procedure for dealing with issues of discipline and the way in which it should be operated. Procedures should:

- Be in writing.
- Specify to whom they apply.
- Provide for matters to be dealt with quickly.
- Indicate the disciplinary action which may be taken.
- Specify the levels of management which have authority to take various forms of disciplinary action; immediate superiors do not normally have power to dismiss without reference to senior management.
- Provide for individuals to be informed of the complaints against them and to be given an opportunity to state their case before decisions are reached.
- Give individuals the right to be accompanied by a trade union representative or by a fellow employee of their choice.

- Ensure that, except for gross misconduct, no employees are dismissed for a first breach of discipline.
- Ensure that disciplinary action is not taken until the case has been carefully investigated.
- Ensure that individuals are given an explanation for any penalties imposed.
- Provide a right of appeal and specify the procedure to be followed.

In addition the ACAS handbook, *Discipline at Work*, states that disciplinary procedures should:

- Apply to all employees irrespective of length of service, race, sex or marital status.
- Ensure that any investigatory period of supervision is with pay (if not with pay this should be provided for within the contract of employment).
- Ensure that, where the facts are in dispute, no disciplinary penalty is imposed until the case has been carefully investigated and it is concluded on the balance of probability that the employee committed the act in question.

Trade unions and disciplinary procedures

An important part of the trade union representative's role where unions are recognised is the representation of members who are subject to disciplinary action. As we have seen, the ACAS Code of Practice emphasises the legitimacy of this. Many disciplinary procedures have been jointly agreed with trade unions, who generally see them as a means of ensuring the equitable treatment of employees.

When it comes to disciplinary rules, trade unions are less likely to want to have a share of control with management. Many trade unionists argue that it is vital to maintain flexibility over this issue in order to protect members' interests, and the formation of rules are a primary responsibility of management.

If disciplinary action has to be taken against a trade union representative, management are advised to discuss the matter in the first instance with either a full-time official or a more senior representative of the union concerned. This is to avoid situations in which action could be seen as an attack upon the union itself.

15.4 The Law on Dismissal

Since the early 1970s when the concept of 'unfair dismissal' was introduced by legislation a significant body of caselaw has developed around the whole disciplinary process. An employer must satisfy an industrial tribunal hearing a claim on the fairness or unfairness of a dismissal that the reason for the dismissal was one of those 'admissible' under the Employment Protection (Consolidation) Act 1978. Once this has been done a tribunal must then be satisfied that the dismissal was reasonable, taking into account equity and the circumstances of the case, including the size and administrative resources of the employer. In deciding 'fairness', industrial tribunals are guided by previous decisions of the Employment Appeal Tribunal (EAT), the Court of Appeal, the House of Lords and the European Court.

The involvement of the law and the consequent complexities that can occur in handling disciplinary issues mean that it is important that managers have a basic understanding of the 'do's' and 'don'ts' or where to seek advice. In most organisations Personnel is the department which is normally available to give help on the legal principles and practicalities of handling staff discipline.

It is always good practice to see the legal guidelines as a sound basis for handling disciplinary matters, irrespective of whether the case is likely to finish before an industrial tribunal.

What is dismissal?

According to the law, employees are treated as dismissed if:

- the contract of employment under which they work is terminated by the employer with or without notice;
- a fixed-term contract expires without being renewed;
- they leave their employment 'in circumstances such that [they are] entitled to terminate it without notice by reason of the employer's conduct' – constructive dismissal.

Constructive dismissal

This occurs when management puts pressure on the employee to resign in a way which goes to the root of the contract. The most obvious example is where management materially changes the contract of employment without the employee's consent.

Exercise 2

You are the owner of a chain of five hairdressing salons. Jane Jones is a stylist at one of them. You tell her that in a month's time she will work at another one. Is this constructive dismissal?

To make a claim of constructive dismissal the employee must leave without notice. The best protection for the employer against such claims is to get the employee's agreement to any changes to the contract of employment.

Who can claim unfair dismissal?

If you refer to the checklist of employee rights in Chapter 12, you will recall that certain categories of employee cannot claim unfair dismissal. These are:

- those with less than two years' continuous service;
- those with less than five years' service who work between eight hours and less than sixteen hours a week;
- those who work less than eight hours a week;
- those who 'normally' work abroad;
- those over normal retirement age.

What is fair and unfair dismissal?

Once it has been established that a dismissal has taken place, the employer must prove that the employee was dismissed for one of the potentially fair reasons laid down in law. These reasons concern issues of:

- capability or qualifications for the work which the employee must do;
- conduct;
- redundancy;
- where continuing to employ the worker would be illegal;
- some other substantial reason.

However, showing that the employee was dismissed for a fair reason is not sufficient. The employer must also be able to prove that the punishment – the dismissal – fitted the crime. If the employer fails to show the reason or shows a reason which is not listed above, then the dismissal will be automatically unfair. If a valid reason is shown, then the employer must show that it was reasonable to dismiss the employee in the circumstances. Tribunals will pay careful attention to the facts of the case, including the extent to which fair procedures were followed.

Reasons for dismissal which are automatically unfair

These are:

- dismissal for being a member of or taking part in the activities of an independent trade union;
- dismissal because of race or sex discrimination;
- dismissal because of pregnancy, unless the employer can show that the woman concerned is no longer capable of doing the work she was employed to do.

The dismissal of strikers is fair provided that all those on strike are dismissed and none are re-engaged within three months of the dismissal. It is not automatically unfair to dismiss those who refuse to join a trade union where a closed shop exists, though in this case there are major exceptions.

Remedies for unfair dismissal

Employees who successfully bring a claim of unfair dismissal against their employers are entitled to remedies in this order:

- reinstatement;
- re-engagement;
- compensation.

Reinstatement

If the tribunal orders reinstatement, management must treat the employee as if the employment had not been terminated. Four factors to be taken into account when reinstating a dismissed employee are:

- Back-pay including any pay increases which should have been received.
- The need to preserve the dismissed employee's continuity of service.
- Any benefits to which the dismissed employee is entitled – holiday pay, for example.
- The date by which the tribunal's order for reinstatement is to be complied with.

Tribunals seldom order reinstatement. In making such decisions they take account of the employee's wishes, the practicality of such an order for management and the extent of contribution by the employee to the dismissal.

Re-engagement

In this case the employee must be re-employed but not necessarily in the same job. Again the cases in which tribunals make such an order are relatively few and the same factors are taken account of as for reinstatement.

Compensation

This is awarded if management is not ordered to re-employ the dismissed employee or if such an order is ignored. There are four types of compensation:

- The basic award – equivalent to a redundancy payment.
- The compensatory award – based on an assessment of what the employee has lost in wages, benefits, etc. now and in the future.
- The additional award – if management do not comply with an order for reinstatement or re-engagement.
- The special award – in cases of dismissal for union membership or non-membership.

The basic, compensatory and special awards will be reduced if the tribunal believes that the employee contributed to the dismissal. The compensatory award is reduced also if the employee failed to attempt to compensate for the loss of the job.

Dismissed workers with a minimum of six months' service are entitled to a written statement of the reasons for dismissal. If this has not been given a tribunal can order additional compensation of up to two weeks' pay.

Exercise 3

From your knowledge of discipline and dismissal now, comment on the degree to which these statements are correct.

1 One of the employees you supervise resigned last week. You didn't like her and are relieved that she's left. You have nothing further to worry about.

2 If employees are persistently late you can dismiss them summarily.

3 You discipline a trade union representative for persistent lateness. Because of his position you should consult a full-time union official or senior representative.

4 A local authority manager required to drive a car as part of her job loses her driving licence for a year. She says that her husband will drive her around while she is disqualified. You say that this is unacceptable and dismiss her.

5 A secretary complains to a personnel officer that her boss continually swears at her. The personnel officer thinks that she is a bit of a prude and takes no action.

Now we examine the general approach of the courts and tribunals to dismissal for the potentially valid reasons listed above.

15.5 Capability or Qualifications

This covers employee incompetence (intentional or unintentional), short- and long-term sickness, and lack of qualifications to do the job. If an employee falls below expected standards of performance, management must show that the reasons for the decline have been investigated, warnings have been given and attempts have been made to help the employee to improve. Whether or not it is necessary to offer alternative work will depend on the size of the organisation and the length of service of the employee.

Similar considerations will apply where employees' poor health makes them incapable of coping with the demands of their job. The law on dismissal due to long-term sickness is particularly complex. Obviously warnings that a failure to return to work will result in dismissal would be inappropriate! Employees are expected to be sympathetic and hold the job open as long as is reasonably practicable. This is particularly the case where it is recognised that an employee is disabled. Tribunals will attempt to balance the employer's need for the work to be done against the employee's need to make a proper recovery from his illness.

In cases of short-term absence, warnings of the necessity to improve attendances should be given, though again the circumstances must be investigated. Medical certificates can be requested even for single days of absence. In making a decision to dismiss it is legitimate to take into account the disruptive effect of repeated short spells of absence on the efficiency of the organisation.

The cases on lack of qualification are few since this must be a condition of employment. Most people who lack adequate qualifications are not selected in the first place. An example would be where a trainee fails to pass examinations which are an essential prerequisite to the right to practise. Even then it might be reasonable for the employer to extend the training period.

15.6 **Conduct**

Conduct is not defined in the legislation and a wide range of misconduct has been said to justify dismissal. In general, an organisation's disciplinary rules should set out the behaviour which the employer will consider reasonable. Aside from the basic rules of conduct, such as good time-keeping, following reasonable instructions and reporting-in sick, an employer will normally indicate those behaviours which will constitute gross misconduct and may lead to summary dismissal, e.g. fighting, theft and failure to observe safety rules. If an action is deemed to be gross misconduct, dismissal without notice would be an appropriate response, although it is still necessary to hold an investigation into the case and its circumstances. For less serious cases, warnings would be necessary prior to dismissal. The need for employers to follow their procedures and to treat employees equitably is a vital factor in handling disciplinary issues.

Handling disciplinary issues

Some managers may go through their career without the need to handle a case of staff discipline. Indeed, as we have seen, the ACAS code advises that, except in serious instances, disciplinary action should not be used as a first resort. Rather, employees should be advised of any shortcomings and be given the opportunity to improve. However, it can be difficult to draw a clear dividing line between an informal 'ticking-off' and a formal warning. Time-keeping is an obvious example. It is therefore important to ensure there is no doubt in the employee's mind when the line has been crossed.

For more senior managers this can mean that the actions of their subordinates may well have a bearing on whether subsequent decisions are fair or unfair. This is why it is important to have a good understanding of the disciplinary procedure and be ready to seek advice at an early stage.

Conducting the interview

Most people find that conducting a disciplinary interview is stressful. It is an area in which a manager's knowledge can be severely tested, often due to inadequate preparation. The way in which interviews are conducted has also been subject to the scrutiny of the courts, and there are some basic ground-rules which it is wise to follow:

- Establish whether a prima facie case exists.
- Obtain and read the disciplinary procedure and disciplinary rules.
- Examine the individual's past record and work performance.
- Decide who will be witnesses; take statements if necessary.
- Consider what other investigations (if any) are necessary.
- Contact the full-time officer (or as directed by disciplinary procedure) if employee is a shop steward or trade union official.
- Advise the employee of the interview making clear that it is a *disciplinary* interview, that he/she may be represented, how serious the matter appears and, if proved, the likely outcome.

An important factor in conducting the investigation prior to the interview is to guard against a situation where the person conducting it also becomes 'judge and jury' at the interview.

The legal principles for the conduct of the interview are clear on the need for justice to be done, and to be seen to be done. A useful framework for management to follow is:

- Make an opening statement giving reasons why the interview has been called and indicate possible outcomes (*without pre-judging the issue*).
- Present management's case, calling witnesses or presenting statements as necessary.
- Allow the employee or representative to question witnesses.
- Allow the employee to state his/her case and to call his/her own witnesses.
- Question the employee's witness, if any.
- Allow mitigating factors to be raised.
- Examine any previous disciplinary record (making due allowances for warnings which may have lost their currency).
- Adjourn and take further advice as necessary.
- Decide action to be taken.
- Announce decision.
- Advise employee of appeal rights if disciplinary action is taken.

Following the interview, managers should:

- Confirm decision in writing stating appeal rights and how they are to be exercised.
- Make a full file note of the interview for possible use in subsequent internal appeal or industrial tribunal.

Fairness and discipline

A significant part of employment case law addresses the issue of what constitutes 'fairness' on the part of an employer when handling cases of discipline. These are some of the principal guidelines:

- *Fairness is judged on the facts known to the employer at the time of dismissal.*
  Tribunals will judge the fairness or otherwise of a dismissal on the information which was known to the employer when the decision to dismiss was taken. This means that information which comes to light after a dismissal cannot be taken into account by the tribunal when it is determining whether the dismissal was unfair. It can, however, be taken into account in the calculation of any compensation which the tribunal may award.

- *Fairness can be judged on facts which managers ought to have known before the decision to dismiss was taken.*
  Although facts which are discovered after the decision to dismiss is taken are irrelevant in deciding fairness, tribunals can take account of them if they believe that there are facts which the employer would have known if he had carried out a reasonably diligent investigation before arriving at a decision.

- *Fairness is dependent on circumstances.*
  There is a range of responses which a reasonable employer might take and any of those responses could be fair. In other words, one employer may decide to dismiss in the light of a given set of circumstances, whereas another, faced with precisely the same facts, may decide to issue a final warning. Both decisions would be fair.

- *What do tribunals expect of reasonable employers?*
  In essence, tribunals expect a reasonable employer to:

  – inform the employee of the details of the allegation;
  – carry out an adequate investigation of the facts, including enabling the employee to put his/her side of the case;
  – take due regard to mitigating factors, e.g. past good record, explanations, provocation, genuine error and management fault;
  – act reasonably and in good faith when forming a conclusion on what action to take.

- *Tribunals do not require employers to prove matters beyond reasonable doubt.*
  The manager faced with conflicting evidence is not required to satisfy a tribunal 'beyond reasonable doubt' that the relevant offence was committed by the employee; rather, it will ask whether the employer had an honest belief based on reasonable grounds which he/she acted upon.

- *Tribunals expect managers to follow procedures.*
  If an employer has an agreed procedure for dealing with discipline, tribunals will expect it to be followed. Failure to follow an agreed procedure will be taken into account by the tribunal, although a breach of procedure is not a matter of law such as to make a dismissal decision

unfair in itself. Instead it is one of the relevant circumstances which tribunals must bear in mind when assessing the fairness or unfairness of a dismissal decision.

- *What are the major procedural steps which tribunals will expect managers to follow?*

(a) *Warnings*

In cases of misconduct, other than gross misconduct, tribunals will normally expect the employee to be given an appropriate warning depending on the seriousness of the offence. In this respect, it should be remembered that warnings are aimed as much to effect a change in the employee's performance or behaviour as to point out the consequences if the employee's behaviour fails to improve. The very nature of a warning also presupposes that time will be given for an improvement to be shown. Precisely how much time should be allowed will depend upon a number of factors such as the nature and severity of the offence and the length of service of the employee.

(b) *Adequate disciplinary interviews*

The conduct of disciplinary interviews must be in accordance with the rules of natural justice. This means that the employee must know the nature of the accusation made against him and be given an opportunity to state his case. Such interviews must be in accordance with any agreed procedure and the individual's right to representation must be safe-guarded.

(c) *Representation*

While it is always advisable that the employee should be present during a disciplinary interview his attendance would not be regarded by a tribunal as an absolute requirement, provided that he was adequately represented by, for example, his trade union.

(d) *Opportunity to appeal*

There will normally be an opportunity for the employee to appeal against dismissal to a higher level of management, and disciplinary procedures, except in small companies, will normally provide this. Internal appeals can service to redress injustices or breaches in procedure which may have occurred at an earlier stage.

Exercise 4

Sarah Green is summarily dismissed for her persistent lateness, long lunch hours and occasional days of absence without permission. Would a tribunal be likely to find the dismissal fair?

15.7 **Redundancy**

This is probably the saddest and most difficult problem of the employment relationship with which managers and personnel specialists have to deal. Unfortunately redundancy has become commonplace in our society. The odds are that you know someone who has been involved in such a situation. You may find it helpful to ask them to describe the situation to you. Reflect on the more important considerations for management once it became apparent that redundancy was inevitable. These are likely to include:

- who to make redundant, in which areas of the business and on what date or dates;
- whether retraining of redundant employees would be in the interests of the organisation;
- what compensation should be awarded to those made redundant.

It is necessary for managers to think about these issues whatever the detailed circumstances. In unionised organisations it will also be vital to draw up a programme of consulting the unions. This may or may not involve the negotiation of a procedure for handling the redundancies, if such an agreement does not already exist. Sometimes management takes steps to assist redundant employees to find other work. Most often this occurs where the effects of the loss of jobs on the local community is likely to be severe. In these situations most attention tends to be given to the process of identifying and dealing with those who are likely to be made redundant. However, it is also sensible to consider those who will remain. The shock of redundancy, especially of large numbers of employees, affects future relationships between management and workers.

If you refer back to the checklist in Chapter 12, pp. 150–1, you will recall that the categories of employee who can make claims of redundancy against their employer are:

- those with two years' service or more;
- those with five years' service or more who work between 8 and 16 hours per week.

In addition workers must have been dismissed before they can make a claim. The legal definition on p. 201 applies to dismissals because of redundancy. In the section below we examine employees' rights to redundancy compensation as distinct from compensation for unfair dismissal.

Situations of redundancy

The definition of redundancy covers three main situations:

- where the business ceases to operate;
- where the employer changes the location of the business;
- where the employer requires few employees for the existing work.

The first of these categories has given rise to few problems in the courts. If management wishes to move to another place, the question as to whether workers are redundant will depend on the details of the contract of employment. If this does not require them to move, then they will be able to claim redundancy compensation.

The most controversial redundancy cases have arisen where management decided there is less work for employees to do or that the same work can be done by fewer people. In such cases work may be recognised and technology may be changed with consequent implications for the terms and conditions of employment under which people are employed. The courts have upheld management's rights to reorganise work in the interests of efficiency. In doing so they have argued that redundancy arises only if there is a change in terms and conditions of employment because the employer's need for 'work of a particular kind' has 'ceased' or 'diminished'. Similarly, where the requirement of overtime is reduced, employees are not redundant if management still requires them to do their work as before.

Sometimes the reorganisation of work or change in technology places new demands on employees for efficiency or adaptability.

Exercise 5

A college of further education installs a new and more complex heating system. Previously the heating system was looked after by the college plumber. it is decided that the new system needs the full-time service of a heating technician who can also deal with plumbing problems. The college plumber is declared redundant. Is this decision fair?

Selection of employees for redundancy

The selection of those employees who must leave can be very painful. We looked at the legal restrictions on this in the last section. Very often selection criteria are agreed with trade unions either at the time of redundancy or when redundancy is only a small dark cloud in an otherwise clear sky.

Redundancy is a difficult issue for trade unions. The views of the members are often divided; some will want to leave with the best possible compensation; others will believe that the union should fight all job losses. In unionised workplaces there is likely to be a demand that volunteers should be allowed to go first.

Exercise 6

What are the disadvantages of this from management's point of view?

In a redundancy situation management would prefer to make redundant those who contribute least to the efficiency of the organisation – the 'slackers', the 'passengers', the 'deadwood', etc. This is where many managers and personnel specialists face something of a crisis of conscience, for these people in all probability will be those who will have the greatest difficulty in getting other jobs. In such situations, 'last in first out' may seem to be a fairer criterion. Sometimes criteria are formalised in a redundancy procedure agreement but often management are reluctant to restrict their flexibility to act in this way.

Legally, employers must consult with recognised independent unions about every proposed redundancy. This involves giving, in writing, to the union:

- the reasons for the proposals of redundancy;
- the numbers and descriptions (i.e. jobs) of employees;
- the total number of employees in those jobs;
- the proposed method of selecting employees for redundancy;
- the proposed method of carrying out the redundancies – timing, methods of payment, etc.

Since the Trade Union Reform and Employment Rights Act, 1993, employees must consult with unions with a view to reaching agreement of ways of:

- avoiding the dismissals;
- reducing the number of people to be dismissed;
- mitigating the consequences of the dismissal.

The law also says that consultation over any redundancies must begin 'at the earliest opportunity'. When large numbers of redundancies are proposed, the following timetable must be observed at the minimum:

- If 100 employees are to be made redundant at one establishment over a period of up to 90 days, the consultation must take place at least 90 days before the first dismissal takes place.
- If between 10 and 100 workers are to be made redundant at one establishment over a period of up to 30 days, then consultation must take place at least 309 days before the first dismissal takes place. If management does not observe this timetable, employees made redundant are entitled to additional compensation. This consists of payment for the 'protected period', i.e. the 90 or 30 days specified for the above categories. Tribunals reduce this amount by earnings or payments in lieu of notice paid during this period.

The Department of Employment must also be notified in writing using a similar timetable.

Retraining or redeployment of redundant workers

Another option for management, if the need for workers is reduced, is to consider the possibility of retraining for other work in the organisation or elsewhere. In addition some workers may be able to be redeployed without further training.

Retraining for work elsewhere can be an expensive option, especially where unemployment is high or workers' skills have become obsolete. Some employers offer job search and career counselling facilities to redundant employees. The objectives of employers in providing such services include:

- concern about the future of such individuals;
- relieving the anxieties of redundant employees;
- enhancing the reputation of the organisation as an employer in the long run.

Sometimes external consultants are used by employers to assist redundant employees. The reasons for this are:

- Individuals need a broad perspective of the job market to define their career goals and sharpen their job search skills.
- The expertise of external consultants should be very helpful in this process.
- External consultants may be more objective about the redundant employee's skills than the employer.
- External consultants may be able to assist with others in a similar position.
- The resources offered by external consultants are likely to be greater than those available to an individual employer – exploration of the job market is likely to be assisted by typing, computing, library and research facilities.

The speed of technical change tends to mean that adaptation to the demands of new jobs will be a permanent feature of employment. The need for a flexible labour force should add emphasis to the need for human resource planning to identify areas of redundant skills so that the viability of retraining can be investigated thoroughly.

It may be possible to offer some redundant employees new jobs immediately. In law, if employees accept 'suitable alternative work' they are not entitled to redundancy compensation. For such offers of work to be suitable the following conditions must be met:

- The offer must be made before the old contract is terminated and must take effect within four weeks.
- The offer must be made by the old employer, by management of the same group of companies or by a new employer who is taking over the business.
- The offer can be made orally or in writing and must give the employee information about 'capacity and place...and...other terms and conditions of employment'.
- Sufficient information must be given to enable the employee to make a decision as to the suitability of the new job.

If the employee refuses alternative work which is suitable, the right to redundancy compensation is forfeited. In making decisions as to suitability, the tribunal takes account of the employee's personal circumstances, including travel, housing, domestic problems or loss of friends.

Exercise 7

A secretary works for a fashion business in Mayfair, London. The firm moves to new premises above a sex shop in Soho. She refuses the offer of alternative employment there on the grounds that she is opposed to 'money-for-sex' activities and finds the new place of employment distasteful. Is her refusal of the new job unreasonable?

Employees who are offered a new job have the right to try it for a period of four weeks. During this period they can leave at any time and claim redundancy compensation. It is then up to the tribunal to decide whether the new job was suitable and whether its rejection was reasonable.

Redundant workers also have the right to 'reasonable' paid time off to look for other work or for retraining while under notice of redundancy. This is only available to workers with at least two years' service. Even if employees are offered alternative work, they are entitled to this. There is no legal definition of what is reasonable. It would depend on the circumstances such as the amount of work available and the time and travel involved in looking for it. In practice the amount of time off given tends to be rather limited.

Redundancy compensation

Scales of minimum compensation in cases of redundancy are laid down by law. The amount of the payment depends on the employee's age, length of service and weekly pay. Only those who have two or more years' service have a legal entitlement to be compensated in this way. Many organisations have paid more to redundant workers than the statutory minimum. Employees have the right to a written statement from management explaining how the compensation has been calculated.

Those who remain after a redundancy

In redundancy, most attention is focused on the plight of those who must leave. Management should not forget those who will continue to be employed. The announcement of redundancy especially if large numbers of people are involved, usually sends tremors throughout the organisation. Those who stay may feel that their employment with the organisation is no longer permanent and that their career prospects have been affected adversely. Management must systematically assess the nature of these changes and immediately should set about the rebuilding process in ways which convince remaining employees that they have a future.

The implication of our discussion is that sometimes redundancy will occur. But is it inevitable? If you refer back to Chapter 2, you will recall that through human resource planning it should be possible to alert management to the possibility of redundancy. Then the need to shed labour can be reduced or avoided altogether by some of the following measures:

- stopping recruitment;
- halting overtime;
- encouraging early retirement;
- introducing job-sharing;
- developing retraining programmes.

15.8 Legal Restrictions

An employer may fairly dismiss an employee whose continued employment would be against the law. This covers such cases as drivers who become disqualified from driving, or employees who do not have a work permit.

15.9 Some Other Substantial Reason

This last 'catch-all' category has been used to cover reductions in wages or changes in hours of work which are argued by the employer to be vital if the business is to survive, the dismissal of temporary employees who have been employed to replace staff absent because of medical suspension or maternity leave, and irreconcilable conflicts between employees where the dismissed employee can be shown to be the main instigator of the trouble.

15.10 Retirement

The normal retirement age is 65 for men; women can retire at 60 or can continue to work up to 65. As we have seen, early retirement has become much more prevalent as many organisations have slimmed down their labour forces. In this section we shall look at the process of retirement and in particular at pension schemes.

Occupational pension schemes

This is a complex subject on which managers and personnel specialists require specialist advice from actuaries and investment advisers. Here we are only scratching the surface. Pensions are probably the most important employee benefit. There are many reasons why organisations seek to provide the best possible occupational pension scheme for employees. These include:

- to help the recruitment and retention of employees, especially more senior and older employees;
- to demonstrate that the organisation is a good employer – this should assist the commitment of employees;
- to enable those who retire to enjoy financial security in their later years.

Contributory and non-contributory occupational pension schemes

Most pension schemes require employees to contribute part of their earnings – usually 6 or 7 per cent – to the fund from which they will later receive a pension. These are contributory schemes. In this sense pensions are a form of deferred earnings. Other schemes are non-contributory in that their full cost is paid by the employer.

Contributory schemes generally provide a better range of benefits because more money is available. Also, employees are often more appreciative of benefits for which they have paid.

By contrast, non-contributory schemes are often cheaper to administer, are flexible and very attractive to employees since no deductions are made from pay. Trade unions are generally not in favour of non-contributory schemes since they may act as 'golden chains' which tie employees to the organisation because benefits are forfeited on leaving.

Who is covered?

It is common to find schemes which cover both staff and manual workers; however, senior management often have a 'top-hat' arrangement in which the scheme is topped up with a non-contributory arrangement.

Benefits

The most obvious benefit is a pension on retirement. Other benefits are:

- a lump sum on retirement;
- death-in-service benefit;
- pension for widows or widowers.

In addition, pension schemes can be more or less inflation-proofed by allowing for increases in response to changes in the cost of living. This is a very desirable feature, although it can be expensive.

Personal pensions

Employees have the choice of taking out a personal pension plan rather than joining their employer's pension scheme. However, this will result in the loss of the employer's contribution to the pension.

Provisions for early retirement

One way of avoiding compulsory redundancy is for employees nearing retirement age to retire early. Many organisations also allow employees in poor health to leave early. Pension schemes have to cope with this eventuality. Normally, such people can draw a pension immediately but, as their contributions will have been less than those who retire normally, their pension will be smaller. Some employers are generous in the pensions which are paid to older workers who retire at a time of redundancy. Lump-sum payments may also be made. The early retirement option will not always be seen in such a rosy light. For management it is an expensive option because of the need to pay pensions early. In addition, it cannot always be assumed that older employees have outdated skills and knowledge. In many cases such people's years of experience are of value to the organisation. Early retirement is usually voluntary. Thus management gives control of the selection process to employees. This may mean that the more useful older employees will leave while others whom management would wish to lose stay.

Provisions for late retirement

Sometimes employers want to retain the services of certain employees beyond retirement age. The rules of pension schemes usually provide for such people to receive an enhanced pension without further contributions either from them or from the employer.

In conclusion, it is dangerous to generalise about people. Not all older employees are ready to retire. To attempt to encourage all this group to leave before normal retirement age is a superficially simple way of coping with redundancy. Good personnel practice demands that the needs of both organisation and individuals concerned must be carefully analysed before starting on this path.

16 The Future is Not Far Away

In this book we have examined the techniques available to personnel specialists and line managers in their search to maximise the contribution of people to business success. We have stressed the need for such techniques to be used within a framework of corporate objectives which in their turn determine organisational requirements, both qualitative and quantitative, for human resources. This book recognises that there are few, if any, easy solutions to people management problems. Each organisation is unique, both in terms of its context (political, economic, social and technological) and by virtue of its culture, systems and structures.

16.1 What of the Future?

Managers in employing organisations are finding themselves faced with more and more questions about the long-term survival of the business because of increasing demands from those who have a stake in it. These 'stakeholders' include:

- the customer;
- shareholders;
- employees;
- suppliers;
- the state;
- the community or public opinion.

Competitive pressures also are intense in many sectors of the economy. New technology provides both threats and opportunities for organisational success.

To improve their position in the market place, many organisations are building strategies based on product and service quality. They are re-structuring the organisation so that it is more flexible and responsive to customer needs and demands.

All of this leads to questioning of established practices not least in the area of human resource management.

You may recall that in Chapter 14 (p. 185) we discussed management's twin objectives of control and commitment in its relationships with the workforce. A necessity to achieve both these goals, rather than one or the other, will be vital in future. Management is concerned both to control the output of available human resources and to build an organisational culture which fosters commitment, responsibility and the development of individual potential. Managerial competencies supportive of this sort of organisational culture include:

- the ability to analyse the organisation's environment;
- proactivity, the anticipation and creation of change;
- leadership and vision;
- the development of organisational structures and processes which promote learning and creativity;
- the development of flatter, decentralised, self-organising work places;
- facilitation, networking and remote management;
- the use of information technology to create new products and services and to support flexible and innovative organisations;
- the bringing together of key stakeholders from different sectors of society in alliances and networks which enable old problems to be tackled.

16.2 The Future: The Challenge for Personnel Management

Assisting management to become more efficient and more effective in both controlling and motivating the workforce presents personnel specialists with considerable challenges in the development of appropriate policies and practices. The most important of these is to ensure that management sees human resource policy as integral to business policy rather than a mere adjunct to it. The presence of a personnel specialist at board level should facilitate such perceptions.

16.3 Developing Mechanisms for the More Effective Control of a Workforce

A significant aspect of the challenges presented to management for the future is that of planning more systematically both its demand for and means of acquiring an adequate supply of human resources.

During the recession many organisations have used new technology and better management techniques to reduce unit labour costs. The capabilities required to undertake a particular job are more thoroughly analysed than in the past. Terms such as 're-skilling', 'upskilling', 're-profiling' etc. all indicate a determination by management to sustain higher levels of efficiency in future.

The importance of developing more flexible employment contracts to minimise overheads and ensure that the size and nature of the workforce can be adjusted with changes in demand for the goods or services produced by the organisation, is increasingly recognised. The use of self-employed people on a contract for services basis and annual hours arrangements are two mechanisms now often used for this purpose.

Changes in the population structure of Britain also emphasise the advisability of the search for more flexible contractual arrangements with employees. The number of school leavers is declining. The greater of these reductions will take place in the next few years. At present the impact of this on labour supply is being masked by relatively high levels of unemployment. Employers should not be seduced into believing, however, that labour supply will continue to be non-problematic. Economic growth would bring with it renewed competition for staff, making it vital for organisations (in particular those with a traditional reliance on the recruitment of young people) to identify new recruitment sources. Strategies to achieve this are likely to include:

- reducing entry qualifications;
- career break schemes;
- job sharing;
- mature entrant schemes including retraining facilities;
- childcare facilities;
- increased emphasis on equal opportunity policies to encourage non-traditional recruits (e.g. men into nursing).

Many employers learned a great deal about these practices during the late 1970s and early 1980s. If the current recession comes to an end and labour shortages again become the order of the day, it will be vital for this learning to be utilised to cope with the emergent labour supply problems.

The need to control employment costs to ensure organisational survival is likely to produce pressure for 'tougher' personnel policies. Personnel specialists will be expected to develop mechanisms to deal with poor performers through redundancy, early retirement or retraining schemes. Disciplinary procedures will place greater emphasis on 'capability' issues. Selection and appraisal must further the aim of ensuring consistently high individual and organisational performance. In the area of collective relationships between management and staff, the need to control employment costs is likely to mean an emphasis on the de-recognition of trade unions and the associated efforts to impose or negotiate out ineffective working practices previously included in collective agreements.

16.4 Encouraging Employee Commitment

Conventional wisdom seems to suggest that the necessity to control the workforce need not be synonymous with ruthless exploitation. There is growing research evidence to suggest that good relationships with employees are at the heart of successful organisations. This is not a focus on people for its own sake; rather, good employee relations are seen as a necessary precursor to good customer relations and organisational survival. The more rapidly changing world of the employing organisation places increased reliance on employees capable of exercising judgement to cope effectively with uncertainty. There is recognition that rules cannot and should not be developed to fit every circumstance. Rule-bound organisations encourage conformity rather than creativity. Encouraging committed individual initiative is a key issue for managers and personnel specialists.

For many organisations this raises fundamental questions about organisational culture, managerial roles and management style. There is increasing evidence that employers both large and small are making more conscious and planned attempts to alter the attitudes, values and routine ways of behaving at work. Management responsibility is being pushed down to lower levels and teamworking is being encouraged. In some cases such culture change is leading to the removal of one or more tiers in the managerial hierarchy. More detailed changes in employment practice aimed at employee commitment include:

- selection techniques capable of identifying those with the capacity for innovation, initiative and flexibility;
- greater emphasis on employee involvement in managerial decision-making;
- improvements in employee communications and consultation;
- payment systems which encourage initiative and high individual performance;
- special development programmes for employees with potential.

16.5 Flexibility: The Key to the Future

We have identified the advisability for management of pursuing the twin aims of controlling the workforce and gaining its trust and commitment. Pursuit of these goals is often accompanied by the realisation that an organisation can become over-structured and that valuable resources can be diverted to maintaining organisational structure rather than fulfilling organisational purpose. Over the last few years large numbers of organisations, both public and private, service and manufacturing, have been forced by the recession to undertake a radical reappraisal of their structure and organisation. In some cases this has led to redefinition of core business. Some organisations have then more explicitly divided their workforce into:

- Core staff – employed to execute the prime business of the organisation.
- Staff contracted to supply specific services – necessary to support and complement core services without forming an integral part of them.

- Flexible staff – a pool of suitably qualified and experienced people who can be called upon at short notice.

Such trends are likely to continue in the future and are beginning to raise questions about the role of the personnel function. For example:

- Is it restricted to the development of appropriate personnel policies and practices for the employment of core and flexible staff or does it also have a legitimate role in the formulation of contracts for the supply of support services?
- How different should human resource policies be in respect of core and flexible staff?

All staff will have long-term careers but must be prepared to develop new capabilities according to business needs. Indeed, flatter organisation structures are already changing assumptions about vertical career progression through organisational hierarchies. The control of labour costs and the need for flexibility in numbers and types of people employed will lead many organisations to make more transient contractual arrangements with other people. Job security will be limited; others will have contracts for services only. Agencies or sub-contractors may be used more wisely, particularly for specialist tasks, to maintain flexibility.

Recognition of these trends and the design of jobs and careers is indicated by the growth of 'portfolio' employment. Just as architects and artists develop portfolios to demonstrate the range and excellence of their work, other people are beginning to develop a range of activities and accompanying capabilities, which are undertaken in parallel. The growth in self-employment and the prevalence of part-time working, particularly by women in the UK, may mean that employers have the opportunity to employ or contract for services with individuals who also work for other employers or are proprietors of small businesses. Whether this already detectable change in the nature of employment is a response to employment policies designed to encourage flexibility of labour or an indication of wider social changes related to orientations to work and changing lifestyles, is an interesting topic for debate. Whatever the case, it suggests that the opportunities for managers and personnel staff, to meet both the needs for a flexible workforce and the desire of some individuals to have a more flexible attachment to employing organisations, will increasingly exist.

16.6 The Implications for the Personnel Specialist

Increased emphasis on the need for organisational flexibility to cope with changed business requirements will have profound effects on personnel specialists.

- First, such people will require increased expertise in the management of organisational change.
- Second, personnel specialists will need to acquire a greater understanding of and involvement in corporate decision-making.
- Third, expertise in very specific aspects of the management of the employment relationship will be needed, such as compensation or recruitment or dealing with staff who work from home or sub-contractors.
- Fourth, personnel specialists will seek out and employ external consultants to assist in the resolution of difficulties arising from the heightened complexity of the employment relationship.

At the beginning of this book we identified a number of roles for personnel practitioners:

- audit;
- executive;
- facilitator;
- consultancy;
- service.

In future it will be necessary to add visionary and magician to the list!

Answers

Chapter 1

Exercise 1
1 Executive.
2 Facilitator.
3 Audit.
4 Consultancy.
5 Service.
6 A combination of consultancy and service, i.e. helping line managers to reach selection decisions and providing information on conditions of employment, etc. There may also be elements of the facilitator role. Pre-selection planning and post-interview discussion may provide the specialist with an opportunity to give managers informal feedback or guidance on the use of selection techniques, such as questioning skills.

Exercise 2
1 False.
2 False.
3 True.
4 True.
5 True.

Chapter 2

Exercise 1
The numbers of people who can be persuaded to work for a company will be influenced by the nature of the work and the terms and conditions of employment offered as compared with those in competitor organisations. The rate at which existing employees leave the company will be influenced by similar factors.

Exercise 2
No. They cannot control the birth rate, for example! Most companies also cannot control the demand for their goods, nor can they control government policies. However, many large companies do attempt to influence government thinking through the use of parliamentary lobbyists and related devices.

Exercise 3
You should have been able to see that, in the following five years, 25 per cent of the pilots will retire. Since it costs over £500,000 to train a pilot, the company has a serious problem.

Exercise 4
The promotion prospects of more junior staff would be very limited. They might leave or become very demoralised.

Exercise 5
Many researchers believe that it takes two to five years to become really effective in a managerial job. If a lot of managers are still learning to do their jobs, it is unlikely that their departments will be as effective as those with more experienced managers.

Exercise 6
Index = number of leavers ÷ average numbers employed = $725 \div 2400 \times 100 = 30.2$ per cent. Thus the labour turnover indeed was 30.2 per cent for January for Lyttlewood Enterprises. This should give management much cause for concern unless of course it has prompted employees to leave because of redundancy or early retirement.

Exercise 7
The answer is 300 since that is the number of people employed one year ago.

Exercise 8
Our sample employee found the job boring, as a consequence looked for another job, found one with better pay and gave this as the reason for leaving.

Exercise 9
They should investigate the attractions which the rival firm is able to offer to employees, and also the aspects of working in their own organisation which may be prompting staff to leave.

Exercise 10
No. Remember, we said that stages 1 and 2 can be carried out in parallel with each other. Stage 2 is by far the more difficult stage of the process.

Exercise 11
Managers directly responsible for that work.

Exercise 12
Labour turnover is highest during the early weeks and months after the date of engagement. Remember the 'induction crisis'! Hence, if no new staff are recruited, the turnover rate will fall dramatically.

Chapter 3

Exercise 1
It should describe:
- the job;
- its place in the organisation;
- the circumstances under which it is performed;
- the objectives to be achieved by the job holder;

and it should be:
- a useful working document;
- up to date and relevant.

Exercise 2

Casual callers or writers of letters and recommendations from existing employees. 'Word of mouth' recruitment has been tested legally. In 1981 the Commission for Racial equality issued a 'non-discrimination notice' on a bakery, F. Broomfield Ltd. The Company had recruited by word of mouth only and this was found to be discriminatory against the recruitment of black people as existing staff were white and recruited their relations and friends who were also white.

Exercise 3

- The audience to be reached.
- The nature of the job.
- The desired image of the employing organisation.
- Cost-effectiveness.
- Time required to fill the vacancy.
- Past experience.

Exercise 4

- To get the right person for the job.
- To establish or maintain an image as a good employer.
- To make the process as cost-effective as possible.

Exercise 5

1 A closed question. It does not yield much information and may be irritating to the candidate if the information is included on the application form.

2 A multiple question. The answer to the first part could be on the application form. The second part is a leading question. The questioner seems to be assuming that the next job was a 'better' job, or that the acquisition of a qualification prompted the change of job. It might be more effective to ask, 'Why did you change your job in 1973?' If reasons other than qualifications are given, the next question could be, 'How did you feel when you became professionally qualified?'

3 A very open question. the answer is likely to need probing.

4 A probing question. The information that the candidate did not like a particular job would be too vague to be helpful in any judgement about suitability for a job.

5 A leading question. Is the interviewer revealing any bias?' It could be re-worded, 'Why did you spend three years working in West Africa?'

6 A problem-centred question. You should be critical of its relevance, unless you assume that it was used to interview astronauts!

7 A direct and fairly meaningless question. If you are looking for a decisive individual, it is probably better to ask indirect questions. For example, the candidate could be asked to describe a difficult situation recently encountered at work.

Exercise 6

1 Audit
2 Executive.
3 Facilitator.
4 Consultancy.
5 Service.

Chapter 4

Exercise 1

1 The numbers of new employees likely to enter the hotel in the foreseeable future for whom a formal induction course would be necessary.

2 The minimum viable group size for such a course.
3 The maximum period of employment before which a formal induction course would become superfluous.

Chapter 5

Exercise 1
There are several possible solutions. One way would be to translate safety notices and other information into relevant languages. For illiterate new employees it might be possible to use clearly understood symbols. Another alternative would be to provide safety training in the relevant languages. A further possibility would be to offer English language training.

Exercise 2
If the existing workforce is predominantly white, the relations and friends whom they introduce to the organisation are also likely to be white. Ethnic minorities are unlikely, therefore, to be afforded equal access to jobs.

Exercise 3
A female actor in a part written for a female character in a play.
A female matron in an all-girls' school.
A male lavatory attendant in a men's toilet.
A male chauffeur for a job in Saudi Arabia (where women are prohibited from driving by law).

Exercise 4
Statutory law.
Case law.

Save Easy Building Society

1 *The advertisement*   Under section 38 of the Sex Discrimination Act 1975, there should be nothing in the wording or presentation of advertisements for jobs to give the impression that only men or only women are required. Hence, John Baker's heading 'Mums please note', as well as being patronising in tone, is also illegal in that it implies that the vacancy is open only to female applicants.
2 *The telephone enquiry*   The Race Relations Act 1976 specifies that individuals should not be treated less favourably than others on grounds of race. Only if John Baker could show that the exclusion of a black applicant was a genuine and necessary condition of employment, and not merely convenient, would his action be legal. His rationalisation about the feelings of his clientele *is* merely a convenience. His perception of the clarity of her intonation on the telephone *might* constitute reasonable grounds for rejection. However, the onus would be on him to prove *both* that clarity of expression was necessary, because of the amount and nature of the telephone work involved, *and* that the applicant did not measure up to the demands of the job in this respect.
3 *Rejection of the fifty-five-year-old applicant*   This is legal. There is no age discrimination legislation in the UK. Interestingly, his action would have been illegal in the United States.
4 *Questioning about domestic circumstances*   According to the Sex Discrimination Act, John Baker should not treat applicants less favourably on grounds of sex or marriage than he treats or would treat other persons. If the female applicant in question had made a complaint to an industrial tribunal, John Baker would have been required to show that his question indicated an intention to discriminate on grounds of parenthood rather than sex.

5 *John Baker's concern about trade union activists* His rejection of a candidate because of her past role as a trade union representative is illegal. Applicants for jobs are protected from discrimination on the grounds of trade union membership by the Employment Act 1990.

6 *The change in Mrs Best's hours of work* Employers are required to give employees a written statement setting out the main terms and conditions of their employment. However, this statement is not the only facet of the contract of employment. The contract was made at the time that Mrs Best accepted the offer of a job as part-time cashier/typist. At that time the hours of work were as stipulated in the advertisement, i.e. 11.00 a.m. to 3.00 p.m. John Baker's decision to change them without her consent might be construed as a constructive dismissal (see Chapter 15, p. 201). However, this is unlikely given the seemingly minor nature of the change.

In any case Mrs Best does not have two years' service (the current qualification period for unfair dismissal compensation – see p. 151). Therefore she cannot make a claim against him to an industrial tribunal. She could bring an action against him in the county court, but in view of her length of service any compensation would be likely to be minimal. The court would be unlikely to order her reinstatement. If other similar work was difficult to find, she would probably choose to stay, and after arguing, put up with the change. However, such an unhelpful or even dishonest way of managing staff is unlikely to lead to harmononious working relationships and an efficient office.

Chapter 6

Exercise 2

No, we can all think of people who earn a great deal of money but whose negotiating behaviour demonstrates that they are far from satisfied. As indicated earlier, the reason for this seems to lie in the nature of our consumer society.

Exercise 3

No. This is one of the 'hygiene' factors. Employees must feel the level of their renumeration is fair for the job they are asked to do if this is not to be a source of dissatisfaction. However, even if employees are paid much more than the market rate, this will not be a source of motivation.

Exercise 4

Of course, the organisational psychologists would refuse to accept that money can be a major motivator for highly paid workers. However, they would be prepared to see it as a symbol of success and affluence in life generally and of recognition at work. Thus money may satisfy several intangible needs.

Exercise 5

In autonomous group working the focus or unit of analysis is the group rather than the individual.

Exercise 6

These include:
- inadequate training;
- threats to job security;
- the failure to clearly define supervisory or middle management roles and work to get the 'ownership' of these people.

Exercise 7

Personnel specialists provide a service to 'internal' customers when they assist line managers to select staff or when they give advice on the implications in employment law of managerial actions.

Exercise 8

National and organisational culture in the UK is in some ways similar to that of the United States. In other ways it differs. Some British people, in particular more traditional managers, see American gurus as introducing unhelpful 'heights' into organisations and therefore may reject interesting and innovative ideas because of the style in which they are delivered.

Exercise 9

1 False.

2 True.

3 True.

4 False.

5 False.

Chapter 7

Exercise 1

By focusing on actual job behaviours rather than on personality traits.

Exercise 2

Discretion. It would be unwise to apply a results-oriented approach where post-holders have little or no ability to influence the nature of their tasks.

Exercise 3

1 Personality characteristics;

2 Required job behaviour;

3 The achievement of pre-set goals and objectives.

Exercise 4

1 (a) Failure to brief George adequately on the purpose of appraisal schemes, and in the past, presumably, to monitor the operation of appraisal systems.

(b) Failure to train George in appraisal, including interviewing techniques.

(c) Failure to ask George how he had managed to complete the 'key objectives' section of the form prior to the interview!

You could also have queried the wisdom of requiring George to undertake personality trait rating and to communicate his assessment of potential to employees.

2 Remember the quotation at the beginning of this chapter: 'the good people don't know what they should be doing or how well they are doing' and 'nobody finds out the bad people'. In addition, the communication of their perceived lack of potential to many employees increased dissatisfaction and had an adverse effect on production. A cautionary tale indeed!

Chapter 8

Exercise 1

Item 4 does not fit with Fred's intention to recruit workers for the shops from the open market. Actions in breach of declared policy are likely to be very damaging to employee morale. Fred should advertise new posts within the manufacturing company before attempting to recruit new employees, unless he wishes to change this aspect of company policy.

Exercise 2
1 They may be out of date.
2 Job descriptions are often a statement of what ought to be rather than what is.

Exercise 3
Some characteristics listed in personnel specifications cannot be developed to achieve optimum job performance. Examples are job experience and interests.

Exercise 4
1 Off-the-job training at the place of work.
2 On-the-job training at the place of work.
3 External training programmes.

Exercise 5
1 Off-the-job training at the place of work.
2 On-the-job training at the place of work.
3 External courses.
And:
1 Teacher-centred approaches.
2 Learner-centred approaches.

Exercise 6
It might be. Alternatively it could be that rising unemployment has made dismissed employees more reluctant to take up cases for fear of being labelled as potential troublemakers by possible new employers. or the company's increased success rate in tribunal cases could be due to the increased quality of its representation.

Chapter 9

Exercise 1
In the 1970s organisation development tended to focus on the development of consensus within organisations. It is now recognised that this is not realistic. Different individuals and groups within organisations have different issues. The goals of employees, for example, will by no means always coincide with those of shareholders.

Exercise 2
There will be more emphasis on the development aspects of the role and on assisting managers to make appropriate decisions about people management problems. There will be less need for personnel specialists to 'police' terms and conditions of employment and procedures (discipline, grievance, etc.).

Exercise 3
The consultancy role – helping management to manage change effectively, *not* acting as an expert consultant giving prescriptions about employment law, recruitment and selection practices or pay and reward systems.

Exercise 4
Prescribing remedies – though organisation development practitioners often do get involved in diagnosing problems or 'surfacing' organisational data.

Exercise 5
(a) Job descriptions are likely to contain a brief summary of the purpose of the role and its core responsibilities rather than a long list of tasks. Person

specifications will emphasise the need for flexibility and proactivity in the face of change. They may go so far as to suggest that the prime focus of the appointment will be to the organisation or one of its component parts rather than to a fixed job. In the selection process there is likely to be more emphasis on perceived cultural 'fit' between the organisation and the appointee and rather more concern with the general capabilities required of staff at a particular level or unit rather than more detailed capabilities related to a current job.

(b) Again there will be more emphasis on such things as flexibility, proactivity and innovation in procedures for determining pay increase, bonuses, etc. Job evaluation systems are more likely to have a general focus on a particular level of work or group of activities rather than a narrow focus on a specific job. They are likely also to relate strongly to the competencies required to perform effectively.

Chapter 10

Exercise 1

In the 1990s organisations must be able to respond quickly and flexibly to changes in demand for goods and services. This means that employees also must be flexible. They therefore must have 'learning how to learn skills' which enable them to continuously adapt to changing organisational circumstances.

Exercise 2

The development is concerned not only with learners as workers but also with them as people. It should be relevant to their overall sense of themselves and not just to the part of them which is involved in work. Good development is also specifically focused on the requirements of the particular organisation, the business which it is in and the context (markets, social, political and technological circumstances). Good development does not assume that the development requirements of staff in one organisation are the same as those in another. It assists employees to respond positively to the changing circumstances – both internal and external – of their organisations.

Exercise 3

A competency can be defined as 'the observable combination of knowledge, skills and attributes that enables optimum performance'. Criticisms of the competency-based approach to management development include:

- a concern that it leads to a focus on rules and procedures at the expense of learning;
- the view that the reality of managerial work does not stack up with the artificial component parts suggested by the competence movement, e.g. financial management or people management;
- a concern that comptencies tend to emphasise the maintenance of the status quo whilst increasingly the real job of managers is to create change;
- the recognition that different people achieve the same outcomes in different ways – and that this is not necessarily recognised or facilitated via a competency-based approach.

Exercise 4

Management development approaches which meet the needs of a particular organisation require a diagnosis of these specific needs of managers within that organisation to be undertaken. This takes longer, is more complex and therefore more expensive than the packaged approach. However, it is now widely accepted that management development is only of use if it is geared to particular organisational circumstances and their implications for managerial work.

Exercise 5

- An analysis of the matches or mis-matches between the demand for likely supply of managers in three years' time.
- An evaluation of the options for closing the gap between demand and likely supply (or dealing with over-supply).
- Implementation of the human resource plan including monitoring and review procedures.

Exercise 6

In some ways this is a trick question since line managers, potential participants and developers all have a role to play in the assessment of managers' development needs. Line managers may take the lead in assisting their staff, often via the appraisal process, to think through their development needs in the light of their recent performance. Developers may take the lead in suggesting ways in which development needs can be met or, from time to time, assisting both line managers and their staff to think through their development needs as well as the means of meeting these.

Exercise 7

These services can be very expensive when provided to individuals. Some line managers may feel that the provision of these services undermines their own role in management development. Equally the presence of these services provided by third parties may encourage some line managers to abdicate the responsibility for the development of their own staff.

Exercise 8

- Trainees are responsible for their own learning.
- Trainees have the right to analyse their own learning needs.
- Trainees have the right to design their own training programmes.

Chapter 11

Exercise 1

1 False. Probably most organisations do provide such services; small companies will be the exception.

2 False. Counsellors should encourage clients to reach their own solutions. In practice, of course, many managers will be tested to act in the way suggested in this statement!

3 True.

4 False.

5 Probably false. Whilst such facilities are unlikely to motivate employees to be more productive, they are equally unlikely to demotivate them. Sports and social clubs may be an aid to recruitment and public relations in the locality. They also may assist in the prevention of occupational stress.

Chapter 12

Exercise 1

The instructions to interviewers are directly discriminatory; the written test is indirectly discriminatory. The CRE, in its investigation, found that Asian applicants did disproportionately badly; the test did not measure relevant abilities and the standard of English demanded was not necessary for effective job performance. The company should devise a more appropriate test.

Other actions taken by Bradford Metro since the CRE investigation include:

1 The introduction and implementation of an equal opportunity policy;

2 A programme of language training for Asian employees to improve their chances of promotion;

3 Training for managers and supervisors in managing a multi-racial workforce.

A higher proportion of Asians and West Indians are now inspectors.

Exercise 2

No, since the job will involve work in countries whose laws or customs make it impossible for a woman to do the job effectively.

Exercise 3

The Act applies to every male and female employee regardless of length of service or hours worked per week. (If you could not answer this, refer to the checklist of employee rights at the beginning of this chapter.)

Exercise 4

1 Maternity leave.

2 Statutory maternity pay.

3 Paid time off for antenatal care.

You may have also listed the right not to be unfairly dismissed because of pregnancy. This is covered in Chapter 15.

Exercise 5

She would be regarded as having acted unreasonably, if the job was broadly the same and carried the same pay and other terms and conditions of employment. An argument that she did not like the manager would not be reasonable. However, if the job was not at the same location or required her to work substantially different hours her refusal would probably be judged reasonable.

Exercise 6

You should ensure that they are suspended on full pay, or offer them suitable alternative work, until a doctor authorises their return.

Exercise 7

1 Clearly this claim is not covered by the definition of 'like work' or 'work rated as equivalent' following a job evaluation study. Whether it is 'work of equal value' would depend on the view of an independent expert. Even then she might not get equal pay if Fred could show that there was a 'genuine material difference' between her work and that of the storekeeper.

2 Her unmarried status is irrelevant. She is entitled to maternity leave. Fred can refuse to have her back as his secretary if it is not 'reasonably practicable' for him to do so. In that case he must offer her 'suitable alternative work'. That is, the work which she is offered must be 'not less favourable' than if she had not been absent.

3 Whether or not the training course is a trade union duty would depend on whether the course is recognised by the union to which the steward belongs and whether it is relevant to his duties as a shop steward. Fred can ask to see the syllabus.

4 In law this would be classified as a public duty. Hence she is entitled to reasonable time off without pay in order to fulfil the demands of the role. It is likely that the small amount of time she is said to need here would be considered reasonable.

Chapter 13

Exercise 1
Through an 'any other duties as required by management' clause in a job description.

Exercise 2
It is not, particularly in the case of managerial or professional jobs, where the individual to some degree defines the nature of the tasks performed. Nevertheless, for job evaluation purposes, it is important to attempt the distinction.

Exercise 3
There is no indication as to how much more important one job is than the next in the hierarchy.

Exercise 4
In many ways this is a trick exercise since, without an intimate knowledge of Colin's Cars, you are unable to weight the factors. However, this would be a useful exercise for members of the working group to undertake to come up with some trial weightings. There is no correct answer. All that can be said is that the right weightings are those which ultimately produce an acceptable ranking of jobs.

Exercise 5
No points would be allocated to level 1, 10 to level 2 and so on up to the maximum of 40 at level 5: a job that fitted level 3 would therefore be given 20 points.

Exercise 6
Job *A* is overpaid and job *B* is underpaid, since in theory the introduction of the job evaluation scheme should be self-financing in that the cost of bringing green circle jobs up to the line of best fit should be balanced by the savings derived from reducing the pay associated with red circle jobs.

Exercise 7
Analytical methods – see Chapter 12, p. 169.

Exercise 8
By reference to the relative importance of the factor to the organisation.

Exercise 9
No, there is always a range of rates paid by different employers, either because the duties performed, even where the job title is the same, vary somewhat or because wage and salary policies of employers differ, as suggested on pp. 163–5.

Exercise 10
'Piecework' is literally work for which payment is by the piece of work produced.

Exercise 11
Payment by results systems give employees considerable control over output. If they wish to limit production, either for individual or group reasons, they can do so. Also employees are likely to become very discontented if their bonus earnings are reduced by shortages of components.

Exercise 12
Our discussions have suggested that the motivation to work is very complex and that, while money is an important source of motivation, it is not the only one for all workers at all times.

Exercise 13
It is paid for achieving and maintaining a standard performance.

Exercise 14
Management should determine this policy as part of its overall remuneration policy and wage and salary administration practices.

Chapter 14

Exercise 1
This is because of the predominantly financial objectives of work organisations.
Exercise 2
You might call it a 'protective practice'. In other words, for you this would be quite legitimate behaviour.
Exercise 3
As an integral part of the process of drawing up these plans. You should recall from the discussion in the earlier part of this chapter that personnel and employee relations should be facets of general organisational decision-making.
Exercise 4
No. Where management is concerned to encourage employee commitment rather than rely solely on strategies of control, line managers should focus on managing by consent rather than via authoritarian techniques.
Exercise 5
Access to the 'organ-grinder' rather than the 'monkey' may become part of the negotiating process. The resultant demoralisation of management's negotiating team is likely to have a very disadvantageous effect on workplace employee relations.
Exercise 6
It is likely that the line manager most immediately concerned with the work group will wish to concede the claim, to get the service operating again. Personnel specialists, on the other hand, supported by more senior line management, should have an eye on the longer-term issues.

Chapter 15

Exercise 1
In attempting to answer these questions you probably found that you not only needed a knowledge of the law but also information on the procedures for dealing with disciplinary cases in the organisation concerned. Here are some brief answers to the questions. The actions which managers should take in such circumstances are covered in more detail later in this chapter.
1 There were two main points which you could have covered here. First, guidance on the processes to be followed prior to dismissal should be found in the organisation's disciplinary procedure. Secondly, employees can be dismissed immediately if they commit 'gross misconduct'. There is no universal definition of this term. Again, the relevant reference document is the disciplinary procedure.
2 Not all employees can bring such claims against their employer. We shall examine this area of the law on unfair dismissal later in this section.
3 This is incorrect. According to the ACAS Code of Practice. *Disciplinary Practice and Procedures in Employment*, and the ACAS advisory handbook,

Discipline at Work, employees have a general right to be accompanied by a trade union representative or by a fellow employee. Whether this means that the latter can speak on behalf of the 'accused' is usually defined in the organisation's disciplinary procedure.

4 Whether or not a tribunal would find dismissal to be fair in this case would depend largely on the nature of the employee's job. Those expected to be trustworthy and of great integrity, such as security guards or cashiers, tend to be treated differently from junior clerical staff, for example.

5 It is not very difficult to dismiss employees fairly if procedures are followed and justice is seen to be done.

6 Most disciplinary procedures would make it clear that this is gross misconduct. Dismissal would be justified provided that the employee's action could be proved beyond reasonable doubt.

Exercise 2

To decide this it would be necessary to examine Jane's contract of employment and the effect on it of your conduct. If the contract says that she has been employed as a stylist at any of your shops and it is customary for staff to move around in this way, then you may be in the clear. By contrast if the contract states that the location of her employment is the salon in which she is currently working, she has worked there for a long time and stylists are never expected to move, then your case will be very weak.

Exercise 3

1 Depending on the circumstances of the case this might be constructive dismissal.

2 Since this would not be gross misconduct such dismissals would be unfair.

3 The action in this case conforms with the ACAS Code of Practice and with the ACAS advisory handbook, *Discipline at Work.*

4 Dismissal because it would be illegal to continue to employ her is unlikely to be fair, though it would depend on the particular requirements of the job. However, the authority would not be expected to come to an arrangement with her husband!

5 It would be wise to investigate this complaint, since if it goes to the 'root of the contract' it might be construed as constructive dismissal.

Exercise 4

No, since this would not be gross misconduct.

Exercise 5

The courts have tended to back employers' rights to change work in the interest of efficiency. In this case the college authorities would have to show that different aptitudes, skills or knowledge were required for the new job than for the old one.

Exercise 6

Those who volunteer are likely to include some people who would find it easy to get other jobs, people whose skills management would wish to retain. The problem for management of accepting this process of self-selection is that it means surrendering control to workers.

Exercise 7

The industrial tribunal said it was and refused her application for a redundancy payment. They said that her refusal to work near a sex shop was based on a personal whim since the commercial exploitation of sex was no greater in Soho than in Mayfair. Possibly it was a little more discrete in the latter area! In this case it was felt that the employee's personal circumstances did not make the refusal of the offer of alternative work reasonable.

Further Reading

Chapter 1
J. Storey, *Management of Human Resources* (Blackwell Business, 1992).
S. Tyson and A. Fell, *Evaluating the Personnel Function (Hutchinson, 1986)*.

Chapter 2
M. Bennison and J. Casson, *The Manpower Planning Handbook* (McGraw-Hill, 1984).
J. Bramham, *Practical Manpower Planning* (Institute of Personnel Management, 1982).
C. Hayes and N. Fonda, *Strategy and People: The Prospect Centre Perspective* (The Prospect Centre, 1988).
IBM Statement on Human Resource Planning, The (Institute of Personnel Management, 1986).
B. Pettman, *Manpower Planning Workbook* (Gower, 1984).

Chapter 3
C. Lewis, *Employee Selection* (Hutchinson, 1985).
P. Plumbley, *Recruitment and Selection* (Institute of Personnel Management, 1985).

Chapter 5
D. Lewis, *Essentials of Employment Law* (Institute of Personnel Management, 1994).

Chapter 6
C. Handy, *The Age of Unreason* (Arrow, 1990).

Chapter 7
C. A. Fletcher and R. Williams, *Performance Appraisal and Career Development* (Hutchinson, 1985).

Chapter 8
E. Moorby, *How to Succeed in Employee Development* (McGraw-Hill, 1994).
T. Pont, *Evaluating Training Effectiveness* (McGraw-Hill, 1993).

Chapter 9
D. Megginson and M. Pedler, *Self Development* (McGraw-Hill, 1992).
M. Pedler and T. Boydell, *Managing Yourself* (Fontana/Collins, 1985).

Chapter 11
R. Plant, *Managing Change and Making it Stick* (Fontana, 1990).

Chapter 12
As for Chapter 5.

Chapter 13
M. Armstrong and H. Murlis, *Reward Management* (Kogan Page, 1991).

Chapter 14
P. B. Beaumont, *Change in Industrial Relations* (Routledge, 1990).

Chapter 15
C. Handy, *The Empty Raincoat* (Hutchinson, 1994).

Index